The Effects of
the Nation

The Effects of the Nation

MEXICAN ART IN AN AGE OF GLOBALIZATION

Edited by
Carl Good and
John V. Waldron

 Temple University Press

PHILADELPHIA

Library of Congress Cataloging-in-Publication Data

The effects of the nation : Mexican art in an age of globalization /
edited by Carl Good and John V. Waldron.
        p. cm.
    Includes bibliographical references and index.
    ISBN 1-56639-865-7 (cloth : alk. paper) — ISBN 1-56639-866-5
(pbk. : alk. paper)
    1. Arts, Mexican. 2. Arts, Modern—20th century—Mexico.
3. National characteristics in art. 4. Art and society—Mexico.
I. Good, Carl, 1965– . II. Waldron, John V., 1960– .

NX514.A1 E36 2001
700'.972'0904—dc21   00-066672

Contents

The Effects of
the Nation

Introduction

Ungoverned Specificities

Carl Good

> If you ask whether "national literatures" should be eliminated
> in favor of "global" perspectives, I'm inclined to say "yes"—
> as long as I don't specifically think about [my own] Australian
> literature and its long and ultimately successful struggle for an
> identity of its own.
>
> Judith Ryan, "Shrunk to an Interloper"

This collection brings together a diverse group of essays focused on all aspects of Mexican visual art, literature, and criticism. Each essay also is preoccupied directly or indirectly with "the nation" and specifically with Mexico. Such a project—hovering in the thematic vicinity of the nation, or rather of a specific nation—is anachronistic at a time many have characterized with the word globalism. The paradox is reflected in the title of the collection, with "globalization" hooked onto the end of it like its caboose (or perhaps its engine). Critics in both the humanities and the social sciences appear more concerned today with theorizing the end of the nation as a disciplinary pretext or conceptual frame. In U.S. departments of Spanish such concerns characterize the work of many active critics, such as George Yúdice, Jean Franco, Alberto Moreiras, Doris Sommer, George Beverly, and Gwen Kirkpatrick, to name a few examples—albeit in very different ways, but often with a strong debt to the work of Fredric Jameson, whose own eye has been roving increasingly southwest toward Latin America. Despite the significant conceptual and lexical variations that distinguish them, these critics tend to agree that studying literature and culture as delimited in some way by national histories and spaces is no longer viable given the changes brought about by globalism in international economics, politics, and culture.

The ten chapters that follow are likewise concerned with the problems and challenges of something like globalism. Nonetheless—and without suggesting that they are all written out of a common orientation or that they would all agree with the claims of this introduction (they are not and they would not)—they tend to hold back from embracing globalism as a theoretical frame, choosing instead to continue lingering with this ambiguous, singular—even perhaps *prohibitive*—something called, not just "the nation," but "Mexico." When they speak directly or indirectly to the challenges of globalism, they do so not by taking a point of departure in the theoretical impasses established by the dialectical framework of a (primarily North American) globalist critical discourse, but by commencing out of a fascination for the singularities and effects of rhetoric and images that continue to be associated with a specific nation and that the globalist discourse seems incapable of approaching. For despite its much-vaunted concern with singularities, that discourse is more concerned with those singularities that have been, so to speak, preconditioned by a dialectical framework as negative objects of mourning and that thus pose little rhetorical threat to, or seduction for, that framework and the descriptive critical gaze that maintains it.

At the same time, these chapters also are cautious about the risks of reestablishing or defining national difference or even of somehow assuming "the nation" as an organic entity. For as soon as "Mexico" is identified as different from x or simply defined in any way, it becomes a problem that pertains not to "itself" but to the very discourse that desires the definition in the first place. Instead, the collection participates in what we could say Mexico always already has been: the effect of a deterritorializing of itself. The chapters move consistently and conceptually toward Mexico's many borders—and not only the geographical ones—in an effort to treat "Mexico" as an open sign of something that owes its effect to its possibility of evoking itself from outside of its own borders. Such a possibility—that "Mexico" speaks outside of itself—has many consequences for critics of Mexican history and art, with the current emphasis on the "borderlands" in cultural criticism being only one of them.

The studies in this collection thus risk the possibilities of not succumbing to a double hazard: on the one hand, the tedious nostalgia of looking back at the fictive stability of the nation seen as a cultural–historical organism and, on the other, the aggressive insensitivity of a critical discourse of globalism that risks subsuming into its general scope the specificities—not of negative objects of description but precisely of imagined discursive points of departure—that risk getting lost when the nation is abandoned as an open concept or form.

The latter hazard is becoming more real for writers in the contemporary North American academy, where the problems associated with globalism have come to compose one of the most prominent critical orientations on the academic market. Although globalism began to emerge into the general critical consciousness about a decade ago, it is still a hot topic in all its variations, not only for area studies but also increasingly for national literature departments as well. Its academic prominence could be described in a very general way by pointing first to its referential stimulations and then to its institutional conditioning factors. On the referential side, globalism critics perceive that the fiction of a national cultural–political center is no longer able to hold (what some would refer to as) the field of cultural production in its sway, no longer organizes that production in the face of transnational market forces and the seduction of the communications media with their proliferating, borderless marketing mechanisms: satellite television, cellular phones, advertising, and the Internet. Critical interest thus migrates toward matters associated with the fluidity of national borders, transnational (preferably round-trip) movements of people, linkages of geographically disparate regions by larger economic and technomedia factors, but also (often in a gesture of "contestation") toward smaller-scale cultural montages, such as urban centers, interest groups, and consumer cultures. Echoing Néstor García Canclini's 1995 argument in *Consumidores y ciudadanos* (*Consumers and Citizens*), many of these critics suggest, with different nuances and emphases, that the contemporary economic (dis)order is redefining citizenship itself around economic consumption rather than political conduct. Such formulations frequently stress a priority of affect and barter over decision and risk: a *feeling* of citizenship as a return on economic exchange rather than the *exercising* of citizenship as either a passion or responsibility in the face of an indeterminable future.

On the institutional side of the issue, globalism critics can point to the decline in the strategic value of traditional area studies to U.S. interests in the wake of the cold war, a trend that has undermined institutional justifications for focusing on nations as principles ordering the history of art and culture. Alberto Moreiras summarizes how the situation is perceived from this institutional perspective:

> The traditional aim of "understanding the foreign other," which was always defined from a US- or Eurocentric perspective that became consubstantial to the area studies enterprise, is today about to be replaced by a new goal: the new code words refer to the integration of problem-oriented scholarship and area-based knowledge in the context generated by the exponential increase in the speed and spread of processes of global integration and fragmentation. Traditional area studies were excessively dependent upon reflection on local cultures in view of their particularity and uniqueness. Its reconfiguration as area-based knowledge purportedly promotes the critical and dynamic study of historical localities in terms of the processes of globalization and fragmentation that affect them. (1996, 60)

Such a scenario is seen to have consequences not only for area studies but also increasingly for departments of literature as well, since the latter, which have always tended to be organized around national and regional cultural histories, participate—albeit with some important distinctions—in the same institutional framework as area studies and increasingly compete for the same funds and favors. Of course, not everyone would agree that institutional interests must be thought of as necessarily determining what kind of work goes on in academic departments. In a short article on the challenges posed by transnationality and corporate ownership of the university, J. Hillis Miller (1995) suggests that what is currently at risk is the university's role as the site of production of the "ungovernable." His metaphor is a reminder of what is at stake in an era when the work carried out in universities is increasingly under pressure to both justify itself economically and subordinate itself to larger institutional interests. Insofar as academics see their work as at some level framed by the institution, they lose not only a notion of their own ungovernable activity, but also, more important, the effects of such an activity on the future of the institution itself.[1]

Putting such a considerable objection to one side for the moment, we could also point out the paradox that emerges from the notion that academic work is framed by institutional and national interests. If such a framing is the case, then we are far from having escaped the concept and the effects of nationness and are, in fact, mere accomplices—or pawns—

of yet another of its ruses. Nationness is not disappearing if what is obliging us to shape our work around the increasing fluidity of national borders is itself a nation—the very nation that cradles our institutions in its ever-increasing complexity, transformation, and juridical decentering. In fact, most globalism-oriented critics have not ignored this problem, often organizing their conceptual schemas around the dilemmas posed when globalism is thus seen as the latest face of a North American cultural domination. That domination is precisely the crux of the problem as posed, with the "ideology" of capital never seeming to wander very far from the proper name of the United States. Within this perspective, some theorists conceive of globalism as a recasting of the national rather than the story of its disappearance. Examining the question of sovereignty, prominent theorist of globalism Saskia Sassen argues that the national system of governance is being reconfigured rather than eliminated, pointing out, for example, ways in which the dispersal of economic production has not been accompanied by a corresponding redistribution of institutions and profits: "Globalization is not global. It occupies extremely structured spaces in countries" (1996, 107–108). Sassen also notes that the free trade of goods and capital has not brought about legally sanctioned free trade on the labor market, and such obstacles to free flow continue to speak of the insistence of national boundaries. Nonetheless, national domination does not disappear from the formulation: Sassen ultimately identifies globalism with a hegemonic imposition of the Anglo-American juridical system that accompanies the reconfiguration of national sovereignty.

The acknowledgment that globalism imposes itself as a version of national domination could be used to argue that nothing has really changed: If the nation has not disappeared but merely continues as a problem of domination—the laws of one powerful nation imposed on its neighbors, such as the Roman Empire's juridical invasion of the Iberian peninsula or Spain and England's of the Americas—then something like globalism always has been at work and there is no reason to rethink anything in light of world-historical changes. In terms of trade and economics, as well, a glance at the prevalence of "global" phenomena in past centuries might lead us to a similar conclusion. A recent *New York Times* article cites some interesting data to suggest that, in fact, the world economy was just as, or more, "global" a century ago: Labor today is less mobile than it was in the last century when 14 percent of Americans were foreign born compared with 8 percent today and when immigrants moved around the globe without passports; international trade tariffs often were lower and the export market was at least as important as it is today (in 1879, 95 percent of Germany's imports were still free of duty, whereas American exports made up 7 percent of the American gross national product, compared with 8 percent today); and according to an International Monetary Fund report, capital movements as a proportion of economic output are significantly lower than what they were in the 1880s. We could go back even further: The same *New York Times* article cites the role played in the Spanish Empire by the Chinese demand for silver in the sixteenth through the nineteenth centuries, a period in which China absorbed half of the world's silver production, thereby playing a significant, indirect role in the mining industry in the Americas as well as the slave trade (Kristof 1999). In an initial series of cautions against assuming too quickly the novelty of globalism phenomena, Fredric Jameson cites from Eric Wolf's *Europe and the People without History* a reminder that "as far back as the neolithic trade routes have been global in their scope, with Polynesian artifacts deposited in Africa and Asian potsherds as far afield as the New World" (1998, 54).

But it is too easy to get lost in a fascination with facts and figures in support of positions favoring either the contemporary novelty or the historical immutability of globalism, both of which lead principally to games of anecdotal ping pong. An argument that globalism is nothing new risks insensitivity to the singular, contemporary effects of historical repetition, whereas an assertion that the world has dramatically changed easily becomes an untheoretical, artless attempt to shape the ghosts of the historically amorphous into an empirical event. Temporality is elsewhere. This is not to turn a blind eye to history, but simply to point out that it never has been easy to grasp change in language of any kind and that a response to it is not found in exemplary constative descriptions hyperconscious of the institutional binds said to condition thought, but out of the very fragmentations and frustrations of those descriptions: in strategic deviations of language that lure thought off of (and are lured off by) its alienating dialectical causeways and into something like the imagination as a recommencement of thought and the open possibility of its effects.

As Jameson himself observes in an article on globalism, the "facts" add little theoretically to the discussion: "the problems [of globalism] lie as much in our categories of thought as in the sheer facts of the matter themselves" (1998, 75). The statement, however, puts a spotlight on Jameson's own categories of thought in relation to globalism, which we could accuse of a failure to be put at risk by passionate deviations of language. Despite initially cautioning against easy assumptions of the "newness" of globalism, Jameson himself ultimately sees globalism as a historical shift located at the intersection of communication and technology and written through by a new phase of a dialectic of capitalist domination marshaled by the worldwide Americanization of culture. He finds this Americanization to be unlike any other national imposition, and in this sense he would not agree that globalization is merely the latest face of national imperialism, positing a "fundamental dissymmetry" between all other cultures of the world and the American culture (1998, 63), the latter of which he characterizes as the "becoming cultural of the economic, and the becoming economic of the cultural" (1998, 60). For Jameson, the imposition of this chiasmatic American econoculture is a fundamental historical break and a symptom of his particular definition of postmodernism.

There is something undeniably compelling about Jameson's description of the postmodern capitalist ideology of Americanization. Furthermore, his concerns should be associated with a genealogy of ethical (at times veering on apocalyptic) preoccupation with the threat to subjectivity posed by worldwide technological, economic, and juridical acceleration, a preoccupation that was perhaps most clearly formulated in Heidegger, recast in Hegelian terms by writers of the Frankfurt School such as Adorno, and treated most recently by Jacques Derrida.[2] But Jameson's argument fails to confront the conceptual challenges of that genealogy, and his reasoning looks very different when we go beyond its constative framework and interrogate its own relation, as an act of language, to the conceptual closures it describes. Ultimately, in this sense, the nimble lucidness of his description is depressed by the monotony of the dialectical suppositions that structure it and that merely replicate some of the most conservative philosophical biases of Western thought.

His *philosophical* treatment ultimately frames the response to globalism with an eventless binary indeterminacy based on a historical teleology that supposes an uninterrupted process of communication from one dialectical phase to another. Jameson believes that the past tells the future exactly where it is going: The mouth of communications technology transmits the (empty) content of a historical drive into the ear of the passive consumer. "The world has changed," it whispers; "there is no longer any change." Like Jameson, we are all hearing things, but what he is hearing in this case has no creative or imaginative effect on thought and ultimately leads only to a conceptual passivity that fails to confront the ironic relation between language and the real. Having defined globalism as an empty communicational concept that is nonetheless new, he posits that it slips in potentially two interpretive directions: In one direction, we have "a message about a new world culture" that is essentially optimism-inspiring, leading to a "postmodern celebration of difference and differentiation" in the expansion of global speech forums of the public sphere (1998, 56–57). In the other direction, the empty signifier of the new communicational concept is filled in pessimistically with a vision of the rigid order of economic production that underlies it: "we begin to fill in the empty signifier with visions of financial transfers and investments all over the world, and the new networks begin to swell with the commerce of some new, allegedly more flexible capitalism" (1998, 56). The latter paints a sinister "picture of standardization on an unparalleled new scale . . . of forced integration . . . into a world-system in which 'delinking' . . . is henceforth impossible and even unthinkable and inconceivable" (1998, 57). What faces the critic, then, is a choice between optimism regarding the new possibilities of communication and pessimism about the rigid division of labor in the new economic order.

Jameson does not just leave the binary to coagulate on its own, of course, but seeks to make "sparks fly" between the two terms, although ultimately what he presents as an indeterminacy in fact sides with a vision of the historical drive of capitalism rather than the open possibility of language and symbolic acts and their effects, precisely because it is the historical drive that his own language maintains as a teleology. Thus manipulated by his own dialectical framework, and despite what is admittedly a nod toward conceptual aperture in the hope of sparks in his final gesture, he has failed from the start to step out of the trap of a historical determinism, leaving completely intact the conceptual categories he otherwise promises to address. His description of globalism is limited by his unwillingness to risk a conceptual and linguistic displacement of the philosophical terms of the teleology that undergirds his argument—a teleology that continues to be such, regardless of its "postmodernism," precisely because its inception is a predetermined dialectical interiority that perpetually dooms its own possibilities to head banging against its own impasses.

Another way of putting this would be to say—recalling Miller's metaphor of criticism as a potentially ungovernable activity—that Jameson too easily allows his perception of a historical dynamic to govern the course of his criticism. The problem is a general one for many critics of globalism, few of whom have paused to consider either the complexity or the simplicity of the problem of whether perceived global-institutional changes should be allowed to dictate criticism's reimagination of its own activity. At issue is the paradox of a criticism that would permit itself to be conditioned by the unfolding of something that cannot itself be grasped outside of a critical framework. The risk is circular: in other words, a criticism too fixated on the "reality" of globalism would become a slave of its own constructions, regardless of "what is going on in the world" in a real sense. Perhaps still reacting against the timid theoretical formalism of two decades ago, much globalist discourse seems to have forgotten one of criticism's most interesting promises: to mingle with the enigmas of history by continuing to imagine and be imagined by the inception of thought outside or on the boundaries of its own teleological tendencies, and thus to seek out its own unassessible effects as history. Such a promise hardly seems possible when a world-historical process such as globalism is taken by critics both as the intellectual starting point to which they must directly respond and the uniform precinct of historical reality in which they are obliged to conceive the limits of their activity. (But we could promise in turn that promises are at their most imminent when they are missing or being broken and there is no need to lament yet.)

Part of the problem for U.S. Latin Americanist critics in the face of the supposed imperatives of globalism is that these imperatives are not external lures but grow almost seamlessly out of—are in large part produced by—trends in our own profession's critical-descriptive practices. Those trends include the tendency to frame Latin American artistic and cultural history as a single, homogenous critical unit, which in addition to making the region so much easier to master critically and pedagogically and allowing for institutional dominion over a more imposing field also has enabled globalist discourse to cast Latin American culture as a realm of specificities forever mourned and affirmed—in a binary dialectical framework—as the negative "other" of a European American symbolic order. The framework often differs strikingly from the ways (note the plural) in which critics in Latin America have conceived of their own national aesthetic–cultural histories and thus ignores a great many effective specificities of (versions of) trends and aesthetic–historical processes. When the standardized chronological "movements" in Latin American literature are put up against the versions of aesthetic and cultural histories in individual countries, the dissonances are pronounced. To take an example that indirectly concerns several of the chapters in this collection, we could point to the ways in which the Latin American "Boom," although coinciding chronologically with a crucial turning point in Mexican art of the midcentury—the struggle by artists against the ideological restrictions imposed by official sanction of the post-Revolutionary Mexican School—is difficult to relate meaningfully to (or more important, has not been related meaningfully to) that struggle. The problem of Latin American regional criticism is an old one and has been debated a great deal, but perhaps not enough at a time when proposals for paradigmatic changes toward globalism—thus seen as an outgrowth of prior homogenizing critical tendencies—threaten to shut off all memory of the problem, despite ubiquitous calls for attention to "specificities" and "singularities." (Although, again, threats also can be invitations and there is probably no need to cry wolf.)

For contemporary globalism discourse never stops calling for a return to specificities while at the same time ignoring the ways in which its own framework subsumes those specificities it ostensibly bears witness for under its own generalized critical categories. Again, this nearly always has to do with an annulment of the specificities within a dialectical framework that condemns them to a permanently mourned negativity, rather than a seeking out of specificities as possible inceptions of thought or as the effect of that which troubles and inaugurates critical language: the homeless intuition that refuses to merely confirm or reproduce prior critical categories. In this sense, the seeming sophistication of globalist discourse often masks the most conservative and unimaginative of critical strategies: the reading of specificities as metonymies of a dialectic of globalism in which the part under examination is assumed to fully express the workings—the historical teleology—of the whole. When the part in question is a work of art or an effective rhetorical instability of some kind, such a strategy can be revealed as the most metaphysical gesture of criticism's attempted mastery of its other, a gesture that has refused to confront or play with the impasses of the philosophical tradition.

A few examples demonstrate this trend more concretely, such as Doris Sommer's use of the term "particularities" in her introductory essay to an issue of the *Modern Language Quarterly* devoted to globalism. Sommer speaks favorably of what she refers to as (borrowing from Derrida) "untranslatable particularities," "as a renewed response to the pressures of dramatic 'globalization.' " But these particularities are further modified as "specificities of time and place" and "particularities of literary context and strategy" (1996, 119), which carefully limits them to phenomena visible to and envisioned by the mastery of the critical gaze and not those that would interrupt that gaze itself with the possibility of another rhetorical point of departure (texts, other critical formulations, rhetorical slippages, art, images, ghostly alterities). Furthermore, the will to mastery is only confirmed by the ostensible political value of these particular particularities: Sommer proceeds to observe that "pride of place may again be working, as it did in the nineteenth century, to safeguard a sense of personal and collective autonomy, even if the political promise of autonomy may not be immediately apparent" (1996, 119), thus protecting and distancing the particularities she seeks from any notion of rhetorical or conceptual risk. And, finally, the gesture toward particularities is further dissolved when Sommer frames them within the categories of a prior critical structure that avoids any risk of contamination by them. For the turn toward "untranslatable particularities" turns out to be merely a new version of the "culturally consolidated formulas of [nineteenth-century] *costumbrismo*" (1996, 120), the operation of which is predetermined by a critical–historical framework that was applied globally over the field of Latin American literary history. The critical language thus promotes "singularities" as a concept without really performatively interacting with them because it is more invested in perpetuating its own institutional–critical frame.

Although Sommer's introductory piece is not intended to be read as an in-depth treatment of the problem of specificities, it is nonetheless symptomatic of a tendency evident among more sustained analyses of the issue. An example of the latter is an essay by Alberto Moreiras, which shows similar problems in the treatment of singularities in North American globalism discourse. Moreiras intelligently critiques a recent version of the tradition that has sought to conceive of Latin America as an organic totality—namely, an attempt by Antonio Cornejo Polar to theorize that totality as heterogeneity—from a perspective interested in identifying the larger ideological–economic agency that writes or frames such formulations. Moreiras thus targets "a certain understanding of local singularity that serves the reproductive interests of the

neoliberal order by fostering consumption of (and thus, not coincidentally, annihilating) difference" (1996, 80). Nonetheless, by limiting
himself to identifying the inscriptions of economic interest and thus
narrowing the possibilities of his analysis within an economic predeter-
minacy or momentum, Moreiras settles himself securely within Jameson's dialectical framework, allowing that framework to totalize the
concept of singularities itself. Despite his brief, poetic evocation of "sin-
gularizing dreams" ("places where a singularity is enacted and an inten-
sity is affirmed, sites of a resistance which is also a withdrawal, a
monadic pulsion, a punctual, discardable identity, or a customized difference . . . virtual expressions of a certain distance, a certain inade-
quacy, a felt disjunction vis-a-vis global incorporation" [1996, 74–75]),
Moreiras is ultimately more interested in running headfirst into the
dialectical impasse set off in his text by italics, which seem to express
critical frustration rather than effect an emphasis: "*the very impossibility
of thinking heterogeneity beyond the processes of globalization that always
already determine it as heterogeneity for consumption*" (1996, 80).

Simply put, regardless of how sophisticated or even poetic the discourse *about* singularity becomes, it is incapable of meaningfully substi-
tuting for the effort to imagine, hallucinate, or enact those singularities
as points of departure of criticism. The observation brings us back to
the description of the chapters that follow, all of which are characterized by such an effort. That is, in all their variety, they share a sense that
criticism finds its effects by allowing itself to be spoken through by—
becoming lost in, interrupted by—the specificity of the topic being
treated, that is, its other, the singular dissonance of image or rhetoric.
And in the process, other ghostly singularities are evoked that have not
ceased to be contiguous with it, in particular "the nation." Although
such a "strategy" cannot be categorically said to escape the theoretical
(or fictional) impasses of globalism or of criticism itself, the performative effects of privileging the imagining of art and singularity in this
sense might be quite different from the effects of the propagation of
mere dialectical rigor.

Ultimately, the chapters in this collection speak and act for themselves, but the convention of the critical introduction calls for a brief
topographical description. Thematically, the chapters roughly follow a
historical chronology through all aspects of Mexican art of the twentieth
century, as traced out in their sequence, a strictly formal arrangement.
This does not mean that they are each pegged to a different time period

and then lined up in chronological order. In fact, their common concern is the possibility of effecting a contemporary critical performative, with the thematic focal point being a kind of secondary preoccupation, which nonetheless inaugurates the possibility of that critical performative. (The selection as a whole is not representational of historical periods, genres, or cultural groupings in any way; rather, its criteria is based on variety of critical approaches.) Although thus maintaining their primary emphasis on the "contemporary," the chapters nonetheless tend to look either "back" (those of the first half of the collection) or "forward" (the second half) in a historical–thematic sense. Thus, although both groups of articles keep one eye idling on the phantasms of globalism and contemporary culture, the arena where the effects of criticism are potentially felt, they focus with the other hallucinating eye—through the singularities that inaugurate its vision—on different directions of the future.

In looking back, the first group concentrates particularly on aesthetic and critical issues associated with modernism of the twenties and thirties, the period that by most accounts marks the inception of the modern Mexican state out of the cultural and ideological fragmentation of the Revolution—a process in which aesthetics played a crucial role—whereas the second group looks forward to themes more commonly associated with that always-provisional term, "postmodernism," to imagine more contemporary points of thematic reference. But rather than thereby establishing an opposition between nostalgia and vanguardism, the two tendencies continually exchange places and should be seen as versions of each other. For example, Karen Cordero Reiman looks back at the muralists of the post-Revolutionary period, but to focus on the representation of corporeal experience in contemporary installation art, whereas Debra Castillo looks forward to border literature, not to take leave of the past but to widen the scope of Mexican literature and criticism to thematics of gender and national borders that perhaps suggest possibilities of fresh critical revisions of earlier, more "centrist" Mexican literature. The effect of the two tendencies thus suggests backward and forward not as diverging strategies but as two variations on an openness to the critical future.

The first chapter in the collection, "Mexican Art on Display," by Olivier Debroise, opens the discussion with what we could call an unconventional overview of twentieth-century Mexican aesthetic–political history, covering a wide chronological expanse from the post-Revolutionary period to the Chiapas rebellion of the 1990s. What is unconventional about this overview is that its lens is not a history of Mexico or of Mexican aesthetics, but a history of the projection of "Mexico" in art expositions, both at home and abroad. But Debroise's focus is more critical than historically descriptive, centering on the dilemma of Mexican art's seemingly inextricable association with the icons of its pre-Hispanic or indigenous past—despite the clearly "constructed" nature of that association—as seen not only in officially sanctioned national art exhibits starting in the 1920s, but also in contemporary Mexican art that often repeats identity cliches despite its critical character. Debroise's conclusions might veer on pessimism, but there is also a critical enthusiasm at work in his call for an interrogation of the specific discursive sources or mechanisms out of which the pre-Hispanic or autochthonous iconicity has emerged in each case in which it is identified, an interrogation he himself puts into motion through attention to details of Mexican aesthetic history—particularly that aspect of this history that shares a border with the United States—that often are left to oblivion by regional historical frameworks.

Despite sharing many of its concerns with Debroise, Juan Bruce-Novoa's study of Mathias Goeritz and the story of Mexican art in the 1950s has a more optimistic assessment of the possibility of a Mexican art that would not simply be reducible to its iconic inscription by the fictive constructs of the national past. Bruce-Novoa examines this crucial period in which many Mexican artists successfully joined a post–World War II international artistic dialogue by refusing to merely serve the nationalist ideologies that had gradually come to coopt the work of artists over the previous three decades. Bruce-Novoa wants to maintain the possibility of speaking of an "artistic expression that is both national and progressively international" by demonstrating how Goeritz's work, in the face of fiercely conservative nationalist pressures, asserts its Mexicanness merely by its own passionate contiguity with Mexican spaces and times rather than by an appeal to the coded, iconic references of a mythical national past.

The two chapters that follow Bruce-Novoa's continue the contemporary critical dialogue with the ghosts of Mexican modernism, but specifically through a deliberate contrast of works and texts from that modernist period and more contemporary periods. Karen Cordero Reiman improvises her own phenomenological approach in contrasting corporeal references in the installation work of contemporary artists Silvia Gruner and Gerardo Suter with works by two of Mexico's most prominent post-Revolutionary muralists, Diego Rivera and Jose

Clemente Orozco. Cordero finds less problematic than Debroise or Bruce-Novoa the issue of Mexican art's references to a national past, and is more interested in utilizing that referential function to illuminate problems of the representation of sensorial experience in the earlier works—an aspect of muralism that has not been discussed much—by means of the contrast with Gruner and Suter, in whose work that experience is critically and ironically foregrounded.

Susan Schaffer likewise contrasts artistic works between the same periods and also brings literature into the discussion. In telling the story of Diego Rivera's abandonment of his Russian lover in Paris, the painter Angelina Beloff, her essay suggests an ironic allegory of the relation between the incipient Mexican nationalist art of the 1920s and European art. Schaffer does not just tell that story, however, but interrogates a conflict of its many narrations, focusing on Elena Poniatowska's aggressive rewriting of Bertram Wolfe's biography of Rivera in her novel, *Querido Diego, te abraza Quiela*. Schaffer's reading of the novel meticulously examines the "palimpsestic strategies" used by its author to ironically subvert Wolfe's representation of Beloff, who, in addition to being Rivera's companion in Paris for many years, also served as the subject for many of his cubist experiments, had a child with him, and was subsequently abandoned by him, along with his engagement with European art, upon his return to Mexico, where he quickly became consumed with the national muralism project. Schaffer weaves together discussions of text and image, demonstrating how Poniatowska's fictive re-creation of the same material worked over by Wolfe both parodies and revises the earlier version in the opening of an ironic space for her subject "in which room is allotted for complexity, contradiction, and evolution."

Jacobo Sefamí's contribution occupies a liminal space between the chapters of the first and the second parts of the collection, with its reading of poetry associated with an event that many critics (at least until the Zapatista rebellion in Chiapas) often have sought to take as a new historical point of reference for Mexican art and culture beyond the Revolution: the 1968 Tlatelolco student massacre. Sefamí seeks to demonstrate that the work of poet David Huerta, often characterized as emblematic of an aesthetic oblivious to concerns of national history, is, in fact, deeply preoccupied with its relation to that history. He shows through careful detail that Huerta, who was himself a witness to the massacre, not only treats Tlatelolco thematically but also allows it to be one of the "animating forces" of his poetry. Sefamí traces this theme throughout Huerta's production in a trajectory in which the "emblematic" function of Tlatelolco is seen to persist as an "allegory of a moment which came to a halt, a space of time which affixed itself to memory."

Danny Anderson leads the collection toward a questioning of traditional assumptions about the Mexican literary canon by examining contemporary struggles for positioning in the politics of the increasingly market- and global-oriented publishing world, recalling that the category of "literature," beyond its critical history as an institution in itself, undergoes continual redefinitions through the disputes and contingencies of the cultural sphere. His examination of recent literary production in Mexico focuses on the complex interactions between shifting social demands, market factors, and competitions for critical legitimacy among Mexican cultural institutions. Anderson's concern is to trouble the facile binary that is produced out of public debates on literature in Mexico: the division of literature into categories of "light" (associated with "feminine" and mass market tastes) and "serious" (associated with disinterested, "serious" aesthetic and formal experimentation). He shows how such a dichotomy ignores a highly productive, contingent, third category or noncategory. This alternative often emerges from what is considered "light" literature and often is associated with female writers, but it is marked by an unpredictable critical power that is formal, thematic, as well as social. Posing important questions about the horizons of literary and cultural production in Mexico, Anderson both implicitly and explicitly responds to factors on the cultural landscape that, despite their differences, are increasingly shared by North American and Mexican contexts.

Rebecca Biron is likewise concerned with the centrism of Mexican literary culture, more specifically with its problematic relation to gender, in her examination of the Mexican literary and media establishment's treatment of writer Elena Garro upon her 1993 return to Mexico following twenty years of exile in France. Just as Schaffer suggests Rivera's return from Europe as an ironic allegory of Mexican muralism's rejection of its own necessary "outside" in a European aesthetic, Biron presents Garro's exile as a metaphor for what she sees as the Mexican cultural establishment's problematic relation to gender. Biron takes as her starting point a contrast between the national eulogies for Garro and her former husband Octavio Paz, who both passed away in the same year. She proceeds to show how Mexican media and literary culture have tended to deny Garro's work a consideration on its own terms beyond the extractions and inventions of biographical allegory, particularly those associated with Garro's relation with Paz. Biron does not linger in her critical observation of this critical-media space but performs a careful reading of Garro's literary texts themselves, working around the cultural misconceptions that have led to "the production and erasure of Garro's voice in contemporary Mexico."

The theme of exile and transnational movement is given a different take in Montserrat Galí Boadella's discussion of Quebecois artist René Derouin. Galí Boadella discusses the history of "travelling artists" in Mexico and the strong romantic impulses behind their fascination with Mexico, in order to contrast them with the peculiar transnational syncretism of the experiences and work of Derouin. She characterizes the latter as a "migrant" rather than a "traveler," given the way Derouin's critical and artistic fascination with Mexico goes beyond a mere romantic distancing, with the country literally becoming the material of his work as well as—in a contrast with Quebec—the object of theoretical reflection on space, culture, and history. Galí Boadella traces out a detailed critical trajectory of Derouin's work, showing its technical and aesthetic development, in the process also reading Derouin's own conceptual observations through his written commentary in personal diaries and exhibition texts.

Debra Castillo interrogates the literary work of another kind of postmodern artist working at the limits of not only national but also gender boundaries. She characterizes the work of Tijuana writer Rosina Conde as marked by a "consciousness of liminality" that "extends itself to all realms of experience," including both the lives of ordinary middle-class people as well as the accented experience of prostitutes and striptease artists. For Castillo, the unhallowed spaces and unstable specificities of Conde's writing, combined with its refusal to accommodate the binaries of interpretive ideological closure, result in a productive instability. Conde's work is a pronounced refusal of erasure on the still-centralized Mexican national cultural scene. It also becomes a locus for questioning the regional and gender binaries that structure discursive constructions of Mexicanness. At the same time, however, Castillo acknowledges that Conde's stories refuse hospitality to their readers; their estrangement effects a productive sense of unease and questioning within the critic's own specific North American institutional context. Castillo thus shows Conde speaking to contemporary issues of criticism in the North American context.

Closing the collection is a chapter that at first might not appear to fit into a collection of this type, although its preoccupation with the Mexico-U.S. border meshes thematically with Castillo's article. "Fitting in," however, is precisely what is at issue, and Rolando Romero's chapter, by not fitting in, perhaps destabilizes lingering tendencies of the collection as a whole to maintain its scope within the geographical and historical borders of Mexico. Romero takes the collection across the border to dialogue directly with critical treatments of the postmodern hybrid in both Mexican and North American criticism, focusing specifically on the conflation of the figure of the Chicano with the place of the "alien" in the film *Blade Runner*. Romero critiques problems of cultural representation in the film and reflects more broadly on postmodernism's "inability to stare cultural hybridity in the face." He questions the tropes of avoidance that often permeate postmodern logic in its relation to that hybridity, tropes that cast the hybrid other as always either past or future but refuse to acknowledge it as an effect in the present, a logic that too easily becomes a convenient avoidance of encounter. In this way, flying in the face of a variety of postmodern formulations, Romero presents a reminder of postmodern criticism's privileging of deferrals over promises and interruptive possibilities. Romero haunts the critical tropes of postmodernism without seeking a resting place among them. He speaks from the outside, and perhaps in this sense, within the collection as a whole, speaks as the deterritorialization and continued effect of Mexico.

NOTES

1. See also Miller's more recent formulation of the challenges facing the academic disciplines of the contemporary university in his 1999 work (coauthored with Manuel Asensi).
2. In one of the most recent examples, an article devoted to religion, Derrida expands the concept of globalism to its widest implications in philosophical, economic, technoscientific, legal, and religious terms, coining the word "globalatinization" (in the French original, "*mondialatinización*") to refer to this "hyper-imperialist appropriation that has been underway now for centuries" (1996, 29) and is now led by Anglo-American language and culture. Globalism, Derrida states, is "at the same time hegemonic and finite, ultra-powerful and in the process of exhausting itself" (1996, 13). It is "running out of breath, however irresistible and imperial it still may be . . . [and] this expiring breath is blasting the ether of the world" (1996, 29).

WORKS CITED

Derrida, Jacques. 1996. "Faith and Knowledge: The Two Sources of 'Religion' at the Limits of Reason Alone." In *Religion*, ed. J. Derrida and Gianni Vattimo. Stanford, CA: Stanford University Press.

García Canclini, Néstor. 1995. *Consumidores y ciudadanos: Conflictos multiculturales de la globalización*. Mexico City: Grijalbo.

Jameson, Fredric. 1998. "Notes on Globalization as a Philosophical Issue." *The Cultures of Globalization*, ed. Fredric Jameson and Masao Miyoshi, 54–77. Durham, NC: Duke University Press.

Kristof, Nicholas D. 1999. "At This Rate, We'll Be Global in Another Hundred Years." *New York Times*, 23 May, sec. 4:1.

Miller, J. Hillis. 1995. "Governing the Ungovernable: Literary Study in the Transnational University." *Between the Lines* 2, no. 2 (Winter): 2–3.

Miller, J. Hillis, and Manuel Asensi. 1999. *Black Holes/J. Hillis Miller: Or, Bustrofedonic Reading*. Stanford, CA: Stanford University Press.

Moreiras, Alberto. 1996. "A Storm Blowing from Paradise: Negative Globality and Latin American Cultural Studies." *Siglo XX = 20th Century* 14: 59–84.

Ryan, Judith. 1996. "Shrunk to an Interloper." In *Field Work: Sites in Literary and Cultural Studies*, ed. Marjorie Garber, Paul B. Franklin, and Rebecca L. Walkowitz, 1–78. New York: Routledge.

Sassen, Saskia. 1996. *Losing Control? Sovereignty in an Age of Globalization*. New York: Columbia University Press.

Sommer, Doris. 1996. "The Places of History: Regionalism Revisited in Latin America." *Modern Language Quarterly* 57: 119–127.

1

Mexican Art on Display

Olivier Debroise

Translated by James Oles

O n the morning of 1 January 1994, Mexico woke up with a terrible hangover. A war had been declared in the southern state of Chiapas by an indigenous army whose leaders wore black ski masks. Before dawn, the rebels had taken various towns and were advancing toward other cities. Taken by surprise, the army seemed unable to stop them. A major confrontation occurred in the marketplace of the town of Ocosingo, where the rebels got trapped by the army, but the rebels quickly vanished into the rain forest. Since the uprising, the Zapatista Army of National Liberation has been negotiating, via the press, with almost all sectors of Mexican society. Perceived initially as outdated Marxist guerrillas, the Zapatistas quickly revealed their generous, even noble, national program of democratic change, which could not be confused with any ideological or millenarist movement previously seen in Latin America, such as Peru's Shining Path or other more recent violent revolts in certain areas of the Mexican highlands. Carrying out the first postcommunist uprising—as Carlos Fuentes had described it—the rebels quickly transcended basic demands for land and welfare, inserting their struggle into the continuing need for a more open, pluralistic, and multiethnic society. The realistic, precise, and often humorous discourse of the Zapatista leaders threatened the foundations of Mexico's strongest and oldest institutions and challenged the boundaries of the cultural discourse current in the country. It not only challenged the institutions, it also radically fragmented the ways Mexicans had been thinking about themselves for the past decades. The Zapatistas became part of a new mythology—they symbolized a different Mexico. Not the least of their reminders was the brutal rediscovery that a quarter of the country's population (more than twenty million Mexicans) was indigenous and still spoke native languages.[1]

As in the nineteenth century, the "indigenous problem" had been obliterated from official Mexican ideology and discourse, buried for decades under a mythical and rhetorical construction developed in the 1920s to unite, through reduction, disconnected ethnic fragments. In this century, an entire political system was constructed around the generally accepted idea of *mestizaje* (miscegenation). A biological and therefore determinist concept, *mestizaje* has been applied to social and cultural issues to define Mexico's difference from Western models by validating the destroyed indigenous substrate.

The idea of *mestizo* culture was broadly accepted as the official discourse because it was simple and even poetic and filled the need for defining what is national in a country built upon ruins. But its very simplicity and appeal erased deeper historical and cultural nuances—and menaces. *Mestizo* identity as nationalism had failed because it dictated a schizophrenia that few individuals really shared, erasing not only crucial differences between multiple ethnic groups, but also the plurality and complexity of foreign immigration, which intensified in the twentieth century. In addition, self-identity is not only determined by blood, language, or religion, but also by an individual's choice to belong to this or that culture.

One of clearest constructions of this ideology took place in the visual arts, which were used to exemplify nationality for the regimes of the postrevolutionary period. The so-called Mexican Renaissance—and, even more, the selection of specific artworks that "revealed" this supposed Renaissance—had been heavily promoted abroad by the Mexican government.

In late 1921, the Mexican government, acting through the Ministry of Trade and Industry, hired an American journalist who had been reporting for the past year and a half about the postrevolutionary struggles for power in Mexico. The journalist, Katherine Anne Porter, proposed putting together an exhibition of Mexican art and sending it to the United States to display to foreign eyes the recent cultural development of the country. None of the famous murals had yet been painted, and the movement, later called the Mexican Renaissance, was just beginning to take shape. Nevertheless, the concept was in the air. The show enthusiastically conceived by Porter drew upon an extremely successful exhibition of Mexican folk art, organized a few months before by the influential landscape painter and political activist, Gerardo Murillo, known as Dr. Atl. That exhibition was the most important and best-received event of the celebration of the Centennial of Mexican Independence from Spain, held in September 1921. Although assembled in a few short weeks, Atl's show was the result of knowledge accumulated over more than a decade by a close group of scholars and artists, most of them from Guadalajara: anthropologist Manuel Gamio; painter and expert on colonial architecture Jorge Enciso; Enciso's brother-in-law, Adolfo Best Maugard; and painter Roberto Montenegro. The exhibition of Mexican popular arts was the culmination of an intellectual project of "national rediscovery" that this aristocratic and well-educated group of intellectuals started in the midst of the Revolution, and that had gained strength in 1915, despite the civil war.

Somehow forgotten as an archaeologist, Manuel Gamio must be considered the primary influence behind the Mexican artistic movement of the 1920s; he shaped the concept of Mexicanness, based on anthropological studies, that marked the whole history of the art in Mexico in the twentieth century. A student of anthropologist Franz Boas at Columbia University, Gamio returned to Mexico with Boas in 1912 to participate in the first American archaeological excavation using stratigraphy. With Boas, he founded the International School of Anthropology, based in Mexico City, and was appointed director when Boas left the country. Gamio then designed an ambitious political program, based on anthropological research, which resulted in his successful 1915 book *Forjando patria (pro mexicanismo)* [Forging a Fatherland (Pro Mexicanism)]. He was appointed director of a new Department of Anthropology at the Ministry of Agriculture, and, despite the war, was able to put his theories to the test in a massive program in the Valley of Teotihuacan, forty miles northeast of Mexico City.

The core of Gamio's project was the archaeological excavation of the ruins, but more than just digging was involved. Anthropological issues, matters of religion and ritual, and sophisticated political aims were also part of Gamio's scope. The goal was more than just acquiring knowledge for the recovery of ancient glories; the project was also designed to restore the pride of the indigenous people who lived nearby. It would also draw an increasing number of tourists to the valley, thus improving the local economy. The study of customs and rituals, such as how local populations reinterpreted Catholicism through the influence of ancient religion, was directed toward a rehabilitation program, a "smooth" but certain and definitive inclusion of these "primitives" into the modern Mexico that was to emerge from the Revolution. As other scholars have shown, despite his good will and progressive philosophy, Gamio failed to fully value the Indians' lifestyle. He was unable to tolerate most of the ceremonies, rituals, and medical treatments that he witnessed, and all he could really praise were the indigenous arts and crafts, such as embroidery and pottery, music, songs, and dances. Contradicting official Mexican history, Gamio admitted the achievements of the colonial period, mainly those of the first years after the conquest, the crucial period of social, political, and cultural blending, and (although with certain reservations because of his anticlericalism) the accomplishment of the Franciscan missionaries. According to David Brading, "The achievement of Manuel Gamio was to reinstate Anáhuac as the glorious foundation of Mexican history and culture, thus reversing a century of Liberal scorn. Equally important, he rejected neo-classical canons in aesthetic judgment, and demanded a revaluation of native-born forms" (1988, 77).

These forms were actually shaped during the first fifty or sixty years *after* the Conquest and implied the blending of pre-Columbian and medieval European styles; Mexico's relative isolation over the following four centuries allowed for their preservation, until individuals such as Gamio would praise them as emblematic of Mexico's identity. His program of integrating the Indians into modern Mexico, however, required the modernization of their craft industry. He declared, for example, that "the Department [of Anthropology] only tries to industrialize the production and sale of pottery according to modern methods, and it allows at the same time full freedom to the potters to express and develop their own artistic taste and personality" (1922, xc). Gamio also argued that Mexican artists should seek inspiration from these arts and crafts. Only if artists worked as "anthropologists" and got closer to the remarkable Indian craftsmen, only if they learned archaeology and understood their past through the eyes of these descendants of ancient civilizations, would Mexico be able to construct a distinctive, and important, art.

Manuel Gamio was the intellect behind Dr. Atl's show of Mexican popular arts inaugurated by President Alvaro Obregón himself on 19 September 1921, in a facility on Avenida Madero in Mexico City. Under Gamio and Enciso's supervision, a group of artists and "agents" in different regions gathered artifacts for the show. Although organized quickly, the Exposition of Mexican Popular Arts can be read as the accomplishment of an intellectual project of national rediscovery. It can also be considered the peak of a neocolonial fashion, much more evident in architecture than in the visual arts.[2]

In the first chapter of the book issued for the show, Atl asserts: "Indian industries cannot be transformed or improved: they are what they are."[3] This axiom contradicts the evolutionary ideas outlined by Gamio and restrains any possible improvement or development. The obsession for maintaining ethnic crafts in a supposed purity would not only imprint tourist discourse but also twentieth-century anthropology in Mexico. Such a nostalgic quest for artifacts frozen in a mythical time, in fact, disavows the craftsman, reducing his task to that of a simple copyist who is unable to create new forms, be influenced, or to prosper; it also widened the increasing gap (fundamentally racial) between artist and craftsman. Paradoxically, the survival and permanence of popular arts are because of, even today, their capacity to adjust to the taste of each period, including the adoption of new techniques, in spite of the reiterated bemoanings of "the lovers of Mexico" in the face of such innovation.[4] The initiative of presenting popular arts in the framework of the Centennial not only responded to cultural zeal, but also was inspired by a deep nostalgia: "[these crafts] will disappear as soon as Mexico definitively enters its period of industrial evolution, to which in fact it is destined by its wealth and its geographical situation," presumed the always determinist Atl (1980, 33).

Atl's incorporations and exclusions in his catalogue are extremely revealing: he, of course, praises pottery, whose study he organized by regions and which takes up about half of the book. Weaving takes second place, followed by crafts "in decadence": lacquerware, feather mosaics, goldwork, ironwork, carpentry, and religious painting (compared, based on the idea of the "copy," with primitive art). Complete chapters are devoted to saddlery (significantly, Atl emphasizes pieces employed in *charrería*, the Mexican nobleman's art of horse riding), vernacular architecture, and illustrated broadsheets.

Without exception, all of the cultural manifestations described by Atl belong to those parts of Mexico where *mestizo* culture was strongest because of communication networks. Atl excludes or forgets "primary" artifacts like those ethnologist Frederick Starr classified at the end of the nineteenth century—ornate Huichol weavings and Otomí or Mixtec tools made from organic material (gourds, canes, reeds, and so on).[5] Thus, Atl's discourse fits intentionally within the neocolonial revival shown clearly in the architectural designs of Vasconcelos's time.

Gamio was the mastermind behind the vogue for Mexican arts and crafts that appeared in vaudeville sets, decorative arts, public festivals, and, of course, the first mural decorations and artistic education programs of the 1920s, particularly the establishment of rural open-air schools, where young students were encouraged to paint what they wanted, how they wanted, in the belief that the "natural talent" of the Mexican race would appear "spontaneously" in their works. Although Gamio was removed from political decision making in 1925, his ideas remained current, with few changes, through the early 1930s. In the late 1920s, under the auspices of the Social Science Research Council, Gamio conducted extensive studies of Mexican communities of the United States: He was a pioneer in that area as well.

Katherine Anne Porter's project for a touring exhibition of Mexican arts and crafts in the United States was accepted because it fit with the Mexican government's desire for diplomatic recognition. For nationalistic reasons, however, a young Mexican painter named Xavier Guerrero, then working on the first mural decorations under the direction of Roberto Montenegro, was appointed its artistic director. Porter was not skilled in curating exhibitions, but she had numerous assistants: She later confessed that Gamio himself supported the show and supervised the selection of objects; painters Adolfo Best Maugard and Jorge Enciso functioned as leaders of the team; Roberto Montenegro helped out, despite having just set up the September show and being busy painting his first mural; and younger collaborators included Miguel Covarrubias, Manuel Rodríguez Lozano, and Carlos Mérida. Diego Rivera himself, who just returned from ten years among the Parisian avant-garde, was apparently involved in collecting artifacts.

While her assistants were selecting the works, Porter wrote, in two weeks, the essay for a now extremely rare catalogue, her forty-five-page *Outline of Mexican Popular Art*, for which photographer Roberto Turnbull provided the illustrations. Then, while the show was being crated in Mexico City, Porter traveled to the United States to find galleries for the exhibition. She later recalled:

> I couldn't get any. I tried the Corcoran in Washington, the Anderson in New York, and in Saint Louis and Chicago, and in all cases they wouldn't let us have the gallery—because the political pressure had been put on, the U.S.

government did not allow the show to come into the country because it was "political propaganda" and the government hadn't recognized Obregón's government. . . . You can't imagine the number of powerful men who were determined that the government was not going to be recognized. And they attacked that show, they wouldn't let us take it into the country. Finally somebody said if we'd bring it to California they would see that we got it going. So we took up there, a great trainload of specimens, but we were stopped at the border.[6] (Hank López 1965, 62)

Porter did not travel with her show to California. But in January 1922, the exhibit eventually was installed at 807 West 7th Street, Los Angeles, by Guerrero and Best Maugard, with the help of the Mexican consul. It was an enormous success: The *Los Angeles Times* reported an average of three thousand to four thousand visitors daily during the two weeks of the display. Then the show was dismantled and the works, which had entered the United States on a special agreement as "property of the Mexican government," were distributed to Mexican consulates all over the country. It should be pointed out that among the beautiful crafts that seduced Californians, the show also included a small selection of modern art: paintings by Adolfo Best Maugard, Xavier Guerrero, and Diego Rivera were hung alongside the embroideries, *serapes,* brilliant pottery, and lacquerware. Although it is uncertain what these paintings were, they seem to have been a sort of footnote to the exhibition, a way of showing that Mexicans still practiced the decorative arts of their ancestors. Based on the work these artists were producing at the time, it can be inferred that the works exhibited contained both "decorative" and popular traits. As far as I know, none of these paintings were ever mentioned in the reviews of the show.

Porter's show was the first significant survey of Mexican art ever presented abroad, and, as such, it set the course for exhibitions of Mexican art abroad and would be repeated, with few conceptual changes, many times over the following seventy years. Porter's enthusiastic *Outline of Mexican Popular Art*, mainly based on Gamio's concepts and her artistic friends' aesthetic taste, would merely be refined by scholars in the late 1920s, becoming canonical between 1928 and 1930, at the beginning of a vogue for Mexico and Mexican arts and crafts that coincided, on the one hand, with a slowdown of artistic activity in Mexico—which allowed artists to shape the history of the movement they had just been involved in—and, on the other hand, with the economic and moral crisis of the Great Depression in the United States.[7]

Porter's attempt soon would be refined by writer Anita Brenner. In the fall of 1928, Brenner was working on a book on folk art, financed by the National University, to be called *Mexican Decorative Arts*. For reasons that remain unclear, this book was never finished, although it formed the basis for her famous *Idols behind Altars*, published in New York in 1929. That same fall, Brenner curated a show of modern Mexican art, financed by the Rockefeller Foundation, for the Art Center in New York. In this case, the show was seemingly designed to prove that Mexican social policy was not "Bolshevist."

Born in Aguascalientes, Mexico, where her father worked for Guggenheim's mining interests, Brenner grew up in Mexico until the Revolution sent her family fleeing to San Antonio. Her journalistic career began in 1924 with an extremely interesting article in *The Nation* entitled, "The Jew in Mexico," in which she explained why there was no "Jewish question" in Mexico. In perfect correspondence with Gamio's program, she stated that "In spite of rabbis, Jewish homes, papers, and clubs, the Jew will be forced into the fiber of the coming Mexico. He is losing himself in a race that is finding itself. . . . Whether he is merchant, teacher, peddler, or artist, educated or ignorant, [he] is becoming as Mexican a Mexican as the descendant of the *conquistador* or the son of the native Indian. He is giving and will give, to the Mexico of the future, not only his work, his money, or his brain, but literally himself" (1924, 212). Brenner was at least speaking for herself, for she became one of the leading promoters of Mexican art, literally giving herself to the cause.[8]

Idols behind Altars, not surprisingly, also recalls Gamio's program.[9] In a much more lyrical, less scientific, and perhaps less prejudiced way, Brenner first sketched a historical synthesis of Mexican history, emphasizing the religious aspects. Her opening chapter, "Mexican Messiah," is the first clear compendium of the ideas about miscegenation, about the cultural exchanges and misunderstandings that were shaped during the colonial period. Brenner's Jewish background gave her the distance she needed to recognize the strengths of indigenous Catholicism, which no scholars such as Gamio—Catholic by upbringing and anticlerical by choice, overwhelmed by the repressive factors of this religion—would have stated. As a journalist and a promoter, Brenner deliberately simplified an extremely complex phenomenon, evidenced by the title of her book: Excavating behind altars, one could find ancient idols still meaningful for the inhabitants; sitting the idol on the altar, a new Messiah will upsurge, Mexico will be reborn. The same concept, though seen as a negative force rather than a positive one, was current among the forces of the Spanish Inquisition as early as the 1570s.

In the second half of her book, Brenner recounts the rise of the Mexican Renaissance, the "reborn Mexico" of her theory. As an active part of the process, she wrote this very first overview of the Mexican Renaissance from a similarly reductionist viewpoint. Clearly, she desired to make it appealing and even exotic to her audience and could not avoid constant references to cultural background, to the "sources" of innate Mexican artistic talent that, according to her, were finally flowing and prospering in postrevolutionary Mexico. As José Clemente Orozco himself observed at the time, she completely banished from her essay any mention of art that did not fit into her scheme: namely, the urban avant-garde movement of the Estridentistas, the open-air schools where young students painted industrial workers and smoky industries rather than idyllic rural landscapes, and so on.

At the Art Center, Brenner intermingled the works of modern Mexican artists (including a few older academic painters who made their last appearance in this show[10]) with folk painting, mainly religious *retablos* (small popular and devotional paintings commemorating miracles) and a few examples of traditional arts and crafts. Thus, reversing the prominence of Porter's Los Angeles exhibit, folk art had become a footnote illuminating the Moderns.

In 1930, at the beginning of an extremely bitter struggle between British and American oil companies over the control of Mexican extraction wells, U.S. Ambassador Dwight Morrow convinced the Carnegie Corporation to sponsor an extensive show of Mexican art at the Metropolitan Museum in New York. Homer Saint-Gaudens, Director of Fine Arts at the Carnegie Institute of Art in Pittsburgh, was appointed curator on behalf of the American Federation of Arts and was sent to Mexico for a two-week adventure in selecting the works. Saint-Gaudens, who seems to have had no previous interest in or contact with Mexico, was fortunate to meet with Count René d'Harnoncourt, an Austrian refugee living in Mexico City and a dealer in antiques and crafts. Count d'Harnoncourt was well known among the painters of the now ten-year-old Mexican Renaissance. In what was a major achievement for the time, works of art were selected, wrapped, packed, and conveyed to New York by Jean Charlot—a French painter who became one of the pioneers of muralism in 1921—and Frances Flynn Paine, a prominent descendent of a wealthy Virginia family, closely acquainted with Abby Aldrich Rockefeller, who was also buying antiques in Mexico to refurbish colonial Williamsburg.

Similar to Porter's previous exhibition, the Metropolitan show was chiefly composed of folk art, but included a representative selection of paintings by modern Mexican artists. As one reviewer stated,

> In two ways the current Exhibition of Mexican Art is unique. First, it is the national expression of a whole people; second, it is the first time that technical skill and material have been subordinated to the content of idea, the interpretation of a single culture. The result is an exhibition that is extraordinarily easy to understand and of wide appeal. In the simple objects, the natural spirit of the Mexican people is naïvely and unselfconsciously expressed; in the more sophisticated and calculated art of Orozco, Rivera, Castellanos, and their compatriots, the simple peasant work finds amplification of meanings. ("Exhibition of Mexican Art," 113)

This deliberate mixture of different works was not praised by everyone: According to reviewer Ella S. Siple in *Burlington Magazine*, the exhibition "was a veritable confusion of Mexican arts, like a country fair in its arrangement, but without any of the local color which enlivens a real country fair. Fine Diego Riveras, all too few, were skied; fine pottery jars were on the floor. It gave one the intimate feeling of having been allowed in the gallery before the curators had started to arrange it, before the judges had eliminated a mass of insignificant clutter" (1931, 157).

Between 1920 and 1928, diverse Mexican artists released a number of aesthetic manifestos, all of which called for the emergence of "modern" art in the nation. "Modern" meant, in part, "universal," and one path to such universality was the incorporation of the "primitive." For Mexican artists, this "primitive" was local and omnipresent, not imported from Africa or Oceania, but it was no less "exotic." Francisco Reyes Palma (1990) has called this process "the nationalization of the avant-garde," and it occurred throughout the hemisphere at about the same time. From Anita Brenner on, however, curators and writers mainly would emphasize the adoption of "primitive" forms and styles, and the continuity of such forms and styles, while practically denying more important and obvious formal ruptures. The "primitive" began to overshadow the "avant-garde," counter to most artists' intentions.

The 1930 Metropolitan exhibit, for example, included and even privileged timeless folk art, archaic ethnosemiotic objects that "represented" the specificity of Mexican culture to the eyes of the "others." Nineteenth-century academic paintings, even those with themes related to Mexican identity, were systematically banished, as were the earliest works of those that had helped forge the Mexican Renaissance: Rivera's symbolist and cubist works, Orozco's political caricatures, Siqueiros's fashionable art-nouveau watercolors. The curators also excluded certain types of folk art, including items made for the tourist trade or those considered too "European," such as the Spanish-style pottery of Puebla, still fashionable a few years earlier. What was praised was the cultural blending of the past, not the present. What was supported was the use of folk artifacts as sources by cultivated, aristocratic Mexican artists: Only they, supposedly, could understand the meaning of these objects because of their contact with the avant-garde.

Even more than Katherine Anne Porter's *Outline*, Brenner's *Idols behind Altars* established a canon for later exhibitions: As in Brenner's book, the Art Center and Metropolitan Museum exhibits showed clearly that modern Mexican painting could not be appreciated fully without "didactic" references to traditional origins, to the legendary past of colonial Mexico and the blending of cultures that distinguished it from all others. Modern Mexican paintings apparently could not stand on their own as the provocative creations of a real avant-garde that defined itself in relation to technical progress (like the futurists) or to political contexts (like the Russian Constructivists).

Although North American experts in Mexican art and cultural history were usually involved in the design of these shows, it was the Mexican government that, for diplomatic and economic reasons, was behind them all. The same formula was repeated at the Museum of Modern Art (MoMA) in 1940, in the context of World War II and the Good Neighbor Policy, and again in 1952, when an even bigger megashow was sent to Paris, at a time when postwar France sought to recover her cultural dominion through the embrace of world art; and yet again with the exhibit "Mexico: Splendors of 30 Centuries" held at the Metropolitan Museum of Art, in 1990, at the beginning of the North American Free Trade Agreement (NAFTA) debates.

This ideology was condemned as populist from the very beginning. Orozco violently rejected the folkloric aspects of official Mexican culture—and Anita Brenner's writings—in the 1920s. Even in 1940, while painting his *Dive Bomber and Tank* in situ at MoMA (a work that may be his most powerful fresco, although it was rarely displayed until recently, because it does not look very Mexican), Orozco viewed his presence as merely that of a "Mexican clown" in an American circus. This antifolkloric stance left Orozco identified with the right, something that had also happened to the Contemporáneos, a group of intellectuals and poets named for their influential literary magazine of the 1930s.

The Contemporáneos called for independence and creative freedom from aesthetic prejudice and identified with French writers, particularly with André Gide's "apolitical militancy" and André Breton's surrealism. The members of this marginal group called for internationalism in culture without denying their Mexicanness; instead, they hoped to unite certain aspects of the European avant-garde with a recognition of their own cultural background. Rufino Tamayo was closely affiliated with these writers and was the first to apply in Mexico the slogan "regionalism is internationalism," bringing the archaic—forms taken from pre-Columbian sculpture—into modernism. Tamayo's position fit perfectly within a Mexican political program that by the 1950s stressed accelerated incorporation into the global economy while simultaneously building impressive museums all around the country to preserve the remains of pre-Conquest cultures.

Not surprisingly, though, Tamayo's retrospective at the Guggenheim Museum in 1979, eloquently called "Myth and Magic"—a title apparently suggested by Octavio Paz—included a selection of pre-Columbian stone sculptures, some from Tamayo's own collection, and the inevitable folk objects, thus following Brenner's canon. In 1916, pre-Columbian sculptures had been juxtaposed with Diego Rivera's cubist works in an almost forgotten show held by Marius de Zayas at the Modern Gallery in New York. De Zayas forced the comparison between cubist Riveras and "primitive" pre-Columbian art, thus drawing a parallel between Rivera and Picasso—even though Rivera had no specific interest in Mesoamerican sculpture at that time—making the comparison arbitrary and even absurd. In the Tamayo show, deputy director of the Guggenheim Henry Berg explained timidly—clearly revealing his naïveté on the issue—that "the relationship between Tamayo's art and these pre-Columbian and popular works cannot be explained in terms of specific individual parallels, nor does this exhibition seek to make such a point. Rather, what is suggested here is that these traditional objects form a visual sounding board which adds resonance to the totality of Tamayo's assembled works" (1979, 6). Was the justification, then, of such a juxtaposition simply poetic? By the early 1980s, the conflict over Mexican identity seemed to have come to an end, resolving itself in the assumption that the two extremities coexisted without conflict: Mexico was a modern nation built on an ancient past, struggling to abandon its third world connotations.

But the debate over identity had a surprising revival in the 1980s, in great part because of the rapid restructuring of Mexican society following an intense economic and social crisis. The political and industrial elites reinforced their power, and to obscure or deny their sale of the entire country to foreign economic interests, they reinforced the nationalist discourse—building even more museums, sponsoring pseudohistorical programs on commercial television, supporting an art market that validated in dollars the treasures of the past, and sending forth all sorts of cultural and artistic proposals that confirm the good health of the national identity. Meanwhile, scholars, writers, and artists had become increasingly suspicious of these official discourses, embarking upon a complete revision of such dogmatic ideological montages, highlighting their theatrical solemnity. Their attempts at decolonization sometimes use the same basic images, but invert the process to show the continuity of interrupted pieces of identity and fragmented memories.

Even in the most recent contemporary shows of Mexican art, such as the Diego Rivera retrospective in Cleveland and Los Angeles, the "Modern Mexican Art" exhibit in Montreal (both curated by Luis Martín Lozano), the massive show of Mayan art presented in Venice in 1999—and in same cases, in the shaping of Chicano and Mexican American exhibitions as well—it seems extremely difficult, if not impossible, to avoid the juxtapositions of folk and high art, to escape from the cliché of the "talented Mexicans" nurtured by their past, to critique this idea of artistic continuity between three or four or more historical eras. No one can escape Gamio, it seems, who in 1929 wrote that "In [Mexico] the stages of civilization which humanity has been climbing since over a hundred centuries ago are reproduced, living and palpitating, before the traveler" (11). Traveling in Mexico or visiting an exposition of Mexican art, the tourist could take in thirty centuries in a single gaze.

Can we distance ourselves from this conventional approach? Can we attempt a new way of understanding Mexican artistic production of the twentieth century, including contemporary art, from our, let us say, "postmodern" perspective? I don't think so.

Mexican artists of the Renaissance of the 1920s, and contemporary artists today, still make constant references to earlier periods—whether pre-Columbian, colonial, or folk—even though a few seem to distance themselves consciously from anything that looks or smells Mexican.[11]

Through the use of an Olmec mask, David Alfaro Siqueiros visually critiqued "ethnography" in his painting of 1939 of the same name; Manuel Rodríguez Lozano and Frida Kahlo collected nineteenth-century *retablos*, which influenced their own work; the contemporary Mexican artist Silvia Gruner takes domestic objects from rural markets and transforms them into installations; and Francis Alÿs, a Belgian artist resident in Mexico since 1990, works with popular billboard painters in series of enameled pastiches of his own diminutive paintings. These and many others are engaged in a discourse on the range and limits of "Mexicanness," on their personal understanding of their inclusion (or even exclusion) from "national identity," what it represents, and how it has been representing.

Such a metadiscourse, such referential art, may justify curatorial projects based on reflexive and revisionist juxtapositions. Rather than unfocused "continuities," curators and scholars might make more precise readings of works by confronting them with their specific sources. A unique, but eloquent, example might be to examine just what precise knowledge Diego Rivera possessed in 1922, when he included the well-known—but often misinterpreted—statue of the Aztec deity Xochipilli in his Education Ministry murals. Did he assume, as we do now, that the god was in a drug-induced ecstasy? What readings and what iconographic sources did he use in his reinterpretation of the great market of Tlaltelolco, depicted in his National Palace murals of 1945?

The example of Siqueiros's *Ethnography*, now at MoMA, is especially revealing. The artist used a wooden mask, found in the state of Guerrero and illegally exported to the United States (in the luggage of an American anthropologist), where it is now housed in the American Museum of Natural History. Siqueiros's painting is not only a commentary on the reuse of artifacts by modern painters who were also collectors—and thus looters—of pre-Columbian artifacts, but also a metadiscourse on the problematic and compromised aspects of anthropology itself. Given recent events in Mexico, understanding anthropology's goals and discourses and its intersection with the visual arts (especially photography) may be more important than just understanding the art itself.

This type of intellectual approach, rather than a purely sensual one, this type of careful deconstruction not only of the sources of the artists but of their goals—and "goals" were extremely important to artists so aware of the political concerns of their art as were the Mexican muralists—is rarely attempted. Official institutions, the sponsors of so much of what happens in the field of Mexican art, are adverse to any strong critiques of their national heroes—the artists—because such critiques go against the diplomatic or touristic objectives of the exhibitions. Complexity also interferes with the almost inevitable linear discourse of these blockbuster constructions that seek to show everything, such as the famous megashow, "Splendors of Thirty Centuries," which toured the United States during the Salinas regime.

Is it really any coincidence that of the more recent Mexican artists, those who have been most promoted and examined abroad in the past few years are those who have been consciously rummaging through Mexican cultural history, using the same sorts of artifacts and cultural references that typified earlier generations? In their paintings, photographs, neoconceptual installations, and performances, these artists incorporate the curatorial discourse I described above—and the same timeless artifacts, the same ethnosemiotic objects, the same approaches to art that are related to craftsmanship and a sort of anonymity (Rubén Ortiz's collective works with low-rider designers in Southern California; Abraham Cruzvillegas's intense workshop with "masters" of folk art from Michoacán; Francis Alÿs's ambiguous relationship with the billboardmakers, to mention a few). Sometimes they work in a deconstructive mode, exploring self-identity, multiculturalism, and gender issues, but more often they work in a nostalgic, poetic, and even devotional way.

The actual inclusion of folk and pre-Columbian artifacts in the work of the Silvia Gruner; the recycling of stereotyped tourist icons by Javier de la Garza; the constant reminiscences of popular kitsch in Julio Galán's paintings; Germán Venegas's sculptural bas-reliefs; the bizarre mixture of New York art world sophistication and Mexico's most prosaic clichés in Guillermo Gómez Peña's performances; the idolatrous bodies in the photographs of Gerardo Suter; the political discourse on the misuse of stereotypes in the media in Rubén Ortiz's films and videos, are just a few examples. It seems as if these artists have coopted the official poetics of representing Mexico and are thus forcing the curators to once again make the same connections, the same juxtapositions, and the same poetical evocations. Some of us realize that this approach is reductive, even inapplicable in certain cases. Few realize that we are playing with the same old clichés, that we are simply restoring the official clichés—and thus official politics—to a privileged position.

NOTES

1. A preliminary version of this essay was presented as a lecture at the Center for Cultural Studies at Bard College, Annandale-on-Hudson, New York, in March 1994, as part of a program for developing the center's curriculum. Although the presentation was originally conceived during the early days of the Zapatista uprising, in reworking this piece five years later it did not seem to me that the role of that rebellion had lost its significance. The Zapatista movement has changed little beyond (and despite) publicity and international legitimization, as demonstrated by recent news from the state of Chiapas. It should be noted that the 2000 presidential elections marked urban Mexico's general frustration with, and rejection of, the cultural politics of the governing party as described in this article.

2. This fashion relates to parallel movements in Southern California around 1914–1915. For San Diego's Panama–California Exhibition, New York architect Bertram Grosvenor Goodhue (who illustrated Sylvester Baxter's seminal work on Spanish-Colonial architecture in Mexico, published in 1901) attempted to underline a Hispanic identity in the young but affluent American state. See Clara Bargellini (1992).

3. I am citing the second issue of the book, published in two volumes in 1922 by Editorial Cvltura, which accompanied the exposition when it traveled to Brazil, and differs in few details from the 1921 version.

4. Fomento Cultural Banamex, one of Mexico's few cultural foundations, recently published a major catalogue of folk art in many aspects similar to Atl's 1921 survey but with a significant difference: The craftsmen and craftswomen are now fully identified as authors, and their portraits have even more importance in the layout of this "encyclopedia" than the objects themselves ("*Grandes maestros*," 1999).

5. See Frederick Starr (1899a and 1899b).

6. See also Enrique Hank López (1981) and Thomas F. Walsh (1992).

7. See James Oles (1993).

8. On Brenner's career, see Susannah Joel Glusker, *Anita Brenner: A Mind of Her Own* (Austin: U of Texas P, 1998).

9. In the early days of her return to Mexico, Anita Brenner worked as a translator for Gamio's research project on Teotihuacan (information obtained from personal communication with Susannah Joel Glusker).

10. Germán Gedovius and Leandro Izaguirre, for example, were still important teachers at the Academy of San Carlos in the early 1920s, and were considered "masters" of Mexican genre painting. They would soon be effaced by newcomers of the open-air schools, and by the muralists.

11. This is the discourse surrounding Gabriel Orozco's success in the mid-1990s. In 1993, Lynn Zelevansky, curator of MoMA's "Projects" program, stated in the introductory pamphlet that Orozco was the first Mexican artist to reject the muralist tradition, which was, of course, completely untrue. Nevertheless, the simple reference drove Gabriel Orozco right back into the sphere of Mexican art that this affirmation tried to obliterate.

WORKS CITED

Atl, Doctor. 1980. *Las artes populares en México.* Facsimile edition. Mexico: Instituto Nacional Indigenista.

Bargellini, Clara. 1992. "Arquitectura Colonial, Hispano Colonial y Neocolonial." In *Arte, Historia e Identidad en América,* XVII Coloquio Internacional de Historia del Arte, 419ff. Mexico City: Instituto de Investigaciones Estéticas, UNAM.

Berg, Henry. 1979. "Preface and Acknowledgment." In *Rufino Tamayo: Myth and Magic.* New York: The Solomon R. Guggenheim Museum.

Brading, David. 1988. "Manuel Gamio and Official Indigenismo in Mexico." *Bulletin of Latin American Research* 7, no. 1: 77.

Brenner, Anita. 1924. "The Jew in Mexico." *The Nation* 119 (27 August): 211–212.

———. 1929. *Idols behind Altars.* New York: Payson and Clark.

"Exhibition of Mexican Art." 1930. *Bulletin of the Museum of Fine Arts* 28 (December): 113–116.

Gamio, Manuel. 1922. *Introduction, Synthesis and Conclusions of the Work: The Population of the Valley of Teotihuacán.* Mexico: Departamento de Antropología.

———. 1929. "The Transcendental Aspect of Tourism in Mexico." In *Mexico: Guía de Turismo* (July): 11.

Glusker, Susannah Joel. 1998. *Anita Brenner: A Mind of Her Own.* Austin: University of Texas Press.

Grandes maestros del arte popular mexicano. 1999. Mexico: Fomento Cultural Banamex.

Hank López, Enrique. 1965. "A Country and Some People I Love: An Interview with Katherine Anne Porter." *Harper's* 231 (September): 58–68.

———. 1981. *Conversations with Katherine Anne Porter: Refugee from Indian Creek.* Boston: Little, Brown.

Oles, James, ed. 1993. *South of the Border: Mexico in the American Imagination, 1914–1947.* Washington, D.C.: Smithsonian Institution Press.

Reyes Palma, Franciso. 1990. "Vanguardia año cero." In *Modernidad y modernización en el arte mexicano,* ed. Olivier Debroise et al. Mexico: Museo Nacional de Arte, Instituto Nacional de Bellas Artes.

Siple, Ella S. 1931. "Art in America—Exhibitions from Mexico and South America." *Burlington Magazine* 58 (March): 157.

Starr, Frederick. 1899a. *Catalogue of a Collection of Objects Illustrating the Folklore of Mexico.* London: The Folk-Lore Society.

———. 1899b. *Indians of Southern Mexico: An Ethnographic Album.* Chicago: n.p.

Walsh, Thomas F. 1992. *Katherine Anne Porter and Mexico: The Illusion of Eden.* Austin: University of Texas Press.

Mathias Goeritz

Emotional Architecture and Creating a Mexican National Art

Juan Bruce-Novoa

En América habrá siempre un arte popular que no reconoce sus orígenes del mismo modo que no se reconoce a sí mismo y por eso es popular, pero que tiene influencia maya, náhuatl, olmeca, inca, y también . . . africana. Pero igualmente hay otra tradición, otra alma americana no menos legítima: la que configurándose en los países del cono sur principalmente que, apartados por completo del pasado indígena, encontraron el centro de su movimiento en la historia sobre la base de la cultura europea a la que, como una acción inevitable, la acción que hace imposible que cualquier cultura tenga un puro carácter flotante y que obliga a la historia de Occidente si no quiere negarse a sí misma a aceptar la existencia de América, tuvieron que asentar sobre su propia tierra.

Juan García Ponce, *Diversidad de actitudes*, 143

t midcentury, Mexico was celebrating three decades of postrevolutionary rule. True, despite the zealous public relations efforts of each presidential regime to stress its roots in the Revolution, the emphasis had been shifting progressively onto the prefix *post* until in 1946 the newly elected president, Miguel Alemán, changed the official title of the ruling party to the rather cynical Partido Revolucionario Institutional. With the title change Alemán accurately, albeit ironically, captured the contradictory thrusts of orderly progress and stability versus the ideal of a pervasive concern for the interest of the popular classes. This was not a simple goal.

Mexico's grand midcentury project of national imaging, the construction of the national university campus, the Ciudad Universitaria (C.U.) reflected the same tension. As the culmination of the Revolution's ideals of educational reform, the new campus would move the nation's university out of the colonial center of Mexico City, where the different schools were housed in disparate buildings, and concentrate them in one location on the city's southern outskirts. The project would demonstrate to the world Mexico's capacity to utilize on a monumental scale the international language of modern architecture and urban planning. At the same time, however, the project would turn its facades over to the muralists for them to cover with images drawn from a well-established catalogue of decorative motifs that had little to do with modern aesthetics. In brief, whereas the architecture was international and modern in design, the surfaces were to be national in their display of local thematics and nostalgic in their heavy use of indigenous imagery. Moreover, the surfaces exuded nationalism in their display of what had become the institutionalized Mexican form of art, muralism. While in the nascent gallery system in the heart of the city a new revolution in cultural production was making its debut, the Institutionalized Revolutionary Party was constructing in C.U. a monument to its self-assured eminence. The government chose to symbolize its right to speak for the nation—its synonymy with the nation—through its display of the artistic equivalent of the enduring, ahistorical popular soul of Mexico.

In March 1947, *Holiday*, a leading U.S. travel magazine, dedicated an issue to Mexico. They commissioned the most renowned Mexican American author of the period, Anita Brenner, to write the central essay as well as some of the accompanying texts. Brenner's title openly announced that the same inner tension between modernization and the supposedly authentic, conservative national soul structured her treatment of the subject: "Mexican Fact and Fiction: A Luxurious Superstructure of Purring Cars and Palaces Is Built upon an Indian World Changed Little since the Days of Cortés" (1947, 22). Brenner's prepolitically correct writing, although refreshingly candid in her scathing critique of Mexican attitudes toward the United States, cannot but leave readers with the impression that for her the "real Mexico" is the indigenous world in which, as her title implies, one can find elements that have resisted the changes of time.

Apropos the magazine's focus, Brenner organized her piece like a guided tour into the known otherness of a foreign culture: "Every year 300,000 Americans cross the border—through the looking glass and into a land where nothing gears with our organized ways and conscientious notions" (1947, 22). Brenner goes on to explain how Mexico tries to give U.S. tourists the security of modern comforts within which they can experience stylized glimpses of pre-Columbian, colonial, and indigenous elements. She finally leads readers away out of the tourist cocoon—"2 percent of the place"—to what she considers normal Mexico: "people, on every level of society, who might be carrying on what they're doing just as well in your home town" (1947, 51). But even so, Brenner recognizes that this modern normality is continually undermined by a general backwardness—"nothing is predictably dependable here" (1947, 25). Eventually, the author takes us to the heart of the real Mexico: "Mexican Village, Old Ways and Crafts" (1947, 111) and then to the archetypal inhabitant, the "Mexican Indian: He's Strikingly Mongolian" (1947, 118). The subtitle declares clearly that the essence of Mexico is non-European in the form of its extreme binary opposite: Asian, a link she goes on to discuss in terms of cultural characteristics as well. Brenner has led readers as far away from the European side of the equation as is rhetorically possible, all in an effort to identify, and identify herself with, an enduring popular presence.

The essay ends with the restatement of the essential contradiction, raised now to the category of "The Mexican Dream . . . being able to live with American comfort, health, efficiency and knowledge, and still keep the Mexican wisdom: the tolerance, and the fundamental belief that jobs, friends, possessions and pleasures are matters of taste rather than of price or position" (1947, 122). Brenner's change in the equation is significant, however: Mexico's traditional conflict between the Hispanic and Indian sectors has now become one between Mexican culture—which we can only assume to be the hybrid product of its traditional European/Asian dynamics—and its U.S. counterpart; that is, a conflict between Mexican national authenticity and the post–World War II internationalization of U.S. culture. We might say that Brenner saw Mexico's midcentury situation already in terms of impending globalization. Implicitly, for Brenner the answer to the threat of U.S. colonization lay in yet another term that would become dear to the critical theorists decades latter, resistance, found in the popular culture sector, what she calls "the native folk and their much more tenacious folkways" (1947, 119).

Brenner's contributor's statement claims that her purpose for writing the essay is to produce better understanding between the peoples of Mexico and the United States. In light of her text, which she recognizes will be read by Mexicans as an attack—"whatever you say about Mexico that isn't *gaga* praise he [the Mexican] takes as dirty low-down insult" (1947, 91)—Brenner, like a modern day literary critic, tries to position herself in a positive light by siding with the underprivileged classes. Her negative observations take aim at that "2 percent" of elite Mexico who court and host the invading Gringos, those who prefer English to Spanish and turn a blind eye to the great authentic base of the Mexican nation. The proof of her position as nontourist, anti-imperialist, antiglobalization intellectual is that her own texts probe through the modern facade and guide readers to that tenacious popular culture.

The material chosen to round out the issue's focus on Mexico further illustrates the point. Brenner herself provides several shorter essays on popular lore: "Dance of the Concheros," "Bullfight," "Medieval Guanajuato," and one on Mexico City that again emphasizes her central leitmotif: "its modernity often conceals its ancient landmarks." In addition there are essays on "Tehuana Women" (Hudson Strode) and "Inside Ixtepec" (Allen Chellas). Even the essays on resorts and sports emphasize their popular quality. One feels Brenner's hand in the editorial decisions, or at least that the editors agreed with her in that true Mexican culture was to be found in the picturesque popular strata of its society.

For our concerns, the most significant article in the issue is the one dedicated to the arts: "Mexico's Explosive Muralists, Their Brushes Cut as Deep as Swords," by Murray Morgan. That Rivera, Orozco, and Siqueiros are praised as heroes comes as no surprise in the context of the rest of the articles. The muralists are depicted as spokesmen of the downtrodden popular sector defined as the authentic Mexico in the accompanying texts. The muralists are placed there as if they were practitioners of popular arts instead of part of that "2 percent" facade presented to tourists in search of Mexican experiences. Despite their ties to international vanguard movements in painting and their close, if often tumultuous, relationship with governmental institutions, they are presented as authentically Mexican, which in terms of Brenner's formulation equals popular. Readers are expected to take the muralists, and implicitly the Mexican school of Art of which they were paragons, to be non-European, the authentic expression of the enduring, ahistorical essence of Mexicanness.

Such claims are contradicted by the facts of sponsorship and patronage that allowed the muralists to function and achieve their status. As Max Kozloff has observed, "North American viewers must be startled by conditions in Mexico that allowed such deeply antagonistic artists as Rivera and Orozco to be sponsored by the authoritarian state" (1993, 68) Actually the muralists illustrated clichéd national themes through European forms on the walls of the wealthy elite of both Mexico and the United States, themes with which their patrons were more than happy to associate themselves as long as they appeared in the form of nostalgic motifs of ahistorical authenticity marking their authors, and by extension their sponsors, as authentically Mexican. Leftist critics still defend the muralists as practitioners of authentic Mexicanness. Shifra Goldman laments the decline of muralism, attributing it to an international, bourgeois, capitalist plot centered in the United States (1981, 29–35). Within the framework of foreign versus national character, the muralists must be defended as the expression of local authenticity in resistance against the globalization of Usonian culture. But in effect, Goldman echoes Brenner: Authentic Mexico is found in the indigenous, popular sector supposedly represented by the muralists, and the U.S. intellectual, caught in the trap of this binary construction, must promote it or become a pawn of U.S. cultural imperialism.

The National Question

The conflict between the international and national is common throughout Latin America. Although it occupies different levels of importance in the national aesthetic discourse in different countries—often depending on the level of indigenous population remaining—the discussion about creating a national art has played a role in all of them. And most often it assumes the same binary structure: the national/positive versus the international/negative. Although I would prefer to dismiss the entire question with the same ease with which García Ponce, in the epigram above, summarizes the coexistence of two equally legitimate traditions, the conflict persists, especially among U.S. critics caught up in an environment of rampant political correctness. Moreover, the situation is the necessary context for understanding the discussion of the change in Mexican aesthetics brought about at the midcentury.

Perhaps Fermín Fevre has provided the most useful, succinct treatment of the question in his essay "Las formas de la crítica y la respuesta del público" (1974). He points out that Mexican muralism constitutes the most serious attempt to create a national art. Yet he quickly points out that the Mexican response followed a thematic route foreign to contemporary aesthetic preoccupations. This seems to leave us at back at the point of discussion above: Progressive aesthetics are international, whereas the pursuit of national thematics is implicitly retrograde. Fevre, whose own preoccupation is the evolution of criticism in Latin American Arts, favors the progressive dialogue with international currents, but in his exposition he raises three points important for our discussion. First, he points out that for years critics failed to question muralism's claims of having created a truly national art. Although he refers to the pioneering efforts of Marta Traba and Emilio A. Westphalen to illustrate that Latin American critics have begun to do so, his statement is still generally valid for U.S. critics who continue to shy away from questioning the value of propopular thematics and blatantly national surfaces.[1] Second, Fevre points out that giving unquestioning support to indigenous and folkloric thematics leads to a fundamental contradiction for postcolonialists:

> Se pretende por una parte que a través de tales referencias se realiza un arte auténtico y contenido social, pero al mismo tiempo, con ese tipo de obras se alienta la avidez del mercado turístico del coleccionista extranjero. Es decir, están destinadas a un consumo limitado y minoritario en donde el interés por ese tipo de obra radica únicamente en su pintoresquismo. Con ello no se hace más que fortalecer una relación de dependencia cultural que precisamente se trata de eludir. (1974, 53)
>
> [On the one hand, an authentic art and social content is supposedly achieved by means of such references, but on the other hand this type of work encourages the foreign collector tourist market. In other words, it is destined for a limited and minority consumption that is interested only in its picturesque qualities. In the process, a relation of cultural dependency is reinforced, which is precisely what was to be avoided.]

This point is key: to insist on keeping Latin America tied to a thematics of picturesque poverty or proletarian struggle is not to support its independence, but rather to promote its cultural colonization. Third, and most important for us here, Fevre argues that there should be a possibility of finding an artistic expression that is both national and progressively international, one that, in the light of point two above, would neither play the populist game nor ignore the national need for self-representation.

Mathias Goeritz and the Nation as Aesthetic Project

In 1949, Mathias Goeritz (b. 1915, Danzig), after half a decade of productive residence in Spain, found himself unable continue his stay. The government's refusal to renew his visa threatened more than to end his sojourn, it also distanced him from the *Escuela de Altamira* in Santillana del Mar of which Goeritz had been the founder. Luckily, that same year he received an invitation to join the faculty of the School of Architecture in Guadalajara, Mexico, although he was neither an academic nor an architect. Since then, Mexico has been his home and base of operations for his dual activities as artist and teacher. From the start he played a major role on both fronts, quickly becoming one of the most significant players in Mexican cultural production of the second half of the century. Although it is always risky to talk of influence, among Mexican artists Goeritz often is often referred to in such terms (Moyssén 1977, 69). It might be more productive, however, to approach him as a mediator/facilitator who centered and gave direction and form to the preoccupations and tendencies of diverse artists who in the 1950s and 1960s redefined the national aesthetic scene, in the plastic as well as the textual arts. These artists have created true landmarks that no consideration of the contemporary Mexican landscape—material and imaginary—can ignore. To anticipate my conclusion, Goeritz and the generation of midcentury created a body of work that, although widely divergent from the thematic nationalism of the school of Mexican art that dominated the first half of the century, has come to be seen as intrinsically linked to the image of Mexico—hence, national art.

Goeritz's arrival in Mexico coincides with the start of the C.U. project. That his activities were viewed as counter to those of the Mexican school that decorated the C.U. walls is clear in the attacks that Rivera and Siqueiros eventually leveled at him in the press (Morais 1982, 31). But it was not the first time Goeritz had worked in antagonistic surroundings. Post–World War II fascist Spain had not received well his abstract work. Franco's Spain might not have Indian tribes and pre-Columbian myths, but that had not kept the Caudillo from fomenting a cult to regional folklorism and national thematics. Within that populist environment, Goeritz had founded the Escuela de Altamira. One could say that in the midst of a national aesthetics based on picturesque regional thematics, Goeritz countered with the proposition of an art that, although linked to a specific historical imaginary mode of expression, utilized the past more as justification of innovation than as a model for imitation—and in the latter sense, taking ancient images as examples of the use of abstraction to purify forms in a way that did not copy any established models, nevertheless maintaining a connection to the archaeological traces of communal activity of a prenational character. Hence, as Frederico Morais points out, Goeritz's orientation was, even before arriving in Mexico, toward the future, the creation of new forms (1982, 14), yet with a communal concern steeped in the sacredness of art's capacity to center human activity, rendering it significant within relentless contingency.

When Goeritz arrived in Mexico, he was faced with the national-versus-international dilemma. Siqueiros's infamous declaration, "No hay más ruta que la nuestra," 'Ours is the only path,' left little room for foreign intervention unless it took the form of collaboration with the Mexican school. However, Goeritz, like the young generation of artists beginning to exhibit in galleries like the Prisse, resisted the institutionalized aesthetics and, because there was no route to follow other than Siqueiros's, opened a new path.

When the newly inaugurated C.U. was starting to attract international attention with its monumental campus, Goeritz was realizing a project that well could be read as counterpunctual resistance to the grandiose central model. Whereas C.U. anticipated—even catalyzed—the impending urban sprawl of the capitol, with its U.S.-style move to the suburbs and use of freeways as access roads, Goeritz's *Museo Experimental: El Eco* (1953) was located on a city street, behind the traditional anonymous walls familiar to the urban dweller of the capitol. Whereas C.U. organized itself to impress the visitor with its panoptic glorification of centralized power—a structure reflecting that of the government that made it possible—the museum purposely played with perspective to disorient visitors. Whereas the former sought to impress visitors with a sense of overwhelming order that reduced them to anonymous participants in the grand plan of the nation state, the latter offered an encounter with the undefined, requiring individual initiative. Whereas C.U. was a public project on grand scale, the museum was private, with no commercial or institutional purpose. The owner of an empty lot, Daniel Mont, offered Goeritz the use of the land and the services of a construction team. Mont's only instructions, "Haga aquí lo que usted quiera," 'Do whatever you want here,' captured the freedom inherent in the project from the start, a feeling Goeritz managed to retain in the spectator's experience of the finished project.

Goeritz was free to apply his concept of emotional architecture. First, he isolated the lot with high walls to create an autonomous space where anything was possible because nothing was preplanned. Hence, the building would be an experience of creation versus the materialization of an a priori model. Working without blueprints, Goeritz improvised orders to the crew, interacting with the space as it took shape. All the walls—exterior and interior—erected and shaped in the act of construction under Goeritz's spontaneous decisions, turned out asymmetric with the purpose of provoking surprise and thus emotion. For example, from a twelve-meter-high yellow wall there emerged, like prehistoric shards, traces of metal reminiscent of cuneiform hieroglyphs from some unknown culture—"*Poema plástico*" Goeritz called it. This wall would later be the site for works by visiting artists: a mural by Henry Moore, the memory of Pilar Pellicer's choreography. As one walked down a corridor, the thirteen-foot ceiling sloped precipitously, producing the sensation of being caught in a funnel that suddenly opened onto the interior open-air patio with its brightly colored rear wall rising as backdrop to an enormous black metal abstract rendition of a serpent. When the Museo Experimental was inaugurated in September 1953, *La serpiente* (the serpent) was the largest abstract steel sculpture in the Americas. The result was a sculpted building, not designed to display art, but to be experienced and explored as an art space itself within which the most important event was the emotion created in and by the visitors in and through their improvised interaction with the building—a decade later this kind of experience would be called a happening.

As could be expected, Goeritz's museum was targeted by the Mexican-School artists. They denounced it as a dangerous example of bourgeois internationalism. Siqueiros and Rivera, with their characteristic arrogance, published a letter replete with personal insults (Morais 1982, 31). Goeritz responded with his *Manifiesto de la arquitectura emocional* in which he strategically set himself in opposition to the infamous dehumanization associated with the international school of modern architecture:

> Existe la impresión de que el arquitecto moderno, individualizado e intelectual, está exagerando a veces—quizá por haber perdido el contacto estrecho con la comunidad—al querer destacar demasiado la parte racional de la arquitectura. El resultado es que el hombre del siglo XX se siente

aplastado por tanto "funcionalismo", por tanta lógica y utilidad dentro de la arquitectura moderna. (Morais 1982, 32)
    [There is an impression that the modern architect, individualized and intellectual, is exaggerating at times—perhaps due to his having lost his close contact with the community—upon wanting to stress overmuch the rational part of architecture. The result is that twentieth-century man feels crushed by so much "functionalism," by so much logic and utility within modern architecture.]

It would have been impossible for Rivera, Siqueiros, and their ilk not to recognize Goeritz's allusion to them and their collaboration in the C.U., where, as it had in so many other government buildings, muralism functioned as an official enterprise—a function of the party in power—in effect, the logical and utilitarian discourse of a totalitarian order. And the implicit accusation of having lost contact with the people hit them in the heart of their populist self-promotion.

    Goeritz's manifesto goes on to state:

[se] Busca una salida, pero ni el esteticismo exterior comprendido como "formalismo", ni el regionalismo orgánico, ni aquel confusionismo dogmático se han enfrentado a fondo al problema de que el hombre—creador o receptor—de nuestro tiempo, aspira a algo más que a una casa bonita, agradable y adecuada. Pide—o tendrá que pedir un día—de la arquitectura y de sus medios y materiales modernos, una elevación espiritual; simplemente dicho: una emoción como se la dio en su tiempo la arquitectura de la pirámide, la del templo griego, la de la catedral románica o gótica—o incluso—la del palacio barroco. Sólo recibiendo de la arquitectura emociones verdaderas, el hombre puede volver a considerarla como un arte. (Morais 1982, 34)
    [A way out is sought, but neither exterior aestheticism understood as "formalism," nor organic regionalism, nor that dogmatic confusionism has truly confronted the problem that man of our time, creator and receptor, aspires to something more than a pretty, agreeable and adequate house. He asks—or he will have to ask some day—from architecture and its modern means and materials a spiritual elevation; simply put: an emotion, just as was given, in its own time, by the architecture of the pyramid, the Greek temple, the Romanic or Gothic cathedral or even the baroque palace. Only by receiving true emotions from architecture will man be able to once again consider it an art.]

One senses that Goeritz has deliberately left out the source of all his references, the Altamira Cave. Something about the Museo Experimental recalls the experience of the ancient, sacred cave, with its play of light and shadow in asymmetric spaces, its images (e)merging from/with the walls evoking a forgotten code of meaning. And in its depth, an ancient cult to animal nature rendered sacred through abstracted imagery. Goeritz sought to provide a new experience, a startling emotion that simultaneously evoked an ancient tradition of communal spiritual orientation.

Let us consider more closely some features of the experience provided by the Museo Experimental: (1) The art space open to collaborative interaction: art as an unusual, surprising experience played out in a community of spectators; (2) art as landmark: the aesthetic object as an intervention in public space that seeks to reorient the spectator toward a relationship with emotional, even spiritual values of human habitation in a transcendent ecology; the art object alters the map of the city with a new presence that redefines space; (3) the renovation of national iconography: art as a dialogue with established codes of imagery to force a reconsideration, not at the thematic level, but on that of poetic evocation; specifically, the monumental, abstract sculpture of the serpent had to resound with significance that turned the subtitle "El Eco" into a reference to the official symbol of Mexico, the eagle and the serpent. Goeritz created a serpent free of the eagle, restored to its prenational, undemonized state—although not entirely, because the wider, social context is unavoidable. Outside the high walls, Mexico City awaited like the predatory eagle and eventually it would close in and destroy the space, forcing *La serpiente* to take refuge in the Museo de Arte Moderno when it opened in the mid-1960s, an ominous prediction of the appropriative capacity of official institutions. But while it stood, Goeritz's museum held open a new possibility whose promise could not be completely obliterated. Not only would elements like the invented hieroglyphs and monumental abstract sculpting return in Goeritz's and others' works, but, more importantly, the project itself also would pass into the communal memory as a significant event marking a key moment in the history of national cultural production. Subsequent work by Goeritz would only add its significance as a generative act.

Goeritz's next opportunity to realize a major project came in 1957 when Luis Barragán employed him to design the entrance to Satélite, a new development on the northern edge of the city. The task required him to incorporate the area's water storage facility into the design. Adapting a motif he had worked with for a number of years, Goeritz designed a monumental sculpture consisting of five concrete towers of unequal height in the center of a traffic circle. William Curtis includes the following description in his authoritative study of twentieth-century architecture:

A cluster of shaft-like monumental towers . . . solid monoliths in reinforced concrete, five in all, rising to 100, 120, 130, 150 and 165 respectively (31, 37, 40, 46 and 50 metres). They were triangular in plan, rough in texture, and originally painted in bold ochres and reds. Experienced from the passing car, they shifted into ever-changing alignments, one moment massive and solid, the next planar and immaterial. Ambiguous in size, the ensemble of coloured, abstract forms generated a field of energy on the scale of the wide central valley of Mexico, and were visible for miles around. (Curtis, 497)

Although critics often associated Goeritz with minimalist concepts, Goeritz's declarations on the spiritual, transcendent purpose of architecture, cited above, distinguishes him from this or any contemporary school that denies art's transcendent potential. Goeritz believes that art can orient experience toward a heightened state of emotion akin to the sacred. In this light we can interpret his statement that *Torres de Satélite* should function as a materialized prayer (*rezo plástico*). Considering how they function, we can appreciate their similarity with traditional axis mundi structures. The towers render an open, communal space a focal point of transit, experienced in repetitive movements that take direction—significance—from their presence; that is, they ritualize the public encounter. Through their play of forms, they demonstrate changing patterns of relationship that, although serving no practical purpose, reflect on the organizational principles that underlie the daily lives of the spectators. And ideally, the mere fact that traffic flows around them makes them resonate with the vibrations of social life that turns the space into a continual field of collaborative interaction.

Most significant of all, the Satélite Towers became an instant icon of modern Mexico City. They rivaled C.U. as a representational image, assuming the status of national metaphor. The architecture that would come to be recognized internationally as the Mexican style—exemplified most aptly in Ricardo Legorreta's work—has more in common with Goeritz's towers than the C.U. Thus Goeritz succeeded once again in creating national art without recourse to the clichéd thematics of popular lore.

Although the next major step in Goeritz's development was the massive project for the 1968 Olympics—*La Ruta de la Amistad*—we should take a brief detour to another project realized at the same time. Ricardo Legorreta's Camino Real near Chapultepec Park was designed as a luxury hotel for wealthy tourists. In concrete terms it represented Mexico to the international elite. Twenty years earlier, such a hotel would have featured a mural by one of the three masters, most likely Rivera who was known for such decorative projects. Goeritz was commissioned to execute a mural in the hotel and the result, within the Mexican context, was surprising and magnificent. He created a richly textured wall of gold, devoid of any representational figures. However, once again it can be read as contextually metaphorical: Instead of the clichéd narrative anecdotes of conquest featured in Mexican school murals, anecdotes that allow the spectator the comfort of distance from the historical moments and figures represented, Goeritz presents the spectator with the unmitigated object of desire that spurred the conquest, gold. By eliminating the anecdote, Goeritz frees the dynamics of greed and desire from historical anchors, allowing it to resonate in the present with the force of emotional experience.[2]

The Route of Friendship (La Ruta de la Amistad) was the centerpiece of the Artistic Olympics planned to accompany the traditional sporting event, a massive collaborative endeavor. Goeritz proposed the construction of a string of sculptures, each designed by a different artist selected to represent, in total, all the major areas of the globe. The sculptures would run beside the new freeway between the central city and the southern outskirts where the Olympic Village was located. By definition the sculptures had to be monumental, large enough to be experienced from passing automobiles. And they were to be abstract in design, thus forming a series of poetic forms with no anecdotal script. Yet, once again, Goeritz intended that the project constitute a landmark of spiritual orientation. The abstract forms ideally would form an evocative experience of sensual forms related in a flowing pattern created by the movement of spectators through space. Implicitly, that movement would harmonize the individually designed pieces, thus metaphorically representing the Olympic ideal.

It would be impossible to miss the significance of La Ruta de la Amistad in the national context. That the major aesthetic project of an event that would represent Mexico to the world was restricted to sculpted abstract forms as opposed to figurative painting signaled that the institutionalized aesthetics had been redefined. In effect, what had been a marginal expression of resistance in the Museo Experimental in 1953 had become, by 1967, the national art. Goeritz and a young generation of artists had transformed the aesthetic landscape of Mexico.

The crowning achievement in what now can be seen as Goeritz's life project came in 1977–1980 in *El Espacio Escultórico*. A collective project with five other artists, the Sculptural Space is the largest sculpture in the

Americas with an outside diameter of 126 meters. On a raised ring sit 64 concrete modules that measure nine meters at the base and rise 4 meters high, forming prismatic triangles separated by a distance of 2.72 meters on the outside and 1.9 on the inside edge. The ring's inside diameter of 98 meters opens a vast pit filled with the twisted, black shapes of the ancient lava bed, stripped of the vegetation that surrounds the ring's outer edge. The contrasts between the junglelike greenery of the approach, the hard-edged construction of the white circle, and the sensuous, tortured shapes of the lava produce the emotional impact Goeritz designed into his Museo Experimental twenty-five years earlier, but now raised exponentially to the sublime. The spiritual character of the Espacio is obvious, forming as it does a perfect axis mundi. Like a monstrous cyclops eye—or vagina dentata or the lost gear of the cosmic engine—the space centers the heavens into a meeting, on the terrestrial plane, with the dark forces of the underground. Horizontally, the division of the sixty-four modules into four sections marks the four directions, structuring the earth into ordered divisions radiating from the center. Again the work echoes ancient sites of sacred orientation while simultaneously reprising the oldest known pyramid in the central valley, that of Copilco a few miles to the south of the Espacio—fusing the universal and local.

The Espacio Escultórico clearly speaks the international idiom of abstraction and geometric constructivism. Yet no one would question its status as Mexican art. It may surprise the tourist, but not as a non-Mexican object. Exactly the opposite: Visitors sense that they have experienced something essentially Mexican, although if one could deposit the entire structure in Brazil or the United States probably nothing about it would intrinsically bespeak Mexicanness. That is the point. Goeritz and his colleagues have managed to domesticate the international idiom. When spoken by Mexicans it produces Mexican art—national work.

Conclusion

Goeritz did not nationalize the international idiom on his own. The contributions of artists, designers, architects, and writers who came of age in the 1950s and 1960s provided the essential context for the acceptance of Goeritz's work. To name a few would do injustice to the many. Suffice it to say that through difficult, sometimes violently acrimonious, struggles, Mexican cultural production freed itself from the tyranny of the institutionalized school of Mexican art. That in the process the new generation allowed itself to become closely linked to official institutions tells us more about the power of the modern corporate state than the aesthetics of the artists involved. The creators of the Espacio Escultórico devised Mexico's largest, most impressive monument in an abstract form that, although it cannot escape official manipulation, remains sufficiently ambiguous to elide efforts to fix it as a clear sign of one or another political ideology. For our concerns, its existence troubles and complicates the discussion of national art, globalization, and local resistance. To retreat to the old binaries should now be impossible.

NOTES

Epigraph: [In America there will always be a popular art which does not recognize its origins, just as it does not recognize itself and for that reason is popular, but which possesses Maya, Nahuatl, Olmec, Inca, and also . . . African influence. But there is also another tradition, another American soul that is no less legitimate: one which came to be configured principally in the countries of the southern cone. These countries, completely separated from the indigenous past, found the center of their movement in history on the basis of European culture. Through an almost inevitable action—the same action which makes it impossible for any culture to maintain a purely floating character and obliges the history of the West to accept the existence of America if it doesn't wish to negate itself—they had to establish this tradition on their own ground.]

1. Guy Brett makes the following observation pertinent to our discussion: "The centres of power have always assumed the right to define and explain the rest of the world. The West assumes, consciously or unconsciously, that it is the 'measure of all things.' . . . These assumptions lead to an unresolvable dilemma when it comes to the presentation of art by Latin Americans in the metropolitan centres. It becomes a complex play of positive and negative. If these presentations stress cultural similarity, they are positive in the sense that they acknowledge that Latin America is part of the mainstream of modern culture, but raise the danger of assimilating the work to a bland 'international art' which makes nothing of the context from which the art comes, and especially the fundamental gap between living standards of the First and Third worlds. If, on the other hand, the presentation stresses difference, it acknowledges that Latin America has a history, cultures, and present conditions different from those of Europe, but raises the danger of defining those differences in telluric, folkloric, essentialist terms. Both sets of alternatives lead inevitably to separate, restrictive categories for the artists. They limit their freedom to concern themselves with any matter whatsoever. No European artists are asked that their work give proof of the 'European identity', but this is always the first thing expected of a Latin American.

This restrictive categorization is so powerful, and the assumption of Eurocentricity so implacable, that it often hardly matters if the response of the West is to praise or condemn" (1990, 10–11).

2. The connection between Goeritz's concepts of emotional architecture and Ricardo Legorreta's work is implicit in the following statement by Legorreta: "Soon after the Camino Real Mexico City was finished I received a phone call from an architect friend, a leader of the international architecture movement, and his comment astonished me. He said that during a visit to the hotel he experienced a particular feeling that caused him great emotion. With some apprehension I asked what emotion that was, and he said, 'The pleasure of getting lost.'

"We architects design too much with our intellects, so our buildings are cold, lifeless, and too predictable. We think that upon entering a place one must know exactly where to go, where the elevators are located, and so on. Yet think of the pleasure people get from seeking. People enjoy Greek Island villages, or Guanajuato, or medieval European towns for the pleasure of what can be discovered, and of getting lost" (Attoe 1990, 35).

WORKS CITED

Attoe, Wayne, ed. 1990. *The Architecture of Ricardo Legorreta*. Austin: University of Texas Press.

Brenner, Anita. 1947. "Mexican Fact and Fiction: A Luxurious Superstructure of Purring Cars and Palaces Is Built upon an Indian World Changed Little since the Days of Cortés." *Holiday* (March): 22.

Brett, Guy. 1990. "Border Crossings." In *Transcontinental: An Investigation of Reality, Nine Latin American Artists*, 9–35. London: Verso.

Curtis, William J. R. 1996. *Modern Architecture Since 1900* (3rd ed.). London: Phaidon Press Limited.

Fevre, Fremín. 1974. "Las formas de la crítica y la respuesta del público." In *América latina en sus artes*, ed. Damián Bayón, 45–61. Mexico City: Siglo Veintiuno Editores.

García Ponce, Juan. 1974. "Diversidad de actitudes." In *América latina en sus artes*, ed. Damián Bayón, 141–153. Mexico City: Siglo Veintiuno Editores.

Goldman, Shifra, M. 1981. *Contemporary Mexican Painting in a Time of Change*. Austin: University of Texas Press.

Kozloff, Max. 1993. "Orozco and Rivera: Mexican Fresco Painting and the Paradoxes of Nationalism." In *Latin American Artists of the Twentieth Century*, ed. Waldo Rassmussen, 60–71. New York: The Museum of Modern Art.

Moys\'en, Xavier. 1977. "Los mayores: Mérida, Gerzo, Goeritz." In *El geometrismo mexicano*, 51–76. Mexico City: Universidad Nacional de México.

Morais, Frederico. 1982. *Mathias Goeritz*. Mexico City: Universidad Nacional Autónoma de México.

Morgan, Murray. 1947. "Mexico's Explosive Muralists: Their brushes cut as deep as swords," *Holiday* (March): 44.

Corporeal Identities in Mexican Art
Modern and Postmodern Strategies

Karen Cordero Reiman

f narration is the art of weaving convincing connections between disparate events and characters, the body is the center of the narrative strategies established in the visual arts, as the site of sensorial experience that permits the construction and reconstruction of meanings in these works.

And yet, it is the very analysis of the works of art themselves which reveals the tenuous, discursive nature of the body as it is constructed by the twin processes of creation and reception. The body becomes the fictional center of the artistic phenomenon: in its simultaneous and often contradictory referentiality to both collective and individual experience, in the historical modulation of the meanings and hierarchical relationships between these different modes of corporeal identification, and in the intersubjective dialogues established between viewer and creator, critic and reader, reader and viewer. The body is a hypothetical entity, which is molded and given form by the dialogical process: at once the condition of creation and the object of its analysis.

The corporeal is particularly relevant to Mexican art of the early and late twentieth century, where persistent artistic representations of the human body are paralleled by that body's centrality in theoretical constructions of social identity. And yet the relationship between these realms of significance rarely has been taken into account. In the former case, the resurrection (most notably, although not singularly, by postrevolutionary statesman and philosopher José Vasconcelos) of the biological phenomenon of *mestizaje* (miscegenation) as a model for the process of construction of modern art in Mexico has important implications for policies and practices regarding race and ethnicity in this century. In more contemporary art, the explicit visual imbrication of personal signifiers with collective symbols inherited from the postrevolutionary educational edifice permits us to reflect on this twentieth-century "tradition" and the construction of bodily discourse in Mexico in more integral ways, thereby endowing the earlier works—through this conceptual crossing—with new meanings and illuminating the historicity of more recent artistic production.

The persistent reading (and writing) of Mexican art as a chronological and unidirectional continuum has discouraged transhistorical comparison, creating a historiography in which the diversity of positions within a given period and the vital dialogue between the art of different periods is opaqued by progressive, linear, and at the same time compartmentalized narratives, in which art is read more as an expression of historical imperatives than as a dynamic aesthetic experience susceptible to re-creation and resignification.[1] The relative absence of apparent bodily discourse in the art of the so-called *Ruptura* (that is, the art of the 1950s and 1960s) has certainly collaborated to divert interpretive efforts from attention to corporeal aspects as a category of analysis that spans the twentieth century, further contributing to the methodological differentiation in the treatment of early- and late-twentieth-century art. In general, the treatment of the body in the primarily figurative modern Mexican art proposed in the postrevolutionary period has been interpreted as "realism" (with all the highly charged ambiguities that term implies), an attempt to register national experience and its historical process in a more direct and democratic fashion. In contrast, the neofiguration and concrete bodily references in the art of the 1980s and 1990s have been interpreted primarily in conceptual or poetic terms. An ideological reading tied to specific historical circumstances and cultural necessities of the postrevolutionary period contrasts, thus, with a globalizing and primarily theoretical reading of more recent art. These counterpointed interpretive strategies widen the historical abyss traced by chronological time, rather than take advantage of the unique possibility that the "presence" of visual art offers for establishing a dialogue between apparently distant phenomena. In this chapter I take up this latter project—that of virtual dialogue—by articulating the narrative strategies used to represent the body in the art of the 1920s and the 1990s and analyzing their relationship to social constructions and experiences of identity to clarify some of the issues at stake in these diverse attempts to objectify the meaning of sensorial and corporeal experience in art, and their implications for processes of interpretation and the construction of historical and critical narratives.

For this purpose, I will take as my primary examples of the construction of corporeal discourse in Mexican art installation work by Gerardo Suter (1957) and Silvia Gruner (1959) and counterpoint it with mural paintings of the 1920s by Diego Rivera (1886–1957) and David Alfaro Siqueiros (1896–1974). In choosing these examples, I do not pretend that they represent in any canonical or paradigmatic way the bodily discourse of modern, postrevolutionary, and postmodern contemporary visual art in Mexico, respectively, although their analysis certainly reveals some characteristics and aspects of those periods. Rather, I consider that their interrelation and comparison from this perspective offers an understanding of these works and suggests modes of signification that would not be readily available in a chronological or traditional contextual framing and that may open new possibilities for the reading of other artworks and cultural phenomena.[2]

The installations of Suter and Gruner emphasize the polysemic and fragmentary nature of corporeal experience in contemporary culture, invoking and simultaneously frustrating the viewer's desire to integrate these disparate elements in a logical, linear narrative, or at any rate in the narrative assumed and fomented by earlier twentieth-century art and art–literature. Their work can be located in the context of Borges's reflections on the fictional forms of memory and history, in the sense that they highlight the role of subjectivity in their narrative constructions, subtly forcing the viewer to question the tropes of nationalist cultural mythology. Among these tropes is the cultural, racial (and narrative) continuity that purportedly constitutes the essence of Mexicanness and is founded on a homogenizing conception of indigenous culture and ethnicity, represented by and articulated in the historiographical treatment of pre-Hispanic art.[3] Celebrated since the nineteenth century as the classical hallowed origin of culture, preconquest art was placed on a similar pedestal by early-twentieth-century art and art history, from publications such as Anita Brenner's 1929 *Idols behind Altars* to the massive and much-discussed exhibit of Mexican art, *Splen-*

dors of Thirty Centuries (1990), sponsored by the Metropolitan Museum of Art, the Mexican television chain Televisa, and the Salinas government, and in which the twentieth century was significantly truncated in the 1950s.[4] Suter and Gruner intervene in that historiographical and iconographic narrative, displacing the viewers' coordinates and catapulting them into perpetual and unstable movement.

In Gruner's 1995 installation *El nacimiento de Venus* (part of the tripartite, trinational exhibition *Triangular*, presented in Guatemala, Mexico, and Sweden) pre-Hispanic figurines crafted in bright pink soap are the protagonists in this operation (Illustration 3.1). The significance of the itinerary and the ephemeral quality of the work are worth noting in this context; it is a piece in process, which has no definitive configuration and is conceived with the changing contexts of international time, space, and culture as variables. The soap was produced by a Swedish machine found in a Mexico City soap factory, which bears the logotype of a swastika and the acronym ASEA (meaning "to clean" in Spanish) (Illustration 3.2). In the Mexico City venue, the tiny pink figurines formed a decorative frieze atop the columns sustaining the arcade of a former convent of the Mercederian order, built in the seventeenth century. In an accompanying video, exhibited beneath the arcade, one of these figurines is progressively diminished by water, while the voice of Silvia's mother punctuates the continuous aquatic soundtrack with her childhood memories of corporeal cleansing in the concentration camp at Ravensbruck. Personal and public references are intertwined through the treatment of objects, time, and space in Silvia's work, forcing us to construct a version of the piece that integrates her images and evocations with our own perceptions, producing a new subjective memory on the basis of disparate objective components. The narrative significance of this work is available only as a reconstruction of sensorial fragments, which lives on—once the installation has been dismantled—only in the memory of the viewer, yet never relinquishes the historical and material specificity of its components.

Entering the dilapidated courtyard of the Ex-Convento de la Merced—a singular but little visited colonial monument in an area of downtown Mexico City now occupied mostly by small textile-related businesses—to see a trinational exhibition of conceptual art is itself a little odd. For me it was my second visit in my then thirteen years of residence in Mexico City; the first had been in 1992, when the space was used for teaching and storage by the Textile Arts Division of the National Institute of Fine Arts

Illustration 3.1. Silvia Gruner, *El nacimiento de Venus*, 1995. Soap. Installation in the Ex-Convento de la Merced, Mexico City (the pre-Hispanic figurines lining the columns are colored bright pink). (Reproduced by permission of the artist.)

(quite appropriately, considering the current context of the building!). This was the second venue of *Triangular*, following Guatemala. Silvia's piece was not immediately visible to me as I circled the patio of the convent. First I noticed the video, on a small screen in a niche in one of the side passages of the courtyard, and only then turned and looked upward, noticing the many tiny fertility figures topping the intricately carved columns. The coloristic contrast was notable, a device which Silvia had exploited in a number of previous works using pink Jabón Zote (Zote brand soap), drawing out what would seem to be every possible nuance and aesthetic potential of this most common of everyday products, visible and obtainable in almost any supermarket, market, or grocery store. Here, as in earlier works in the Ex-Convento of Tepoztlan and the alternative space Temistocles 44, Gruner used the soap as a vehicle for multiple metaphorical associations, among them the very diverse concepts and implications of cleanliness and the extreme associations of the body with physical/spiritual/national hygiene, from the ascetic regime of the sixteenth-century mendicant orders in Mexico (she carved an A into the bars of soap so that they read AZOTE, to flagellate) to the conversion of

Illustration 3.2. Silvia Gruner, *ASEA*, 1995. Color photograph, 51 × 61 cm. (Reproduced by permission of the artist.)

human Jewish bodies into soap in Nazi Germany. The subversive feminine associations of the color in the gray stone architecture, the subtle conflation of a fertility symbol with one of bodily dissolution, and the oral transmission of feminine knowledge and memories along with the physical inheritance of racial identity through the mother are among the references that reverberate in my memory of the piece. It is not a memory that I can fix on an object or an image, but a composite of experiences and reflections, dispersed in time and space and recollected, and transformed here into prose and a selection of illustrations. And surely, what "stuck" is partly the result of the intersection and association of my own memories and identities with Silvia's in spite of our different nationalities and histories: shared discomfort with the stereotypes of femininity, of post-Holocaust Judaism, and of "Latin" heritage, and more so with their awkward combination in one person, made eloquent in a work of art.

Gerardo Suter's multimedia piece, *Bitácora: Disecciones de un topógrafo* (1997), in the Center for the Arts in Mexico City, also addressed the elusive and fragmentary nature of memory, through the installation in a completely darkened room of large, luminous images of androgynous figures, digitally manipulated to engage in repetitive actions. The work alludes to our banal, anguished mental rituals, by means of corporeal and sensorial identification with the anonymous figures, while the contrasting emotional states suggested by each segment of the cycle, and the evanescence of the images themselves, resist any summation.

In contrast to the experience narrated of Gruner's *El nacimiento de Venus*, the spatial experience of the viewer here is more carefully controlled, on the one hand simply by transporting him or her into a world of penumbra, where one's sensorial reception is transformed and limited, and on the other hand by the ordered disposition of a series of works that capture different aspects of the experience of memory, each complementing the anguish produced by the other. The conceptual character of maps, mapping as an impulse to order and control rather than an objective description—a theme much commented on in recent critical literature[5]—is taken up here as Suter assumes the guise of a visual neuropsychologist, dissecting or extracting (constructing, reconstructing) images that highlight and continually frustrate our cultural need to complete the picture, the narrative, to remember the fragments of experience that even in the process of their registration are distorted and blurred. In an initial image, iconic—were it not anti-iconic in its movement—a bald androgynous figure (the protagonist of this series of images) gathers sand from a pile while it continually slips through his fingers. Further on, the figure's head rolls on the sand in a series of five horizontal images, as if it were rolling on a bed pillow during a disturbing dream, but the framing marks a discontinuity and disordering in relation to our narrative expectations, forcing a disconcerting awareness that *we* make the narrative (Illustration 3.3).

The counterpoint between the images functions effectively to highlight this aspect. The most static image, toward the end of the series, entitled *Stratus V*, is a monumental torso against a dark background, in a symmetrical posture—arms outstretched laterally, bending a thin rod that arches overhead—reminiscent of Leonardo's famed study of human proportion after Vitruvius, except that our view of this perfect body is abruptly cut off by a black panel that cuts across the chest, directly below the arms (Illustration 3.4). Subtly punctuated by its division into horizontal panels, this time by thin white lines, it is deceptively tranquil, a promise of a complete image . . . broken. Almost in front of

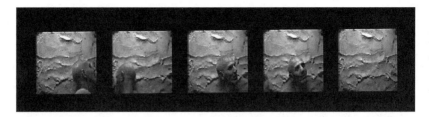

Illustration 3.3. Gerardo Suter, *Stratus III*, 1997. Five black-and-white video projections from the series *Bitácora*, Centro Nacional de las Artes, Mexico City. (Reproduced by permission of the artist.)

it is what for me was the most disturbing and viscerally provocative element of the installation, a digital projection on a circular area of powdered gypsum on the floor: One looks down toward a figure vainly and perpetually struggling to avoid sinking in the sand—on which a line-drawn map from a sixteenth-century codex is also projected (Illustration 3.5). But it

Illustration 3.4. Gerardo Suter, *Stratus V*, 1997. Installation view from the series *Bitácora*. Gelatin silver print on transparent acetate. Five sections, each 400 × 107 cm. (Reproduced by permission of the artist.)

Illustration 3.5. Gerardo Suter, *Stratus II,* 1997. From the series *Bitácora.* Black-and-white video projections on powdered gypsum. (Reproduced by permission of the artist.)

is only an image . . . no use to stretch out a hand and help, no possible relief, and no progression.

Here the play between the flatness and virtuality of the image and its compelling emotional pull is highlighted. Suter, exacting in his technique and in the aesthetic and conceptual structure of the piece, nevertheless courts the ragged borders of the mind and its images, opening up the time and space between the pieces and thus deliberately implicating and drawing the viewer into his work, relinquishing the objective control that the photographic illusion traditionally flaunts and that he has so carefully cultivated. Apparently more anonymous than Gruner, or less evidently autobiographical, he also pushes his obsessions to their limits, making his own vulnerability (and ours) the narrative crux of the work in a different way.

In contrast, the murals produced during the early and mid 1920s in Mexico, in the wake of ten years of armed conflict, reveal the need to control and unify perception and the use of the artistic representation of the body in this sense, as a vehicle for social identification, cohesion, and transformation. These works also reveal, however, the difficulty of this homogenizing effort; the proposals for the creation of a modern Mexican art and for the representation of a quintessentially Mexican body in this period were multiple and diverse, responding to a variety of aesthetic models and political perspectives, thus highlighting the primarily conceptual process through which the visual embodiment of Mexicanness was engendered, and belying later argumentation that it was based primarily on ethnographic observation and mimetic exercises.[6] This experimental quality is particularly evident in the murals painted in the Escuela Nacional Preparatoria, under the patronage of Vasconcelos's Ministry of Education (1921–1924), where the theme of *mestizaje* as a defining trait of Mexican society is explored from a variety of stylistic and thematic approaches. In effect, this monument can be seen, in retrospect, as a type of laboratory in technique, form, and content for what would later be characterized as the Mexican mural movement.[7]

In contrast, the Emergent Man in Diego Rivera's mural *Creación* of 1922–1923 (Illustration 3.6) in the Anfiteatro Bolívar and the figure of Woman in its lower left corner (Illustration 3.7) are visually stable bodies that represent a philosophical and social paradigm by means of the corporeal metaphor of *mestizaje*. The invention of hybrid bodies that incorporate the concept of a *raza cósmica* allows Rivera to offer icons of collective, symbolic identity, in a symmetrical, hierarchical composition

Illustration 3.6. Diego Rivera, *Creación*, 1922–1923 (detail of Emergent Man). Mural in the Anfiteatro Bolívar, Escuela Nacional Preparatoria, Mexico City. (Copyright © 2001 Banco de México and Frida Kahlo Museums Trust, Av. Cinco de Mayo No. 2. Col. Centro, Del. Cuauhtémoc 06059, México, D.F. Reproduced by permission.)

Illustration 3.7. Diego Rivera, *Creación*, 1922–1923 (detail of lower left corner). Mural in the Anfiteatro Bolívar. (Copyright © 2001 Banco de México and Frida Kahlo Museums Trust, Av. Cinco de Mayo No. 2. Col. Centro, Del. Cuauhtémoc 06059, México, D.F. Reproduced by permission of Banco de México and Instituto Nacional de Bellas Artes y Literatura.)

intended to indoctrinate the spirit rather than provoke a visceral, emotional reaction. As an expression of Vasconcelos's program of spiritual nationalism, which sought to suture by means of cultural homogenization the political, social, and economic fragmentation manifest in the armed struggle, Rivera in his mural constructs an ideal Mexican body. The anatomical and compositional stability and the virtual weight and materiality of his figures contrasts notably with, and constitutes a historical foil for, the dematerialization of the image induced by Gruner and Suter, which invokes the dynamic interaction of the spectator.

The visual comparison of the central figure in Rivera's *Creación* and Suter's *Stratus V* clarifies this point. Rivera's Emergent Man engulfs and dominates our personal space, visually and architectonically, citing its religious precedent in collective memory in figures of God the Father, although deliberately transforming both the allegorical and stylistic references to conform a specifically modern iconographic program. The torso emerges from succulent, Rousseau-inspired foliage, his arms opening in a wide V-shape to transform the dynamic triangular format into a modified star. His dark visage, almost masklike in its stylization, seems flat and superimposed on his vigorous musculature, echoing the smaller face that emerges from the jungle below among the primitivizing animalistic symbols of the four evangelists. The bodies of Rivera's protagonists (not only the Emergent Man, but the awkwardly androgynous Woman) express spiritual and social potential through the physical prowess of a clearly conceptual "national body"; the conventional associations of the ideal classical male nude are joined with deliberate stylistic references to a local, indigenous "other" (which does not have anything much to do in fact with any particular aspect of Mexico's nature or culture) locating the artwork and its argument in a precise geographical and ethnographic framework, and subsuming the implied viewer's specificity within the conceptual construct of spiritual nationalism. The sensuality of the volumetric and coloristic construction is seductive yet monumental, compelling yet devoid of intimacy. Just as Renaissance and primitivizing post-Impressionist references are conglomerated here, relinquishing their specificity to construct a common point of mythic reference, the work uses our gestural and iconographic references to draw us away from our subjectivity toward a homogenizing ideal.

Suter's *Stratus V* feeds on the expectations forged by this tradition, in its size, symmetry, and general corporeal gesture, yet it forces us into a more specific and self-reflexive mode of interrelation in which unquestioning identification is impossible. It deliberately separates us from its human subject with a black barrier, makes clear that it is a mere image by the separation into panels, and curiously dehumanizes the hairless, expressionless, and yet aesthetically exquisite figure, enhancing its purism by the coloristic limitation to black and white, which contrasts with Rivera's vivid palette.

A more extreme expression of the iconic stability sought by postrevolutionary culture is present in the monumental figures painted by David Alfaro Siqueiros in the stairwell of the Escuela Nacional Preparatoria in the first half of the 1920s, and in the cycle he designed, in collaboration with Amado de la Cueva (1891–1926), for the Paraninfo of

Illustration 3.8. David Alfaro Siqueiros, *El entierro del minero,* 1923–1924. Mural in the Escuela Nacional Preparatoria, Mexico City. (Copyright © David Alfaro Siqueiros / SOMAAP, México 2001. Reproduced by permission of Sociedad Mexicana de Autores de las Artes Plásticas and Instituto Nacional de Bellas Artes y Literatura.)

the University of Guadalajara a few years later. In *El entierro del minero* (Illustration 3.8) at the Preparatoria, Siqueiros attempts, like Rivera, to construct a "Mexican" body on the basis of ideas and artistic models rather than on the basis of observation of any real body. The umber tones of the dark, squared-off bodies and features of the pallbearers blend with the earthy sepia coloring of the background, contrasting with the brilliant blue of the coffin, which alludes to its transcendent mission. In the Guadalajara mural cycle, which deals with issues of land distribution and the use of natural resources, the umber and sepia tones are applied flatly to areas articulated with black linear drawings, rigid in their symmetry and frontality, almost diagrammatic in the simplicity of

Illustration 3.9. Amado de la Cueva and David Alfaro Siqueiros, *Ideales agrarios y laboristas de la Revolución de 1910*, 1925–1926 (detail). Mural in the Biblioteca Iberoamericana Octavio Paz of the University of Guadalajara, Guadalajara, Jalisco. (Copyright © David Alfaro Siqueiros / SOMAAP, México 2001. Reproduced by permission of Sociedad Mexicana de Autores de las Artes Plásticas and Instituto Nacional de Bellas Artes y Literatura.)

their representation, and yet once again monumental in their dimensions as they loom over the observer (Illustration 3.9). The influence of Renaissance models evident in Rivera is mitigated here by the volumetric compaction and more radical stylization of the figure inspired in pre-Hispanic stone sculpture—seen through the filter of Gauguin and Picasso—in an attempt to create a distinctly autochthonous "classic" style, in which the allusions to movement and the impulse to narration are minimal. The mythical, canonical status accorded to pre-Hispanic art, and in particular to Aztec culture, provided symbolic roots for the homogenizing conception of a "Mexican body," which posited the "Indian" past as the basis of national identity.

In this case, pre-Hispanic art serves as a metaphor rather than referring to specific visual antecedents and their meaning. It is a convenient way of symbolizing the past in apparently immutable form and projecting the implications of that past on contemporary bodies without taking into account the human variables in this construction of history. In other words, it is less problematic, for the aesthetic and political purposes of the period, to imagine a pre-Hispanic man (there are no women in this example) as a sculpture, rather than as flesh and blood. These are figures to be read, not interacted with; they are inserted in modern activities, yet they are codexlike in their spatial disposition and earthy in their coloring.

This essentialist vision invites adhesion, rather than corporeal identification. In spite of the populist discourse of the 1920s in Mexico, the world of art and its creators was basically confirmed—in the incipient realm of art criticism and art historiography—as a sacred, symbolic, untouchable precinct, spatially and temporally distinct from daily life, paradigmatic, rather than interactive, interweaving nationalism with biological determinism in a discursive operation that bore little link to social reality, but constituted itself as an ideological dogma.

The persistent role of pre-Hispanic art and culture in the symbolic constitution of a national corporeal identity, founded on the myth of racial and cultural continuity, is underlined by the fact that both Suter and Gruner often have used pre-Hispanic referents as a point of discursive departure, in their attempt to subvert linear and essentialist constructions of the body and history.

The fact that both artists come from families of European origin (Suter, Argentine-born and a resident of Mexico since 1970, has French, Swiss, German, and Italian antecedents, whereas Gruner is a descendant of European Jews) surely accentuated their consciousness of the contradictions implicit in these essentialist constructions, and their interest in exploring the relationship between the real body and the mythic ancestral body, creating images of disjunction and compenetration that offer new historiographical and narrative paradigms.

Suter in his 1985 series, *El archivo fotográfico del Dr. Retus,* inverted his last name to pose as a nineteenth-century explorer of pre-Hispanic ruins, who with his distinctive photographic framing accentuates a contemporary and subtly erotic reading of their poetic potential, rather than distance and mystery. In later photographic series he juxtaposes nude bodies directly with "primitive" or anthropological artifacts, or echoes the iconic symmetry and heroic corporeal symbolism of the muralists, and even their monumental scale in the format of his prints, but in a veristic photographic idiom that subverts the possibility of mythic seduction. The corporeal identification with the figures makes a distanced reading of the pre-Hispanic content impossible in these hybrid constructions; as in the album of Dr. Retus, the contemporaneousness of the idiom predominates.

The installation *Anáhuac* of 1995, presented in the Centro de la Imagen in Mexico City, marks Suter's departure from the use of photography as a primarily two-dimensional medium and its incorporation in multimedia spatial configurations, which open up new possibilities of corporeal and sensorial interaction. The photographs, printed on translucent acetate, were hung from the ceiling, and a video monitor with a sound track of rhythmic breathing presented alternating positive and negative images of an iconic androgynous figure, superimposed with alternating images of a map of Tenochtitlan from a sixteenth-century codex, and a detail of the *Guía Roji* map of contemporary Mexico City. Nearby, the video *Antigua* represented two nude figures engaged in a dancelike ritual interaction, within a circular frame. The temporal collapse anticipated in formal terms in Suter's earlier work clearly acquires performative dimensions in this piece, incorporating new narrative devices that permit the spectator's physical participation in the construction of new nonlinear narrative and historiographical relationships.

As the corporeal dimension of Suter's work has expanded in this sense, the weight of the pre-Hispanic referents has waned, acquiring an increasingly abstract and ambiguous quality; in *Bitácora* they are reduced to the incorporation of some projected images from sixteenth-century codices and a verbal reference to Aztlán as the object of the fictional topographer's voyage in the accompanying wall text written by the artist. The monumental dimensions of his images continue to evoke the heritage of muralism, but its discourse is intercepted directly in terms of corporeal strategies rather than historical symbolism.[8]

Silvia Gruner, in contrast, has moved from a more abstract and conceptual questioning of canonical structures to a very direct, eroticized, and confrontational symbolic interaction, with essentialist configurations of Mexican art and culture that attempt to "colonize" and control the possibilities of historical and aesthetic dialogue.[9]

In her performance and installation work of the early 1990s she counterpointed the specificity and materiality of the gendered body with scientific paradigms (*Yo soy esa simetría* [*I Am That Symmetry*], 1990–1991;
La medida de las cosas [*The Measure of Things*], 1991). In the following
years, she brought into question the imbrication of these contradictions
in everyday environments in Mexico, and the ensuing fragmentation and
mutilation of corporeal experience in our cultural identity, creating
objects and installations that juxtaposed pre-Hispanic figurines and pottery shards with contemporary domestic artifacts and locks of her own
hair, thus producing new "relics" as the product of a personal archaeology (*Destierro*, 1992; *Fetiches domésticos*, 1992; *La expulsión del Paraíso*,
1993; *Inventario*, 1994; *Reliquias*, 1994; and *Azote-a*, 1994).

The installation *El nacimiento de Venus* (*The Birth of Venus*) (1995), the
photographs entitled *How to Look at Mexican Art* (1995), and the video
In Situ (1995–1996), involve an increasingly probing, more ironic, and
less aesthetically purist exploration and transgression of established and
codified boundaries: the aesthetic and the political, the public and the
private, the sacred and the sexual. In *El nacimiento de Venus*, the tiny pink
soap fertility goddesses demonumentalize pre-Hispanic art, in their
dimensions, in their ephemeral material, and in the feminization of the
subject matter and viewpoint, while the dehumanizing and inhumane
character of ethnic policies, disguised as aesthetics and eugenics in Nazi
Germany and in modern Mexico, are suggested through our interaction
with objects and processes intimately related to our bodies and personal
identity. In *How to Look at Mexican Art* and *In Situ* a worn-through *mol-
cajete* (grinding mortar) and small pre-Hispanic-style clay figurines
become the objects of direct tactile and oral fondling and penetration,
belying and debunking their historical and symbolic aura, and ultimately, the political motivations behind that aura.

The title of the photographic series *Don't Fuck with the Past, You
Might Get Pregnant* (1995) (Illustration 3.10) is at once a light-hearted
challenge to and a powerful condemnation of this historical and aesthetic mystification of the past, as well as an ironic revindication of personal experience and of corporeal and ethical integrity as points of
departure for artistic and historical—as well as personal—analysis and
art making. Here Gruner inverts traditional gender roles and artistic
protagonisms, as she registers multiple views of her finger piercing
through the torso of a small male figurine, reveling in the documentation of her personal archeopornography, the simultaneous violation,

Illustration 3.10. Silvia Gruner, *Don't Fuck with the Past, You Might Get Pregnant,* 1995. Color photograph, 41 × 51 cm., from a series of nine photographs. (Reproduced by permission of the artist.)

exposure, and sublimation of a number of interrelated but usually unarticulated social, aesthetic, and ideological prohibitions.

The decentering and reconfiguration of the corporeal discourse of Mexican modernism in works such as those of Suter and Gruner serve several functions. One is simply to incite us to a consciousness that this canonical art *has* a corporeal discourse, a fact often ignored in the historiographical treatment of art in terms of a body politic rather than a politicized reading of the body. Another is to establish a critical dialogue with that past that breaks down conventional divisions between the personal and political, not only in conceptual, but, more importantly, in spatial and sensorial terms. Finally, it is as a result of what we might term this "deconstructive attitude" that our own bodies, persons, and *personae* are directly and irrevocably implicated in all these works, in a process of cocreation that also implies a commitment, a commitment to critical narratives assumed not as dogmas but as creative and personal, physical as well as mental acts, part of a signifying process rather than an end in itself, at once historical and contemporary, memory and presence, art and act.

NOTES

1. I have further analyzed some of the implications of these historiographical tendencies, particularly with regard to Mexican art of the first half of the century, in my essay "Constructing a Modern Mexican Art, 1910–1940" in the exhibition catalogue edited by James Oles, *South of the Border: Mexico in the American Imagination 1914–1947*, p. 13. For a concise and penetrating analysis of the conceptions of history and historiography, and their narrative implications, see Guillermo Zermeño and Alfonso Mendiola (1995).
2. For a detailed discussion of some of the theoretical implications of the modes of conceptualizing text and context in art history and its historiography, see Mieke Bal and Norman Bryson's article, "Semiotics and Art History" (1991). A broader historical and thematic treatment of corporeal discourse in Mexican art can be found in the exhibition catalogue *El cuerpo aludido: Anatomías y construcciones* (1998).
3. Francisco Reyes Palma in "Dispositivos míticos en las visiones del arte mexicano del siglo XX" (1996) deals with this topic in more depth.
4. For a summary and contextualization of the discussion around the Metropolitan exhibition see Mari Carmen Ramírez, "Brokering Identities: Art Curators and the Politics of Cultural Representation" (1996).
5. See, for example, Steven Pile and Nigel Thrift, eds., *Mapping the Subject: Geographies of Cultural Transformation* (1995); Peter A. Jackson, *Maps of Meaning: An Introduction to Cultural Geography* (1989); Jon Bird, Barry Curtis, Tim Putnam, George Robertson, and Lisa Tickner, eds., *Mapping the Futures: Local Culture, Global Change* (1993); and with specific regard to the art world, Ivo Mesquita's *Cartographies* (1993).
6. The diversity of modernist and modernizing discourse in Mexican art of the postrevolutionary period is studied in detail in the essays contained in the catalogue *Modernidad y modernización en el arte mexicano 1920–1960* (1991).
7. For a more detailed analysis of the diverse artistic and historiographical perspectives in the murals of the Escuela Nacional Preparatoria, see Karen Cordero Reiman, "La invención del muralismo Mexicano" (1999).
8. Additional information on Suter's work can be found primarily in the catalogues of his exhibitions and the corresponding texts: *Tiempo inscrito* (1991); *Códices* (1991); *Cantos rituales* (1994); *Anáhuac* (1995); *Cartografía* (1996); *Labyrinth of Memory* (1999).
9. For additional information on Gruner's work, see her *Reliquias/Collares* (1998), which includes texts by Cuauhtémoc Medina, Osvaldo Sánchez, and Kellie Jones.

WORKS CITED

Bal, Mieke and Norman Bryson. 1991. "Semiotics and Art History." *Art Bulletin* 73: 174–208.

Bird, Jon, Barry Curtis, Tim Putnam, George Robertson, and Lisa Tickner, eds. 1993. *Mapping the Futures: Local Culture, Global Change.* London and New York: Routledge.

Brenner, Anita. 1929. *Idols behind Altars.* New York: Payson and Clarke.

Cordero Reiman, Karen. 1993. "Constructing a Modern Mexican Art, 1910–1940." In *South of the Border: Mexico in the American Imagination 1914–1947* [exhibition catalogue], ed. James Oles, 10–47. Washington, D.C., and London: Smithsonian Institution Press.

———. 1999. "La invención del muralismo mexicano." In *Memoria: Congreso Internacional de Muralismo. San Ildefonso, cuna del Muralismo Mexicano, reflexiones historiográficas y artísticas,* 231–240. Mexico: UNAM/CONACULTA/DDF/Antiguo Colegio de San Ildefonso.

El cuerpo aludido: Anatomías y construcciones. México, siglos XVI–XX [exhibition catalogue]. 1998. Mexico: Museo Nacional de Arte.

Gruner, Silvia. 1998. *Reliquias/Collares* [exhibition catalogue]. Mexico: Centro de la Imagen/Fondo Nacional para la Cultura y las Artes.

Jackson, Peter. 1989. *Maps of Meaning: An Introduction to Cultural Geography.* London: Unwin Hyman.

Mesquita, Ivo. 1993. *Cartographies* [exhibition catalogue]. Winnipeg: Winnipeg Art Gallery.

Mexico: Splendors of Thirty Centuries [exhibition catalogue]. 1990. New York: The Metropolitan Museum of Art.

Modernidad y modernización en el arte mexicano 1920–1960 [exhibition catalogue]. 1991. Mexico: Museo Nacional de Arte.

Pile, Steven, and Nigel Thrift, eds. 1995. *Mapping the Subject: Geographies of Cultural Transformation,* London and New York: Routledge.

Ramírez, Mari Carmen. 1996. "Brokering Identities: Art Curators and the Politics of Cultural Representation." In *Thinking about Exhibitions,* ed. Reesa Greenberg, Bruce W. Ferguson, and Sandy Nairne, 21–38. London and New York: Routledge.

Reyes Palma, Francisco. 1996. "Dispositivos míticos en las visiones del arte mexicano del siglo XX." *Curare* 9: 3–18 (English translation 19–32).

Suter, Gerardo. 1991a. *Códices* [exhibition catalogue]. Mexico: Galería Arte Contemporáneo.

———. 1991b. *Tiempo inscrito* [exhibition catalogue]. Mexico: Museo de Arte Moderno.

———. 1994. *Cantos rituales* [exhibition catalogue]. Mexico: Galería OMR.

———. 1995. *Anáhuac* [exhibition catalogue]. Mexico: Centro de la Imágen/Museo de Monterrey.

———. 1996. *Cartografía* [exhibition catalogue]. Brazil: XXIII Bienal Internacional de Sao Paulo.

———. 1999. *Labyrinth of Memory* [exhibition catalogue]. New York, Americas Society Art Gallery.

Zermeño, Guillermo, and Alfonso Mendiola. 1995. "De la historia a la historiografía: Las transformaciones de una semántica." *Historia y grafía* (Department of History, Universidad Iberoamericana) 4: 245–261.

4

Elena Poniatowska's *Querido Diego, te abraza Quiela*
A Re-vision of Her Story

Susan C. Schaffer

n 1907 the young Diego Rivera landed on European soil, where he would spend the next fourteen years honing his skills as a painter. Financed by a grant from the Mexican government, his journey through "the lands of reason"[1] began in Spain, where he imitated old-world masters for two years. Taking up residence in Paris, Rivera experimented with the latest painterly trends alongside such cosmopolitan artists as Picasso, Modigliani, Jacobsen, Matisse, and Foujita. Finally, only months before his return to Mexico in July 1921, Rivera toured Italy—Siena, Arezzo, Perugia, Assisi, and Rome— where he studied the luminescent Renaissance frescoes that so profoundly informed the new art he would soon help engender in the Americas: muralism. Rivera's success abroad convinced Minister of Education José Vasconcelos to add the painter to a team of artists he assembled to launch Mexico's postrevolutionary mural project. More than any of his collaborators, Rivera received accolades for his sweeping depictions that romanticized the nation's pre-Colombian past and glorified the political struggles of its contemporary workers and peasants. His larger-than-life persona only amplified the mythologizing force of his monumental walls. For decades to come, the name Diego Rivera became synonymous with the country's postrevolutionary ideology.

Despite Rivera's metamorphosis from cosmopolitan modernist to national muralist, in his 1998 *Dreaming with His Eyes Open: A Life of Diego Rivera*, Patrick Marnham characterizes the Mexican's European apprenticeship as "the most important years of his life" (1998, 200). This view has been supported recently by art critics, such as Ramón Favela, who seek to chip away at the entrenched Rivera/postrevolutionary metaphor to reveal a more complex picture of the elements that construct the painter's and, consequently, Mexico's identity. The importance of Rivera's European training is contested, however, by his first biographer, Bertram Wolfe. A North American who worked as an international communist organizer in Mexico City during the 1920s, Wolfe cultivated a relationship with Rivera as a comrade and later dedicated many years to writing the muralist's biography. By publishing a treatment of Rivera's life and works outside of Mexico, Wolfe sought to broaden exposure to Rivera's achievement of promoting socialism through art. Thus, a primary objective of Wolfe's *The Fabulous Life of Diego Rivera* (1963; a rewrite of his 1939 *Diego Rivera: His Life and Times*) is to uphold Rivera as a chief representative of Mexico's new ideology and identity. One way in which the biography serves this purpose is by implying that Rivera's training in Europe was ultimately as bankrupt as the isms he and his colleagues pursued there. According to Wolfe, despite Rivera's attempts to emulate the bohemians, he could never escape his "exotic" Mexican roots: "Travel where he might, always he carried his land with him" (1963, 112). Wolfe believed instead that Rivera's true mission was to return "to his native land to paint 'the revolution' on walls of his own," to develop his "Aztec approach to communism": "the best service he could give [to the Mexican Communist Party]" (1963, 215, 149, 226).

Bertram Wolfe's portrayal of Rivera's life and craft is Manichean in its preference for the "verdant" Americas over Europe. Early-twentieth-century easel painting is a particular target of his scorn, criticized as an expression of elitist nihilism. Commodities handled by bourgeois art dealers and collectors ("esthetes"), these canvases were, in Wolfe's estimation, detached from the workaday world and its struggling masses (1963, 82, 89). It is only when Rivera rejects Europe and easel painting that he learns to communicate to "the people" through his monumental walls. Wolfe even subjects Rivera's romantic ties to this facile equation. On the one hand, his Mexican wives incarnate the color, wildness, and vibrancy of their mutual homeland. Guadalupe Marín, who often modeled in the nude for his early frescoes, epitomizes pre-Columbian fecundity and "femaleness" (1963, 183). Wolfe compares the "great curves of arm and thigh, exuberant breasts and rounded belly" of Marín to "the solidity and grandeur of [a] pyramid" (1963, 183). Frida Kahlo plays "the role of companion, confidante, and comrade" (1963, 252), satiating Rivera's thirst for ideological passion (1963, 183). On the other, Rivera's first wife, the Russian printmaker and painter Angelina Beloff, whom he abandons for Mexico, emblematizes the soberness of Paris and its decadent art. Whereas the British biographer Marnham holds that Beloff "was to shape the course of Rivera's life for . . . twelve years" (1998, 66), Wolfe disregards her contributions to the painter's artistic and ideological education: "The Revolution which took possession of Diego Rivera and made him a painter was the Mexican Revolution, not the Russian" (1963, 421).

Elena Poniatowska, herself a European émigré (as a daughter of Polish immigrants), claims that she wrote her epistolary novel *Querido Diego, te abraza Quiela* in response to Bertram Wolfe's *The Fabulous Life* (Ratkowski 1986, 37–38). The catalyst that incited her to pen an imaginative version of Beloff's relationship with Rivera was Wolfe's Chapter 12, titled "Angelina Waits." In it Wolfe relies heavily on excerpts of letters to Rivera from his first wife in order to show that her reaction to being abandoned was hysterical. Poniatowska conducted her own research on Beloff, however, and concluded that "todo era falso, que Bertram Wolfe era muy descuidado, que inventaba todo," 'it was all false, Bertram Wolfe was careless and invented everything' (1986, 38). This revelation—that the verbal tableau Wolfe crafted of Angelina was as fractured as the cubist portraits Rivera had painted of her—piqued the writer to create through fiction a richer, more complete version of Beloff's story.

In his insightful article on *Querido Diego* (1990), Juan Bruce-Novoa suggests that to appreciate the complexity of Poniatowska's novel it should be read as a subversion of the dominant text: Wolfe's slanted biography. Such an approach allows the reader to see beyond the novel's orthodox veneer to perceive the "ironic subtext of the feminist author" (1990, 118). According to Bruce-Novoa, one of the keys to detecting this alternative reading lies in Poniatowska's use of "palimpsestic strategies" (1990, 117). My aim in this chapter is to identify some of these strategies and to analyze how they allow the novelist to superimpose her fictive version of the events on the texts that comprise Beloff's representation. The three texts of the palimpsest most germane to this inquiry are the portraits Diego Rivera painted of his wife between 1914 and 1918 and Bertram Wolfe's two biographies, the original *Diego Rivera: His Life and Times* from 1939 and its 1963 rewrite, *The Fabulous Life of Diego Rivera*.[2] Together these layers constitute a monumental tablet of inscription that enshrines Rivera at his wife's expense. Yet a close reading of these texts reveals insights that surpass a mere critique of the Beloff-Europe/Rivera-Mexico comparison. Poniatowska, through masterful use of parody and revision, fashions in *Querido Diego* a potent counterdiscourse that elevates Beloff's experience to a position where it may be fully examined and reassessed.

In the absence of a text articulating Beloff's own view of her story, a discussion of how Angelina is "killed into art" (Gilbert and Gubar 1979, 17) may begin with Diego Rivera's portraits of his wife.[3] During his years in Europe, the young artist painted numerous canvases of Beloff. Prior to 1913, as well as after 1917, these paintings are "realistic." Those completed during this span of time were products of the painter's search for a unique style within the parameters of cubism. One of the distinctive features of Rivera's cubist production was his choice of subject matter. Rather than concentrating on neutral motifs, as did fellow members of this school, the Mexican was "extremely personal and biocentric" in his selection of content, as art critic Ramón Favela avers (1984, 70). In particular, Rivera persisted in depicting human subjects despite the criticism that portraiture—an act of reproduction or interpretation—was an anathema to the cubist goal of realizing pure creation. During the period of Rivera's most intensive work on cubist portraiture, 1916–1918, he shared with the classical cubists a preference for ideal forms that were used to "evoke in the spectator a spiritual 'totalizing image' " (1984, 130). But unlike other cubists, Rivera endeavored to "individualize" his subjects by devising, in his own words, an "ensemble of traits that would make a unique and personal facial cipher" (quoted in Favela 1984, 121).

According to Favela, the principal aim of cubism is "to reduce objects to their simplest geometric forms; to arrive at their *essence* rather than attempting to artificially reproduce the photographic appearance of objects" (1984, 56). Although this definition emphasizes the cubists' interest in form, it also suggests that cubist works convey a content. This holds especially true for Rivera's art, often described as synonymous with "fabulación infinita," 'endless fabulation' (Labastida 1994, 76). A brief analysis of two Beloff portraits demonstrates how Rivera

Illustration 4.1. Diego Rivera, *Mujer en verde* (*Woman in Green*), 1916.
(Copyright © 2001 Banco de México and Frida Kahlo Museums Trust, Av. Cinco de Mayo No. 2. Col. Centro, Del. Cuauhtémoc 06059, México, D.F. Reproduced by permission.)

makes use of an "ensemble of traits" to impose on the spectator a paradigm or way of observing the constructed image of his wife (Wilshire 1989, 104). In the 1916 *Mujer en verde* (*Woman in Green*, Illustration 4.1, mislabeled as *Angelina Pregnant 1917* in Wolfe's biographies), round shapes and decorative patterns code the subject as female. The most salient form—the pregnant lower abdomen—is located in the center of the canvas and is silhouetted by light green spaces.[4] In *Angelina y el niño Diego, maternidad* (*Angelina and the Child Diego, Maternity*, Illustration 4.2, mislabeled as *Angelina and the Child Diego* in FL and *Angelina and Diego Jr.* in LT) the abdomen has been replaced by Dieguito, the new focal point of the portrait. Furthermore, unlike the frontal position of the woman's head in *Mujer en verde*, here it bows toward the baby, rein-

Illustration 4.2. Diego Rivera, *Angelina y el niño Diego, Maternidad (Angelina and the Child Diego, Maternity)*, 1917. (Copyright © 2001 Banco de México and Frida Kahlo Museums Trust, Av. Cinco de Mayo No. 2. Col. Centro, Del. Cuauhtémoc 06059, México, D.F. Reproduced by permission.)

forcing the centrality of the infant. In both portraits the "essence" of the female subject has been circumscribed as "mother."

In his biographies of Rivera, Bertram Wolfe agrees that the muralist's cubist paintings constitute more than mere experimentation with form; clearly Rivera's enterprise involves fabricating a content:

> The artist took all these casual fragments, and out of the depths of his own sense of form and structure, put them together into something new, a new pattern, a new solid, a new object—of his own creation. . . . Behold the ultimate in selection, distortion, and rearrangement . . . ! Behold the ultimate in the sovereignty of the creative mind, the artist became architect, constructor, builder, creator of his own universe! (1963, 85)

Wolfe neglects how Rivera's cubist strategies inform his own textual-ization of Angelina Beloff. It is indeed striking the degree to which Wolfe's verbal portrait of Rivera's wife echoes the painter's pictorial image of her. Emulating Rivera, Wolfe centers his description on a lim-ited number of traits. One of the signs he most frequently employs to encapsulate Beloff is the bluebird. The Russian is bathed repeatedly in the color blue and her mannerisms are described as "birdlike":

> Blue-eyed, light sky-blue. Blue jersey or smock, blue suit of trim, resolute lines, covered a slender, not unfeminine figure. . . . Birdlike in her movements and lightness, in the poise of her head slightly tilted to one side when she was lost in contemplation, in the delicately aquiline profile, in the lips always pursed into the shadow of a meditative smile, birdlike in the thin, reed, chirping note of her high monotone voice.[5] (1963, 68)

Wolfe may associate Beloff with light blue because Rivera used this color to depict his wife in several portraits, although the muralist also rendered her in green and white. In any case, blueness supports the biographer's efforts to link Angelina to frigid Europe, both literally in terms of climate and figuratively in terms of ideological and psycholog-ical detachment.

Another feature Wolfe borrows from Rivera to sketch Angelina is that of motherliness. In fact, the biographer turns maternity into a thesis pos-tulated to rationalize Rivera's unlikely attraction to this "sweet and win-some creature" (1963, 67). Wolfe emphasizes that Beloff, six years older than Rivera,[6] served more as the painter's cook, maid, and guardian than as his wife. A final summation of Beloff cements this idea: "Angelina, sev-eral years his senior, gentle, soft, maternal, had played mother along with wife to his young manhood" (1963, 251). Wolfe also deploys the thesis to explain why it was inevitable that Rivera would desert Beloff when their son Dieguito died: "With his death, one of the ties that linked Diego to France (and to Angelina) was broken" (1963, 101).

E. H. Gombrich has called cubism "the most radical attempt to stamp out ambiguity and to enforce one reading of the picture—that of a man-made construction" (1956, 281). Rivera's portraits clearly aspire to this goal. Yet Wolfe surpasses Rivera in loading the static images of Beloff with univocal meaning. A single iconic text, such as a portrait, cannot narrate; therefore its meaning can never be fully stabilized. Nonetheless, according to Kevin Halliwell, slippage of signification may be largely overcome by placing several images in a sequence and accompanying them with a written text (1980–1981, 84). This is exactly what Wolfe does in his biographies. In lieu of photographs, he provides the reader with black-and-white reproductions of four portraits of Angelina Beloff: three cubist and one referential.[7] As noted earlier, some of these are mislabeled or incorrectly dated.[8] Although such inaccuracies, in themselves, falsify the historical record, even more disturbing is Wolfe's selection of the four images. By choosing to include only those portraits that supported his thesis, the biographer accomplished an act of distortion comparable to any Rivera achieved with his paintbrush.[9]

Furthermore, the manner in which Wolfe positions and arranges the portraits in his texts imposes a narrative on them that corroborates his interpretation of the events. First, all four appear on a single page that precedes any textual description of Beloff. To illustrate, in *The Fabulous Life* the portraits are shown between pages 42 and 43, but the related text is not introduced until page 56. This previewing tactic imprints on the reader's mind an indelible visual image of Beloff that later triggers recollection when the textual descriptions are read. Wolfe then places the portraits in a sequence that obliges a chronological reading of them.[10] The sequence as it appears in *The Fabulous Life* serves as an example. By virtue of their cubist style, their dates, and their display on the page, Plates 17, 18, and 20 form a unit that suggests the story of Beloff's pregnancy (Illustration 4.3). On the other hand, Plate 19, the referential portrait, may be decoded as analogous to Wolfe's summation of Beloff as a pitiful mother who had lost a child and soon would lose a husband.

To reinforce Beloff's subordinate role in Rivera's "fabulous life," Wolfe pens a verbal treatment of the paintings. This alphabetic representation, in Barthian terms, "anchors" the univocal meaning of the images (Barthes, 1977). The four paragraphs that compose the textual description—each devoted to one of the portraits—appear in the first chapter dealing with Beloff: Chapter 6, or "Painter's Paris" (1963, 68–69). In them, Wolfe offers details that replicate the version of Beloff's story already "told" by the page displaying the four portraits. Words are now used to further emplot the narrative according to the template he established pictorially: before, during, and after "the birth of Diego Junior" (1963, 69). The descriptors chosen to verbalize the female subject's thorax in the three cubist portraits demonstrate this, especially in *Life and Times*. Here Wolfe codifies the "first" chest and belly as "straight as a board—no sign of her pregnancy showing" (1939, 71). The "second" is described as a "monumental belly," ironically

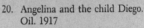

17. Portrait of Angelina. Oil. 1917

18. Angelina Pregnant. Oil. 1917

19. Portrait of Angelina. Oil. 1918 (?)

20. Angelina and the child Diego. Oil. 1917

Illustration 4.3. The sequence of Rivera's portraits of Beloff that appears in Bertram Wolfe's *The Fabulous Life of Diego Rivera.* (Copyright © 1963 Banco de México and Frida Kahlo Museums Trust, Av. Cinco de Mayo No. 2. Col. Centro, Del. Cuauhtémoc 06059, México, D.F. Reproduced by permission of Banco de México and Rowman and Littlefield.)

superimposing Rivera's characteristic monumentality on his wife's pregnant body (1939, 71). The "third" is deemed "deflated" because the abdomen has been supplanted by Dieguito, "the new center" (1939, 72).

The "before, during, and after" template also drives the Beloff narrative throughout the biographies. Chapter 6 could be read as a more detailed verbal description of FL's Plate 17, for it discusses Angelina's background, physical appearance, and early relationship with Rivera before their son was born. Chapter 9 provides the story behind FL's Plates 18 and 19: her pregnancy and Dieguito's death. And Chapter 12 relates Beloff's empty life after Rivera left Paris for Mexico, clearly justifying Angelina's abject look in Plate 19. The chapters treating Beloff appear at such regular intervals—6, 9, 12—that they stand almost literally as framed portraits in a gallery. It is important to remember, however, that the "exhibit" in this gallery does not feature Angelina Beloff, but rather Diego Rivera. The text that fills the lengthy gaps that lie between these "paintings," or chapters, suggests praise for the Mexican master's decision to desert fashionable Europe in favor of the autochthonous West.

The fragmentary structure and distorted content of the biographies clearly reflect Diego Rivera's cubist project. And the chapter that most closely emulates that project is, not surprisingly, the one that so troubled Elena Poniatowska: "Angelina Waits." Here Wolfe rivals the muralist with regard to "selection, distortion, and rearrangement." In Chapter 12, Wolfe brings closure to the two artists' relationship by citing excerpts from Beloff's letters to Rivera after their separation in the early 1920s. Initially, the biographer's extensive use of these letters, presented as historical artifacts, may fool the naïve reader into accepting Wolfe's depiction of "poor Angelina" as a hysteric.[11] Yet Wolfe fragments, refracts, and frames the letters so ruthlessly that the biographer's misogyny no longer remains a matter of subtext. More than carelessly quoting the letters out of context, Wolfe excises portions of them, repeats others, and freely uses ellipsis in an effort to play apologist for Diego Rivera. The text in which the biographer encases Beloff's private communications serves a similar purpose. In the following example Wolfe adds statements by Diego Rivera to his own biased commentary to explain Beloff's exaggerated dependency and pain:

> Her life was not centered in painting as his was, with all else subordinate. "For me painting and life are one," he had written to Renato Paresce in 1920. "It is my dominant passion . . . an organic function more than an activity of the spirit." For her, love and life were more nearly one, painting a

mode of filling in the interstices. He was lover, comrade, son, and the prototype of hero painter. Gladly she had forsworn land and friends and language for his; she had built her life with him as its armature. (1963, 128)

Writing as if he were privy to her innermost feelings and aspirations, Wolfe "deflates" Beloff while inflating the Mexican's greatness. In reality, however, Wolfe suppressed many historical facts and documents that could have presented the Russian in a more positive or, at least, comprehensive light. The biographer offers no samples of Beloff's artistic production, for instance, nor does he furnish excerpts from Rivera's letters to Beloff in which the muralist expresses appreciation of his wife both as a companion and an artist.[12] Ignoring such evidence, Wolfe prefers to deride Angelina:

[Rivera's] silences were eloquent. The cool spaces that lay between the lines of his dispatches of money should have told her. Did she not know him enough to understand how hard it would be for him to say directly, "I do not love you"? Perhaps the Russian way is for lovers to torture each other by lengthy analyses of their altered feelings, but the Latin hints more gracefully when he loves and with more subtlety when he has grown indifferent. (1963, 128)

Wolfe criticizes Beloff for her inattention to the hidden meaning in what Rivera, a master of representation, failed to represent.

Despite working in different mediums, Rivera and Wolfe fashion Angelinas that mirror, as well as reinforce, each other. This alignment of inscriptions largely stems from the intimacy that existed between biographer and subject. David Bromwich (1984) notes that a biographer is prone to developing a kinship with his subject when they share similar experiences. This was particularly true for Wolfe and the muralist since, as *The Fabulous Life*'s concluding note states, "Wolfe lived in Rivera's Mexico for many years and knew the painter well from 1922 until Rivera's death in 1957." Even more, Wolfe appears as a player in the biographies. For example, in the chapter titled "The Communist War on Rivera," he describes and justifies his complicity in Rivera's decision to leave the Communist Party temporarily. Finally, the two collaborated on three books devoted to verbal and iconographic portraiture: *El romance tradicional en México* (1925), *Portrait of America* (1934), and *Portrait of Mexico* (1938). Wolfe himself admits that his friend and coauthor influenced his thinking:

I should put the reader on notice that I owe Diego a great debt, for it was through his eyes that I first learned to see the visible world somewhat as artists see it, and to perceive Mexico's landscapes, people, history as a succession of "Riveras." . . . It was a priceless gift to have had my vision and sensibility enriched by the contagion of his enthusiasms. (1963, 4)

On the other hand, Wolfe contends that he was as "truthful with his pen" as Rivera was "truthful with his brush": "On my 'principal subject' I have done no retouching and exercised no concealment. . . . I have not consciously left anything untold that would signify the slightest modification of the picture I have drawn" (1939, viii, ix). The biographer invokes here the implicit pact between author and reader that, according to Philippe Lejeune (1989), traditionally governs biography.[13] The biographer promises impartiality in return for the reader's pledge to read the text "factually," rather than "fictively" (Abbot 1988, 613). Regardless of Wolfe's disclaimers, however, the drawing metaphors he chooses to describe his activity as biographer belie his neutrality toward Diego Rivera. As Hayden White insists, historical discourse, of which biography is a subset, is hardly an objective medium, differing only from literary discourse in that its referents are "real" events rather than "imaginary" (1989, 24).

Elena Poniatowska shares with Bertram Wolfe a strong identification with her subject. But unlike the biographer, she openly confesses that the voice in *Querido Diego* (1978) is very close to hers: "al escribirlo sentí que me convertí en ella; en realidad soy yo la que le digo a un hombre todas estas cosas, " "As I wrote it I felt like I had become her; it's really me who tells a man all these things' (Ratkowski 1986, 38).[14] Moreover, although she bases her narration on the same evidence as Wolfe—providing, in fact, a more complete historical record of Beloff's life—Poniatowska calls her text a novel. She does not disguise her intent to use fiction to revise Beloff's image and broaden the emplotment of the Russian's narrative.[15]

Poniatowska's re-presentation of Angelina Beloff hinges primarily on a double stratagem. First, she subverts the dominant texts by creating a parody of Wolfe's and Rivera's reductionist portraits. Then she constructs a more variegated, enriched view of the Russian by recontextualizing her story and fictively illuminating the black holes left vacant by her predecessors. In crafting a new text for her subject, Poniatowska knits together a vast number of discursive threads, many of which loop back to unravel the underweave of the palimpsest. The intricate intertextuality of *Querido Diego* problematizes virtually every aspect of the narrative. Issues regarding documentation, translation, focalization, implied reader, and genre pose intriguing research questions and merit in-depth analysis.[16] The three variables, however, that best reveal how Poniatowska superimposes her text onto the palimpsest are space, time, and discourse.

Elaine Showalter characterizes the normative sphere of woman's space as that "of the Other, the gaps, silences, and absences of discourse and representation, to which the feminine has traditionally been relegated" (1984, 36). Throughout the history of representation, women have been inscribed pictorially as objets d'art or verbally as minor players in the biographies of men.[17] Poniatowska employs stealth to contest this inscription. In *Querido Diego* there are unquestionably times when the protagonist's depiction is in concert with Wolfe's and Rivera's. Beloff is occasionally limned as naïve and blind to the obvious, for instance. And the reader recoils when she self-effacingly calls herself "tu [Rivera's] pájaro," 'your bird,' and confesses that "sin ti, soy bien poca cosa," 'without you, I'm really almost nothing' (1978, 58, 17). Nevertheless, this one-sided view is counterbalanced by many other scenes in which the printmaker is assertive, confident, and even defiant. In fact, the reductive features that shape her portrait in the master texts frequently are deflected or debunked in Poniatowska's version, rather than reiterated. The blues with which Wolfe uniformly colors his Angelina often are associated in the novel with Rivera and his "savage" Mexico, whereas Poniatowska's Beloff frequently shades herself and her European world in hues of gray. Furthermore, although Beloff's love for Dieguito is undoubtedly genuine, her innate maternalness is challenged. Before she meets Rivera, Beloff sees children merely as artistic subjects: "Yo nunca me detuve a ver a un niño en la calle . . . por el niño en sí. Lo veía ya como el trazo sobre el papel," 'I never paused to look at a child on the street . . . for the child in itself. I looked at the child as if at a mark on a paper' (1978, 33). After Rivera has left her, in a particularly lucid moment, she rebels against the way she is publicly construed: "hoy no quiero ser dulce, tranquila, decente, sumisa, comprensiva, resignada, las cualidades que siempre ponderan los amigos. Tampoco quiero ser maternal," 'today I don't want to be sweet, tranquil, decent, submissive, understanding, resigned, the qualities which friends always exalt. Nor do I want to be maternal' (1978, 41–42).

Beyond exposing the superficiality of the Beloff clichés, Poniatowska parodies the conventional notion that the subject of a portrait is defined by the sum total of traits with which the painter has articulated her on canvas. The novelist accomplishes this most explicitly by omitting any original reference to Beloff's appearance or age and, conversely, by hyperbolizing Rivera's size. In a clever subversion of male representational strategy, Poniatowska transforms Rivera's "fabulous monumentality" into "gran corpachón," 'big jumbo body' (1978, 15). At the same time, she playfully imitates Wolfe's reduction of Beloff to bluebird by linking Rivera's "gordura" (heaviness) metonymically to his inflated ego and bombastic personality. Poniatowska also undermines traditional portraiture by literally overlapping her protagonist and the master. This occurs in the powerful scene in which Beloff sees herself in the mirror as an engorged Diego. In my mind, it is not coincidental that the following depiction "mirrors" that of her pregnant state in Rivera's *Mujer en verde:* "Me volví hasta gorda Diego, me desbordaba, no cabía en el estudio, era algo como tú . . . mi caja toráxica se expandió a tal grado que los pechos se me hincharon, los cachetes, la papada; era yo una sola llanta," 'I actually got fat, Diego, I poured over, I didn't fit in the studio, I was something like you . . . my thorax expanded so much that my breasts, my cheeks, my neck swelled up; I was one big inner tube' (1978, 23). While this scene visually superimposes Beloff on Rivera, it also implies an assault on Bertram Wolfe, for Poniatowska's verbal transformation of the woman's "caja toráxica" into "una sola llanta" satirizes the biographer's alphabetic description of the portraits.

In *Querido Diego*, Poniatowska does not merely exact revenge on patriarchy's depiction of women, she also opens up for her subject a new dispersive space in which room is allotted for complexity, contradiction, and evolution. Whereas Wolfe maintained that for Beloff "painting [was] a mode of filling in the interstices" (1963, 128), Poniatowska plumbs these fissures, as well as the gaping crevices of the dominant texts, to bring to light the Russian's multifaceted emotional, intellectual, and artistic life.[18] Her Angelina exhibits not only the depression and deficiency Wolfe attributes to her, but also a wide range of characteristics that includes perseverance, confidence, and pride in her achievements. The Beloff that utters the following is absent from the official record: "El lograr mi independencia económica ha sido una de las fuentes de mayor satisfacción y me enorgullece haber sido una de las mujeres más avanzadas de mi tiempo," 'Achieving economic independence has been one of my greatest satisfactions and I am proud to have been one of the most advanced women of my time' (1978, 66).

Concerning Beloff's participation in intellectual and artistic arenas, Poniatowska depicts the protagonist as grappling with her art. This struggle illustrates not her lack of talent, as Wolfe alleges, but rather the process—punctuated by moments of fecundity and paralysis—that all artists, including Rivera, undergo. In rebuttal to Wolfe's assertion that her art was "unimportant" (1963, 129), Poniatowska devotes fully one third of the novel to Beloff's formation as an artist and her work as a successful painter and printmaker. The Russian's dedication to art is further highlighted by the parallels Poniatowska draws between Rivera's and Beloff's work regimens: Both devote such long hours to their vocation they forget about basic needs such as eating and sleeping. The most audacious illustration of the novelist's effort to equate Beloff's artistic commitment with Rivera's appears in the fourth letter. For this epistle, Poniatowska appropriates an anecdote Wolfe (1963, 57) introduces as proof of the muralist's passion for painting, and protagonizes it instead with her subject. In *Querido Diego* it is not Rivera who visits the Louvre, then stops by the Galería Vollard to admire the Cézanne canvases on display. Beloff is the one who is so mesmerized by the paintings that she spends three hours lost in their contemplation. Soon after this artistic epiphany, Angelina, not Diego, is bedridden with pneumonia. It is significant that Poniatowska applies the Rivera anecdote to Beloff as an introduction to the scene in which the Russian replaces Rivera's canvas with her own and returns to painting. In palimpsestic fashion, Beloff's act of usurping Rivera's privileged position at the easel mirrors Poniatowska's confiscation and revision of Bertram Wolfe's text. Such treatments of space exemplify how *Querido Diego* becomes a forum for the exploration of both absences and presences (Heilbrun and Stimpson 1989, 62). By toying with the gaps so prevalent in the master texts, Poniatowska undermines stereotypical caricature and supplants it with the creation of a vital "subject-inprocess" (Moi 1986, 16).

Another variable that sheds light on Poniatowska's subversive stratagem is that of time. In particular, a comparison of her use of sequence to that of Wolfe's informs our inquiry. As was noted earlier, the biographer organizes his account chronologically, upholding a convention in historical discourse that fosters linear narration. In contrast, Poniatowska relates the same tale—albeit with a different focus—using what Kristeva (1986) has termed "women's time." Unlike chronology, which typically spotlights the salient events of public life, "women's time" accentuates the personal and the private. It postulates a temporal dimension that rejects linearity, codified by historians as objective, and embraces what Kristeva calls "free and fluid subjectivity" (1986, 208).

Throughout *Querido Diego*, Poniatowska's applies "women's time" to counteract intransigent official time. The novel begins where Wolfe's story of Beloff ends: with separation and abandonment. As Nancy K. Miller (1980) has noted, in traditional biography there are only two possible outcomes for women: marriage or death. Poniatowska defies this fatal emplotment by converting Beloff's figurative demise into a beginning. To chart Angelina's evolution from this starting point, the novelist skews Wolfe's "before, during and after" template at every opportunity. Although the text marks time linearly from "19 de octubre de 1921" until the epilogue's 1935 anecdote, thus ostensibly tracing Beloff's life after Rivera, the actual sequence of events rarely obeys chronology and is frequently interrupted by flashbacks. For example, Poniatowska devotes four letters—2, 3, 7, and 10—to detailing out of any predictable order the Russian's formative years as a promising art student, her pregnancy, Dieguito's illness, and Rivera's affair with Marievna.[19] The fact that crucial events, such as the child's death, are narrated several times further violates chronology.[20] Poniatowska also scrambles time within the letters themselves to fortify her revision of Beloff. The maximum expression of this is found in the penultimate letter, labeled "2 de febrero de 1922," where despite the sense of temporal unity this date confers on its content, the events related in the letter span the entire history of the Beloff/Rivera odyssey. Moreover, its narrative is sequenced in accordance with Beloff's mental travel through time. Of particular note is the way in which the novelist selects events for this letter and maps them out on a sinuous route complete with flashbacks and shortcuts to the future. She first excises fragments from Wolfe's Chapters 6, 9, and 12, then reorders and inserts them into her own imagined story relative to Beloff's various psychological positions. When examined in the light of the biographies, Poniatowska's unconventional sequence suggests the arbitrariness of Wolfe's chronology, as well as his careless documentation of dates and sources.[21]

Alternative use of time in *Querido Diego* also fosters the expansion of Beloff's story so that moments of importance to her inner life may be recorded. By shuffling past, present, and future, Poniatowska allows the psychological to occupy the same authorized space as the "factual." Imagined occurrences, in particular, constitute a major portion of the text. Beloff re-creates the past by verbalizing how her life might have been had her son lived and Rivera not left her: "Imaginaba yo a Dieguito asoleándose, a Dieguito sobre tus piernas, a Dieguito frente al mar," 'I imagined little Diego sunbathing, little Diego on your lap, little Diego by the seaside' (1978, 13). Likewise, she actively envisions a present and a future: "te imagino alrededor de una mesa intercambiando ideas," 'I imagine you around a table, exchanging ideas' (1978, 60) and "dentro de poco enviarás por mí para que esté siempre a tu lado," 'very soon you will send for me so that I may be always at your side' (1978, 14). This blurring of "real" and imagined events provides more than a window into Beloff's psyche or another usurpation of a Riveran attribute, namely, fabrication. It also sets up Poniatowska's challenge against the objectivity of Bertram Wolfe's account. Although the "factual" use of tenses is requisite in biography, giving priority to the preterite, Wolfe often resorts to the present and, more surprisingly, the conditional to insert his own commentary into the historical narrative. Poniatowska's abundant use of the hypothetical in *Querido Diego* may be understood to parody that found in *The Fabulous Life*. Compare the conditional tenses employed in these two passages, keeping in mind that the first is extracted from a biography, the second from a novel:

> If [Angelina] could have seen the paintings [Rivera] was doing on Mexico's walls while she sat in their Paris room grieving, she would have known that he would never return. (Wolfe 1963, 128)

> Mi mayor alegría sería ver entre mi escasa correspondencia una carta con un timbre de México. [My greatest happiness would be to see a letter with a Mexican stamp among my meager pile of mail.] (Poniatowska 1978, 24)

To break the linguistic code of the dominant palimpsestic layers, Poniatowska manipulates discourse subversively in *Querido Diego*. She utilizes this ploy most extensively in the final third of the novel, after having laid a largely imaginative foundation that yields a more balanced view of the printmaker. Letters 8, 11, and 12 are the site of Poniatowska's most ingenious verbal battle, and her principal adversary is Bertram Wolfe. To attack him discursively, Poniatowska implements a stratagem similar to that used to refute other aspects of the official texts: Poniatowska cannibalizes passages from the biographies, translates them either literally or paraphrastically, then inserts them in her novel. Especially subjected to this operation is all of the language that composes Chapter 12—including fragments of Beloff's letters as they are cited by the biographer, Wolfe's paraphrase of other portions of Beloff's letters, and his own commentary.

The eighth letter offers a good example of how Poniatowska reframes Beloff's story, for it is the first to quote heavily from the July 22, 1922 letter cited in "Angelina Waits" (Chapter 12 of Wolfe, 1963).

Letter 8 begins with Beloff's most rebellious stance against Rivera and with the realization of her abandonment: "Diego no es un niño grande, Diego sólo es un hombre que no escribe porque no me quiere y me ha olvidado por completo," 'Diego isn't a big child, Diego is just a man who doesn't write to me because he doesn't love me and has completely forgotten me' (Poniatowska 1978, 42). This introduction differs markedly from the one Wolfe employs to present the same Beloff letter. The biographer first characterizes the letter as "fateful," then states that Beloff wrote it because she had "failed to thank [Rivera]" for three remittances of money he had generously sent her (1963 124, 125). Whereas Poniatowska emphasizes Beloff's strength, Wolfe insinuates her weakness and lack of good manners. The authors also differ in the way in which they close their citation of the July 22 letter. Wolfe concludes by chastising the Russian (as if he were addressing Beloff in person) and by launching into a litany of rhetorical questions that exposes his prejudice against her:

> Poor Angelina! Love cannot be compelled by pity. After years of intimate life with Diego, did she not know him well enough to perceive that all was over? Had he not refused to tie again the bond which had broken with the death of their boy? Had he not let her know that his passion had long yielded to a feeling akin to the fraternal? Had he not even brought to her, as to an unusually knowing friend and confidante, tales of his new passions for other women? (1963, 127–128)

Poniatowska, on the other hand, ends her incorporation of Beloff's letter with words that could be read as a defiant response to Wolfe's outburst:

> Recibo de vez en cuando las remesas de dinero, pero tus recados son cada vez más cortos, más impersonales y en la última no venía una sola línea tuya. . . . Debería quizás comprender por ello que ya no me amas, pero no puedo aceptarlo. (1978, 43)[22]
> [Every so often I receive remittances of money, but your messages are shorter and more impersonal every time; in your last one there wasn't even one line from you. . . . I should probably understand from this that you no longer love me, but I can't do so.]

In passages such as these, the reframing of Wolfe's language transcends disclosure of how Beloff unjustly is encased in Rivera's portraits and his friend's biographies. Poniatowska implies that the secondary meanings of the verb "to frame," including to shape, construct, devise, contrive, deceive, or falsify, aptly describe patriarchal inscription in general.

In addition to debunking official discourse through recontextualization, Poniatowska penetrates the code itself and exposes it to new meanings. Wherever the biographer employs ellipses, paragraph indentations, or blank spaces to mark quotations, Poniatowska takes advantage of the seam to rip it open and inject her own text. The final letter, dated "22 de julio de 1922," illustrates this tactic. Upon comparing the following passages, note how the novelist fills in the blanks left by the biographer to remind the reader of Rivera's dependence on his wife (the ellipses are Wolfe's; italics indicate Poniatowska's changes and additions). Wolfe:

> It seemed to me that despite everything there still remained between us those very profound bonds which it is not worth while [*sic*] to break definitely, that still each of us might be useful to the other. . . . What hurts is to think that you no longer have any need of me at all—none at all. (1963, 125)

Poniatowska quotes the same passage, but inserts new material in the ellipsis following "—none at all," rendering the final sentence thus: "Lo que duele es pensar que ya no me necesitas para nada, *tú que solías gritar: 'Quiela' como un hombre que se ahoga y pide que le echen al agua un salvavidas*" (1978, 71), 'What hurts is to think that you no longer have any need of me at all—none at all . . . *you who used to yell, "Quiela" like a drowning man who screams for a life preserver.*'

In other instances, Poniatowska does not wait for Wolfe to supply the space for her to insert a revision, but pries open her own gap in the biographer's quotation of Beloff's letter to add language that dramatically improves the status of its speaker, as the following example demonstrates:

> One might surrender, take a job as a governess or stenographer, or anything else for eight hours a day, general *abrutissement*, play or movie on Saturday, promenade in Saint-Cloud or Robinson on Sunday. I don't want that. So I accept the tail of the line in application for the work I am seeking, poverty and worry if necessary, and your Mexican pesos. (1963, 127)

In Poniatowska's version, italics indicate her changes and additions (the English translation is cited first):

> *Nor any line from you in the remittances of money. If I had told you that I would have preferred a line to the money, I would only be partly lying; it's true that I would prefer your love, but thanks to the money I have been able to survive; my economic situation is terribly precarious and I have thought of leaving painting,* to surrender, take a job as a governess or stenographer, or anything else for eight hours a day, general *abrutissement*, play or movie on Saturday,

promenade in Saint Cloud or Robinson on Sunday. I don't want that. *I am disposed to continue in the same situation, in order to be able to dedicate myself to literature and accept the consequences: poverty,* affliction and your Mexican pesos.

Tampoco una sola línea en las remesas de dinero. Si te dijera que hubiera preferido una línea al dinero, estaría mintiendo sólo en parte; preferiría tu amor es cierto, pero gracias al dinero he podido sobrevivir, mi situación económica es terriblemente precaria y he pensado en dejar la pintura, rendirme, conseguir un trabajo de institutriz, dactilógrafa o cualquier otra cosa durante ocho horas diarias, un *abrutissement* general con ida *al cine o al teatro* los sábados y paseo en Saint Cloud o Robinson los domingos. Pero no quiero eso. *Estoy dispuesta a seguir en las mismas, con tal de poder dedicarme a la pintura y aceptar las consecuencias:* la pobreza, las aflicciones y tus pesos mexicanos. (1978, 70)

It could be argued that such infiltration violates Beloff, not Wolfe, because he claims to cite verbatim from the Russian's letter. However, what is being contested is not the missive's content, but the biographer's fragmented use of it. Wolfe's usurpation and distortion of Angelina Beloff's personal property for the purpose of depreciating her and, alternatively, defending Rivera's actions is Poniatowska's true target.

Many readers of Elena Poniatowska have observed that at the heart of her production is a desire to enfranchise voices muted in traditional texts. Works such as *Tinísima* (1992) and the earlier *Querido Diego* (1978) demonstrate that also central to her literary project is a commitment to overcoming univocal representation. The challenge is daunting, for as Nisbett and Ross have observed in *Human Inference* (1980), once an image is planted it becomes almost impossible to root out. The "real" Angelina Beloff fell prey to this psychological principle when, in 1986, she added her voice to the palimpsest by publishing her *Memorias*. Although Beloff contradicts much of the official record, the author of the memoir's epilogue, Raquel Tibol (1986), ignores the differences and, in giving her final assessment of the Russian, reverts back to the master texts. Tibol diminishes Beloff, stating that her memories "están teñidos por la gris melancolía y el soterrado dolor provocados por el fracaso de su relación con Diego Rivera, único hombre con el que convivió y a quien amó irremediablemente durante su larga existencia," 'are colored by gray melancholy and concealed pain brought about by the failure of her relation with Diego Rivera, the only man she ever lived with and whom she loved irremediably during her long life' (1986, 93). She corroborates this by citing not only a translated fragment of Beloff's 22 July 1922 letter taken from Wolfe, but many of the same sources upon which the biographer relied. The epilogue, in effect, nullifies Beloff's words by superimposing on them another layer that affirms the dominant texts.

Poniatowska's own epilogue to *Querido Diego* provides a subtle recipe for combating acts, such as Tibol's, that perpetuate stereotypes. The novelist begins by ostensibly commending Bertram Wolfe, "a quien estas cartas le deben mucho de su información," 'to whom these letters owe much of their information' (1978, 72). The anecdote that follows confirms this acknowledgment, for it is extracted from the conclusion of Wolfe's chapter, "Angelina Waits." In it, Wolfe alleges that when Beloff finally traveled to Mexico in 1935, Rivera walked by without recognizing her in Bellas Artes. Poniatowska's research, however, revealed this account to be apocryphal (Ratkowski 1986, 38; Bruce-Novoa 1990, 129). By repeating it in her epilogue, together with a veiled invitation for the reader to consult *The Fabulous Life of Diego Rivera*, she supplies a major clue to a palimpsestic reading of her novel, a reading that manifests Wolfe's bias.[23] Moreover, knowledge of the anecdote's spurious nature throws doubt on the validity of the biographies as a whole. Poniatowska's act of crediting Wolfe is thus recast as an effort to discredit.

In "The Laugh of the Medusa," Cixous insists that "woman must put herself into the text—as into the world and into history—by her own movement" (1981, 245). The question is, How can one "seize the occasion to speak" when inscription is so firmly entrenched that the listener is loath to hear (1981, 250)? Elena Poniatowska's answer is to appropriate, then sabotage, the methods adopted by the status quo to fabricate representations. Specifically, in *Querido Diego* she usurps Bertram Wolfe's own stratagem to expose his biographies as works more akin to "fabulación infinita" than to history. At the same time, Poniatowska makes full use of her talents as a researcher and a novelist to rescue details overlooked by her predecessors and to bridge the gaps of the historical record with her imagination. The net effect of Poniatowska's endeavor is to provide in *Querido Diego, te abraza Quiela* a more calibrated, and perhaps more genuine, version of Beloff and her story.

NOTES

1. In *Dreaming with His Eyes Open: A Life of Diego Rivera*, Patrick Marnham uses "The Lands of Reason" as a title for the biography's Part II, which centers on Rivera's apprenticeship in Europe.
2. The following abbreviations will be used to cite the three major works analyzed

in this paper: QD (*Querido Diego, te abraza Quiela*), LT (*Diego Rivera: His Life and Times*), and FL (*The Fabulous Life of Diego Rivera*).

3. Although Beloff wrote her version in *Memorias*, it was not published until 1986. Furthermore, according to Berta Taracena in her introduction to *Memorias*, Beloff destroyed most of her correspondence with Diego Rivera (1986, 13).

4. In Wolfe's biographies the portraits appear in black and white, thus enhancing considerably the effect of highlighting the abdomen.

5. Wolfe attributes the bluebird analogy to Ramón Gómez de la Serna (1963, 68).

6. Other sources, such as Raquel Tibol in her epilogue to Beloff's *Memorias* (1986), maintain that the Russian was seven years his senior.

7. Although numerous photographs of Beloff have been reprinted in books treating Rivera, such as *Rivera: Iconografía personal* (1986) and Florence Arquin's *Diego Rivera: The Shaping of an Artist* (1971), none appear in Wolfe's biographies. Neither is there a photographic record of Beloff in Rivera's autobiography *Confesiones de Diego Rivera* (the second edition is written by Luis Suárez in 1975). Curiously, however, in Wolfe's works as well as in *Confesiones* photos of Rivera's other wives are displayed.

8. The painting titled *Portrait of Angelina 1917* offers another glaring example. According to Favela (1984), this portrait is actually a rendering of a family friend, Berthe Kritosser, completed in 1916. It is interesting to note that Wolfe "mislabeled" the "real" Beloff as well. According to Poniatowska, "Diego nunca le decía a Angelina Beloff 'Quiela' sino 'Gela.'" "'Diego never spoke to Angelina Beloff as "Quiela," but rather as "Gela.'" (Ratkowski 1986, 38). This is confirmed by the letters Rivera wrote to Beloff. For examples, see "Cartas inéditas" (1986) and Rivera Marín and Coronel Rivera's *Encuentros con Diego Rivera* (1993).

9. Although Rivera painted numerous "realistic" portraits of Beloff, Wolfe elected to reprint only one: an image that supports his thesis that Beloff was despondent over the death of her son and anticipated that Rivera would leave her as a result. The picture Wolfe projects of Beloff might have been altered considerably had he selected another portrait, such as *Angelina Beloff, 1918*, a work that portrays her as a Goyesque "Maja vestida" (Rivera Marín and Coronel Rivera 1993, 137).

10. Here is a list of the portraits as they appear first in *Life and Times*, then in *The Fabulous Life*:
    LT   Plate 14 = *Portrait of Angelina 1918*
          Plate 15 = *Portrait of Angelina 1917*
          Plate 16 = *Angelina Pregnant 1917*
          Plate 17 = *Angelina and Diego Jr. 1917*
    FL   Plate 17 = *Portrait of Angelina 1917*
          Plate 18 = *Angelina Pregnant 1917*
          Plate 19 = *Portrait of Angelina 1918* (?) [The question mark after the title of Plate 19 appears in the original text.]
          Plate 20 = *Angelina and the Child Diego 1917*

11. For more on woman as hysteric, see Hermann (1989).

12. For examples of both, see "Cartas inéditas" (1986) or *Encuentros con Diego Rivera*

(Rivera Marín and Colonel Rivera, 1993. Samples of Rivera's letters are also found in Marnham's biography (1998).

13. Lejuene's thesis (1989) centers specifically on autobiography, but applies to biography as well.

14. This ambiguous reference to "un hombre" invites us to rethink the title of the novel as *Querido Bertram, te rechaza Elena*.

15. Originally, Poniatowska wanted her text to be "un libro muy realista con fotos de Diego Rivera y de Angelina Beloff, cuadros, su cuadro cubista de la maternidad, para que fuera como un reportaje," 'a very realist book with photographs of Diego Rivera and Angelina Beloff, paintings, his cubist portrait titled "Maternity," so that it would be like a reportage' (Ratkowski 1986, 39). However, her editors would not comply with this wish. The addition of images certainly would have altered *Querido Diego*, producing perhaps an effect similar to that found in *Tinísima* (1992); it also would have constituted an interesting counterpoint to Wolfe's use of image in the biographies.

16. Claudia Schaefer, in her article "Updating the Epistolary Canon" (1992), addresses some of the implications of Poniatowska's choice of genre.

17. For more on woman as objet d'art and as a subordinate player in the biographies of men, see John Berger (1977) and Carolyn Heilbrun (1988), respectively.

18. For an analysis of Poniatowska's depiction of Beloff's emotional life, see Steele (1985) and Bruce-Novoa (1990).

19. Poniatowska uses dates, not numbers, to label the sections of her novel. I have numbered the letters to facilitate their discussion. It should also be noted that the twelve texts are not even letters in the truest sense of the word, because they lack a salutation (other than the one implied by the title). In many ways, the texts read more like journal entries, as Steele (1985) has noted, than correspondence.

20. Even the final letter, dated "22 de julio de 1922," in which fragments from Beloff's 22 July 1922, letter are cited, only superficially coincides with Wolfe's Chapter 12. Poniatowska has radically altered the order and nature of the events originally inscribed in the biographies.

21. The fact that Poniatowska lifts quotes that Wolfe attributes to others and has Beloff or others "speak" them also serves to take the biographer to task for his less than rigorous documentation.

22. For more on the dialogical in *Querido Diego*, see Bruce-Novoa (1990).

23. The record on when Poniatowska discovered the anecdote to be apocryphal is murky. Nevertheless, even if she made this discovery after she wrote the novel, it still suggests a palimpsestic reading once the reader has knowledge of the anecdote's falsity.

WORKS CITED

Abbot, H. Porter. 1988. "Autobiography, Autography, Fiction: Groundwork for a Taxonomy of Textual Categories." *New History* 19: 597–615.

Arquin, Florence. 1971. *Diego Rivera: The Shaping of an Artist.* Norman: University of Oklahoma Press, 1971.

Barthes, Roland. 1977. *Image, Music, Text.* New York: Hill and Wang.

Beloff, Angelina. 1986. *Memorias.* Mexico: UNAM.

Berger, John. 1977. *Ways of Seeing.* New York: Penguin.

Bromwich, David. 1984. "The Uses of Biography." *Yale Review* 73: 161–176.

Bruce-Novoa, Juan. 1990. "Subverting the Dominant Text: Elena Poniatowska's *Querido Diego.*" In *Knives and Angels: Women Writers in Latin America,* ed. Susan Bassnett. London: Zed.

"Cartas inéditas de Diego Rivera a Angelina Beloff." 1986. *Plural* 15: 56–63.

Cixous, Hélène. 1981. "The Laugh of the Medusa." In *New French Feminisms,* ed. Elaine Marks and Isabelle de Courtivron, 245–264. New York: Schocken.

Favela, Ramón. 1984. *Diego Rivera: The Cubist Years.* Phoenix, AZ: Phoenix Museum.

Gilbert, Sandra M., and Susan Gubar. 1979. *The Madwoman in the Attic: The Woman Writer and the Nineteenth-Century Literary Imagination.* New Haven, CT: Yale University Press.

Gombrich, E. H. 1956. *Art and Illusion: A Study in the Psychology of Pictorial Representation.* Bollingen Series 35. Princeton, NJ: Pantheon.

Halliwell, Kevin. 1980–1981. "Photographs and Narrativity: A Reply." *Screen Education* 37: 79–86.

Heilbrun, Carolyn. 1988. *Writing a Woman's Life.* New York: Norton.

Heilbrun, Carolyn, and Catherine Stimpson. 1989. "Theories of Feminist Criticism: A Dialogue." In *Feminist Literary Criticism: Explorations in Theory,* ed. Josephine Donovan, 61–73. Lexington: University Press of Kentucky.

Hermann, Claudine. 1989. *The Tongue Snatchers.* Trans. Nancy Kline. Lincoln: University of Nebraska Press.

Kristeva, Julia. 1986. "Women's Time." In *The Kristeva Reader,* ed. Toril Moi, 187–213. New York: Columbia University Press.

Labastida, Jaime. 1993. "Diego Rivera por el mismo." In *Encuentros con Diego Rivera,* ed. Guadalupe Rivera Marín and Juan Coronel Rivera, 5–9. Mexico: Siglo Veintiuno. Rpt. in *Plural* 276 (1994): 72–79.

Lejeune, Philippe. 1989. *On Autobiography.* Trans. Katherine Leary. Minneapolis: University of Minnesota Press.

Marnham, Patrick. 1998. *Dreaming with His Eyes Open: A Life of Diego Rivera.* New York: Alfred A. Knopf.

Miller, Nancy K. 1980. *The Heroine's Text: Readings in the French and English Novel, 1722–1782.* New York: Columbia University Press.

Moi, Toril. 1986. "Introduction." In *The Kristeva Reader,* ed. Toril Moi, 1–22. New York: Columbia University Press.

Nisbett, Richard, and Lee Ross. 1980. *Human Inference: Strategies and Shortcomings of Social Judgment.* Englewood Cliffs, NJ: Prentice-Hall.

Poniatowska, Elena. 1978. *Querido Diego, te abraza Quiela.* Mexico: Era.

———. 1992. *Tinísima.* Mexico: Era.

Ratkowski Carmona, Krista. 1986. "Entrevista a Elena Poniatowska." *Mester* 15: 37–42.

Rivera, Diego, and Bertram D. Wolfe. 1925. *El romance tradicional en México*. Mexico: n.p.

———. 1934. *Portrait of America*. New York: Covici, Friede.

———. 1938. *Portrait of Mexico*. New York: Covici, Friede.

Rivera: Iconografía personal. 1986. Mexico: Fondo de Cultura Económica.

Rivera Marín, Guadalupe, and Juan Coronel Rivera, eds. 1993. *Encuentros con Diego Rivera*. Mexico: Siglo Veintiuno.

Schaefer, Claudia. 1992. "Updating the Epistolary Canon: Bodies and Letters, Bodies of Letters in Elena Poniatowska's *Querido Diego, te abraza Quiela* and *Gaby Brimmer*." In *Textured Lives: Women, Art, and Representation in Modern Mexico*. Tucson: University of Arizona Press.

Showalter, Elaine. 1984. "Women's Time, Women's Space: Writing the History of Feminist Criticism." *Tulsa Studies in Women's Literature* 3: 29–43.

Steele, Cynthia. 1985. "La creatividad y el deseo en *Querido Diego, te abraza Quiela*." *Hispanoamérica* 14: 17–28.

Suárez, Luis. 1975. *Confesiones de Diego Rivera*. 2nd ed. Mexico: Grijalbo.

Tibol, Raquel. 1986. "Epílogo." In *Memorias*, Angelina Beloff, 93–98. Mexico: UNAM.

White, Hayden. 1989. " 'Figuring the Nature of the Times Deceased': Literary Theory and Historical Writing." In *The Future of Literary Theory*, ed. Ralph Cohen, 19–43. New York: Routledge.

Wilshire, Donna. 1989. "The Uses of Myth, Image, and the Female Body in Re-Visioning Knowledge." In *Gender/Body/Knowledge: Feminist Reconstructions of Being and Knowing*, ed. Alison M. Jaggar and Susan R. Bordo, 92–114. New Brunswick, NJ: Rutgers University Press.

Wolfe, Bertram D. 1939. *Diego Rivera: His Life and Times*. New York: Alfred A. Knopf.

———. 1963. *The Fabulous Life of Diego Rivera*. Chelsea: Scarborough House.

5

"Un octubre manchado se detiene"

Memory and Testimony in the Poetry of David Huerta

Jacobo Sefamí

Translated by Carl Good

He aquí que toco una llaga: es mi memoria
[Behold, I touch a wound: it is my memory]

Rosario Castellanos, quoted in Elena Poniatowska, *La noche de Tlatelolco*

n *La otra voz: Poesía y fin de siglo* (*The Other Voice: Poetry and the End of the Century*), Octavio Paz inveighs against economic globalism:

> Today literature and the arts are exposed to a different danger. What threatens them is not a doctrine or an omniscient political party but an economic process, one that is faceless, soulless and directionless. The market is circular, impersonal, impartial and inflexible. Some will assure me that the market is just in its own way. Perhaps. But it is blind and deaf, it does not love literature or risk, and it does not know how to choose. The censure it imposes is not ideological: it has no ideas. It knows of prices, but not of values. (1990, 125)

Some would differ with Paz over his assessment of the ideological factors behind the imposition of the market, given that we are speaking of a capitalist mechanism derived from the hegemony of transnational corporations, but many would resonate with his assessment of the negative effects that economic globalism represents for literature and, more specifically, for poetry. For example, market considerations led many of Mexico's most prestigious publishers, such as the Fondo de Cultura Económica, to limit their production of books of poetry at the end of the 1980s and the beginning of the 1990s. However, a long-standing tradition of influence by intellectuals in the political realm in Mexico has kept the balance tipped in favor of writers: Today poets are still being printed and new publishing houses with a passion for poetry continue to appear, for example, Verdehalago, Sin Nombre, El Tucán de Virginia, Aldus, UNAM (The Ala del Tigre Series), UAM (Margen de Poesía Series), and CONACULTA (Práctica Mortal, Los Cincuenta, and the Fondo Editorial Tierra Adentro Series). Even the Fondo de Cultura Económica has come back with numerous volumes of poetry and anthologies. It is a paradox in Mexico that although the hegemony of the market might exert an ever stronger force on the economy, poetry appears live and well.[1]

But another of the consequences of so-called globalism is that critical discourses—around the world—have begun to debate the social, political, and cultural effects of the market, and this debate has tended to marginalize the study of phenomena as rooted in the local, national, and even regional (such as Latin American) level. Simultaneously, literature itself is often marginalized as a separable category of study in favor of a focus on the analysis of the complexities resulting from the advance of capitalism. Studies interested in the circumstances of a single country at a given historical moment, in direct connection to certain discursive strategies, increasingly find no place in this new critical environment and would appear threatened with elimination by the enthusiasm for the "global."

Such studies, however, in the degree to which they insist on the historical specificities of the local, could be seen as acquiring a status of resistance in the face of the hegemonic threats of globalist discourses. I would argue that a careful analysis of the work of contemporary Mexican poet David Huerta, for example, necessarily participates in such a resistance. At first sight, David Huerta[2] would appear a strange candidate for a discussion of the local, given his having inherited a preoccupation for language that connects him with similar poetics in different parts of Latin America, in affiliation with French poststructural theories and in the tradition of Cuban neobaroque poet José Lezama Lima. Huerta is, in this sense, a figure who illustrates "cosmopolitanism" (or "universalism," albeit not "globalism") in the world of Mexican and Latin American poetry.

Despite these large levels of cosmopolitan connections, my reading of Huerta's work is interested in demonstrating that the specificity of the local is the source of his poetry. Huerta's local preoccupations are demonstrated by a wide variety of cultural or sociological or both themes in his work. This chapter will address the infamous student massacre at Tlatelolco on 2 October 1968, in an effort to understand how a local event (one that is simultaneously inscribed in an international context) affects the work of a poet who would otherwise appear to be more interested in French theory or neobaroque experimentation.

As a participant in the student movement at the time, David Huerta (b. 1949) witnessed firsthand the horrifying events of the Tlatelolco massacre. Although references to the event in his poetry are sporadic and do not actively draw attention, I suggest that the incident underlies much of Huerta's poetry and serves as one of its animating forces. As Huerta himself stated in an interview with Silvia Palma, "Tlatelolco engendró muchas cosas que no eran testimonio explícito del evento, entre ellos, mi libro producido a lo largo de diez años," 'Tlatelolco engendered many things that were not explicitly testimony of that event; among them, my book [*Incurable*, 1987] produced over a ten-year period' (1992, 3).[3]

Huerta's first book, *El jardín de la luz* (*The Garden of Light*, 1972), resonates with readings of other poets: Octavio Paz, in particular, and also Jorge Guillén, José Gorostiza, Borges, the early poetry of Efraín Huerta (David's father), and the early José Emilio Pacheco. Huerta's poems feature words such as "silencio" (silence), "mirada" (gaze), "palabra" (word), "luz" (light), and "espejo" (mirror) in tight, self-reflexive lines, as can be seen at the end of the first poem in the collection: "La mirada brilla en el centro/ del silencio," [the gaze shines in the center/ of silence]. The notion of silence as the supreme product of analogy is common in Paz's work. Take, for example, this line from *Blanco:* "aguzar/ silencios/ hasta la trasparencia" [to sharpen silence into transparency]; or another from *Ladera este* (*East Slope*): "Los signos se borran:/ yo miro la claridad," [The signs are erased/ I gaze at the clarity]; or a third example, from *El mono gramático* (*The Grammatical Monkey*):[4] "La visión de la poesía es la de la convergencia de todos los puntos. Fin de camino . . . : la visión vertiginosa y transversal que revela al universo no como una sucesión, un movimiento, sino como una asamblea de espacios y tiempos, una quietud" [The vision of poetry is that of the convergence of all points. End of the road . . . : the vertiginous, transversal vision which reveals the universe not as a succession, a movement, but as an assembly of spaces and times, a stillness]. Huerta falls back on these themes in the first part of *El jardín de la luz.* Two examples: "Ella se abría, quizás, y de sus párpados/ la claridad nacía como una fuente./ Ella fue la quietud para tus ojos" [She opened, perhaps, and from her eyelids/ clarity was born like a fountain] ("Serena," [Serene]); and "La claridad abre las alas;/ en su vuelo perfecto/ el aire desanuda/ la transparencia de la brisa" [Clarity opens wings;/ in its perfect flight/ the air unties/ the transparence of the breeze] (*La claridad y el vuelo* [*Clarity and Flight*]).

Despite this general "mimetic" tendency, however, *El jardín de la luz* also includes a poem about the massacre, bearing the title *Testimonio.* The poem sits in the very middle of the collection, demonstrating its centrality. Although it makes no concrete allusion to 1968, its title echoes the subtitle of Elena Poniatowska's famous book, *La noche de Tlatelolco: Testimonios de historia oral* (*The Night of Tlatelolco: Testimonies of Oral History,* 1971).[5] Once the poem's principal referent is established, the small anecdote recounted there becomes clear. Although it uses the same type of vocabulary—tending toward analogy—as the other poems of the volume, here the "mimetic" enchantments are broken:

> No hubo piedad para la luz.
> En lo más hondo de la desesperanza
> dolía esa tarde el miedo.
>
> El abismo del aire
> fue un tatuaje de llamas,
> un brusco vértigo de ráfaga.
>
> Sobre los labios de ceniza
> brilló como un cristal
> una limpia blasfemia
> y en la garganta atroz
> florecieron las súplicas.
> De súbito,
> el ciego arrasamiento
> giró sobre sí mismo;
> la tarde se detuvo.
>
> En la hierba ruinosa
> creció la inolvidable
> cicatriz: guirnalda
> de silencio que arde
> inscrita en la memoria
> de aquella rota claridad. (1972, 55)

[There was no pity for the light.
In the depths of despair,
fear anguished that afternoon.

The abyss of the air
was a tattoo of flames,
a sudden vertigo of fire blast.

On the lips of ash
a clean blasphemy gleamed
like a crystal
and in the awful throat
pleadings flowered.
Suddenly,
the blind razing
spun around on itself;
the afternoon halted.

In the ruined grass
grew the indelible
scar: wreath
of silence
which burns
written in the memory
of that broken clarity.]

If light is the motive of song, if clarity is the target of peace, in this poem fire ("un tatuaje de llamas," "vértigo de ráfaga") undoes the harmony, leaves a mark, a wound. The spiritual calm from which the light is issued is violated. From this point onward, Huerta will refer to "la tarde" emblematically, almost as an allegory of a moment that came to a halt, a space of time that affixed itself to memory. The wound, in fact, signifies that the body cannot forget; memory (as stated in the epigraph at the head of this essay) is a wound that does not heal. The preterite dominates the poem, fixing the event in the past, but in the final stanza the past burns into the present a wound that cannot be erased. The poem does not use personal pronouns: The speaker's experience is collective, belongs to many others. The presence of this collectivity in the poem provides grounds (albeit exaggerated) for considering a reading of nationalist motifs in the poem. Such a reading emerges, in particular, from the image, "guirnalda de silencio" [wreath of silence]. The word "guirnalda" may evoke the rhetoric of the national anthem: "para ti las guirnaldas de oliva,/ un recuerdo para ellos de gloria,/ un laurel para ti de victoria,/ un sepulcro para ellos de honor" [for you the wreaths of olive,/ a memory of glory for them,/ a laurel of victory for you,/ a tomb of honor for them]. If in the anthem the wreaths celebrate victory, the wreath of silence presents an empty, disenchanted vision of history: The heroic deeds of 1968 end in death.

In *Cuaderno de noviembre* (*November Notebook,* 1976), Huerta chooses a much longer verse; his poetry now takes leave of its former transparency and becomes more opaque. It could be said that French theory (Barthes, Derrida, Deleuze, and Guattari) exerts a force on much of the poetry of this collection as well as that of later volumes—*Huellas del civilizado* (chapbook, 1977), *Versión* (*Version,* 1978), and *Incurable* (*Incurable,* 1987).[6] Simultaneously, Huerta's poetry in these collections recalls other poets, particularly José Lezama Lima (of whose work Huerta has made two anthologies, the first published in 1977),[7] José Carlos Becerra (who died in 1970 and whose complete works were published in 1973);[8] and, as can be seen particularly in *Huellas,* Rodolfo Hinostroza (through his 1971 collection: *Contranatura*).

Cuaderno is composed of fifty poems with neither titles nor any apparent interconnections other than their self-referentiality. The title of the book as a whole may allude very indirectly to Tlatelolco: It is the notebook that is written in November, the month following the massacre, a kind of "hangover" of the event.[9] Clearly, most readers of the volume would contest this, but in fact one of the themes in much of Huerta's poetry from *Cuaderno* onward is that references elude us, fleeing in a general collapse of everything, even language itself. We could add that the very materiality of the word "*novi*embre" (November) contains the two words "*no vi*" [I didn't see]: nonacceptance, denial as a mechanism of questioning.

The presence of Tlatelolco is latent in many images throughout *Cuaderno* (poems 13 and 14, for example), even if it would be unjustified to propose a univocal reading linking the entire collection to this event. Poem 2 provides another example. Unlike *Testimonio,* the elements here are more nebulous: the absence of a title that would anchor the poem; the density of the images; an imprecise anecdote; a single, unfolding, extremely long and almost unbreatheable sentence. If *Testimonio* depersonalizes to encompass the tragedy, Poem 2 emerges from personal experience, that of an individual who survives and emerges from death: "Yo volvía entre la magnitud confusa, rodeado por la sombra del reino, por el minuto que pasaba/ con sus naufragios y sus tintas" [I returned in the confused magnitude, surrounded by the shadow of the kingdom, by the minute which passed/ with its shipwrecks and its inks] (1976, 13). The utterance of the word "I" is a result of the speaker's survival: This "I" appears in the midst of the confusion, the lack of identity, the vastness, which death comprises. More than question the violence of the moment or recount the massacre, the text centers on the speaker's perplexed surprise at being among the living. The subject splits into two: one witnesses the stage of death, experiences action; the other seeks to understand but remains astounded, immobilized by incredulity. The poem ends with the trauma of the survivor who questions the very fact of his having evaded death: "la fisura del frío sucesivo,/ una irresponsable agitación que sobrevivía en la inquietud de los pies/ como el escozor de la huida frente al arma de fuego/ y como la sonrisa en un charco de luto, prisionero entonces en el aire que me excluía" [the fissure of the successive cold,/ an irresponsible agitation which survived in the restlessness of the feet/ like the searing pain of the flight from the firearm/ and like the smile in a puddle of mourning, prisoner then in the air which excluded me] (1976, 14). Fear spurs the flight, but the action seems involuntary, reflexive, the result of an innate "mechanism" that distances the subject from the danger.

Except for the phrase, "huida frente al arma de fuego" [flight from the firearm], the poem does not directly refer to 1968. However, the subject coins a vocabulary—almost a code—to evoke the event. For example, with "la fijeza de la misericordia y el color de la tarde" [the fixity of mercy and the color of the afternoon], the stasis of the afternoon is once again insisted on ("la tarde se detuvo" of the previous poem) as a way of allegorizing the tragedy.[10] Then, too, the word "plaza" is masked with a second word, "playa" (beach), which also alludes indirectly to the tragedy: "ese mecanismo que yo era estaba ahí también, junto a los otros, en una playa ligera y sin sentido" [that mechanism that was I was there also, together with the others, on a light and senseless beach (playa)] (1976, 14). With the flash of nearly blinding light, the "playa" reproduces the dazed effect of the subject who witnesses the massacre. (In addition, the texture of the sand allows for the possibility that that which is written there be erased, or at least emerge out of the confusion of uncertainty.) Huerta has remarked in several interviews that his reaction to Tlatelolco was articulated belatedly because of his inability to recover from the shock of the massacre. The fixity of a moment in memory coexists with an incapacity to recuperate and clearly articulate the particularities of the event: "regresaba con una delicia de animal, suspendido en el tamaño de mi persona y enmascarado/ por un gesto borroso" [I returned with animal delight, suspended in the size of my person and masked/ by a blurred gesture] (1976, 13).

The trail of "phantasmal" references to Tlatelolco takes us to a "textual fragment," *Detalles* (*Details*), from *Huellas del civilizado* (1977), Huerta's next volume of poetry. *Detalles* is written very much in the Poundian style as used by Hinostroza in *Contranatura* (1971): a weaving that features a wide diversity of linguistic textures. The poem itself has no unifying theme other than a certain synchrony of mental effects in the poetic subject. The effect is similar to that of a hallucinatory or drunken "trip." The fragment that alludes to Tlatelolco is the following:

> las fotografías no amarillean
> pero la ciudad se derrumba con dulce violencia
> no es el fin del mundo ni el comienzo
> dicen que lo peor es seguir así
>
> luego las calles los carteles los gritos
> y Debajo Del Asfalto Está La Playa, decían
> los motines y el resplandor de las patrullas policíacas
> la siniestra humillación de todos
> pero nosotros esperábamos otra cosa
> una diluida esperanza después de tantos golpes
> hasta la tarde casi noche en la plaza
> una demostración de fuerza
> y, decían, el foco de la subversión ha sido sofocado
> los periódicos que comprábamos con ansiedad
> el miedo como una mancha en cada esquina
> en cada gesto
>
> y los amigos pasaban de un tema a otro
> yo no sabía qué decir
> a no ser qué hora es? quién dijo eso? (1977, 6–7)
>
> [the photographs do not yellow
> but the city collapses with sweet violence
> it is not the end of the world nor the beginning
> they say the worst is to continue like this
>
> then the streets the posters the cries
> and Under the Asphalt Is The Beach [Playa], they said
> the riots and the gleam of the patrol cars

the sinister humiliation of everyone
but we awaited something else
a diluted hope after so many blows
until the afternoon nearly night in the plaza
a demonstration of force
and, they say, the focus of the subversion has been stifled

the newspapers that we purchased anxiously
fear like a stain on every sidewalk
in every gesture

and friends went from one topic to another
and I didn't know what to say
except what time is it? who said that?]

The fragment appears in the poem like a hallucination or nightmare, the memory of an event that cannot be forgotten but that has not been confronted or resolved. The text, however, is much more explicit; its concreteness recalls the moment as seen through the disaster that the massacre represented for the generation to which the subject of the poem belongs: "the city collapses." Reactions to the massacre vary a great deal; in the poem the I is characterized by extreme dumbfoundedness and alienation; the possibility of a global examination of the situation is null; its responses are limited to rhetorical questions. The image is, in fact, that of the subject sketched through the different poems on Tlatelolco: the one who remains perplexed and incapable of response, the one who cannot articulate its own vision of the events. However, the poems themselves are proof that the subject has expressed itself, although its reaction is delimited by a denial ("no vi"), a reduction (no sé qué decir), or a tangential vision of the massacre (an indirect, and, sometimes disguised, discourse).

David Huerta's most explicit text on 1968 is entitled, *Nueve años después* (*Nine Years Later*), written in October 1977 and published in *Versión* (1978). This is the only poem in the entire book printed in italics; it is also separated from the remaining poems by its own title page, which reads, *Un poema fechado* (*A Dated Poem*). The title of the volume, *Versión*, could allude to 1968, because it presents its own version of the events by means of this dated poem. The text returns to the scenario of poem 2 of *Cuaderno:* the "I" as a survivor of the tragedy who relates his experience. The differences between the two poems are notable, however. Here, in *Nueve años después* the references are clear, the sentences are brief, and the poem's greater length permits a more complete development of the images. The title implies that the events have traumatized the subject into muteness and that only now ("nine years later") can he unburden himself (a possibility that would not be absolutely faithful to the larger context of Huerta's previous poems, as commented on above).[11] The poem focalizes the massacre from the speaker's perspective, establishing a sharp division between the I and others. This division builds in complexity, however, with the I taking life almost against its will, as if it were betraying others by saving itself and not dying. The tension leads to the subject's constant estrangement in the face of its own body: the voice that sounds like that of another person, the legs that run independently, the blood that circulates despite the death that the "I" presupposes. This estrangement is also produced out of perplexity in the face of the death of others: "Todo el silencio de mi cuerpo abría sus alveolos/ frente a los cuerpos arrasados, escupidos hacia la muerte por el ardor de la metralla:/ esos cuerpos brillando, sanguíneos y recortados contra la desmenuzada luz de la tarde" [All my body's silence opened its alveolae/ before bodies struck down, spit towards death by the heat of bullets:/ those shining bodies, bloody and cut out against the shredded light of the afternoon] (1978, 45–46). Images of the massacre pursue the subject everywhere: "Respiraba imágenes y desde entonces todas esas imágenes me visitan en sueños,/ rompiéndolo todo, como caballos delirantes" [I breathed images and since then all those images visit me in dreams,/ breaking everything, like delirious horses] (1978, 45). By relating a concrete experience, the poem takes recourse to a predominantly narrative discourse. This narration, however, is permeated with the subject's self-questionings of why and how he is to write about the tragedy: "Hablo con mi sangre entera y con mis recuerdos individuales. Y estoy vivo . . . Yo no quisiera hablar del tamaño de aquella tarde,/ no poner aquí adverbios, gritar o lamentarme . . . ¿Dónde podría poner mi vivir, mis palabras/ sino ahí, nueve años después, en esa cólera fría . . . Es verdad que escuché la metralla y ahora esto escribo . . . Hablo de estos recuerdos inmensos porque tenía que hacerlo alguna vez, así o de otra manera" [I speak with my blood intact and with my individual memories. And I am alive . . . I would not want to speak of the size of that afternoon,/ or to put adverbs here, or shout or complain . . . Where could I put my living, my words/ if not there, nine years later, in that cold cholera . . . It is true that I heard the gunfire and now I write this . . . I speak of these immense memories because

I had to do it sometime, one way or another]. The text's primordial conflict is how to speak of a painful experience with a certain calmness; the discourse's strategy of eliminating adverbs apparently is designed to avoid a description of the how, when, and why of the massacre. The speaker instead takes up adjectives, especially in relation to subjectivity: "mis manos estaban fúnebres de silencio . . . mis huesos estaban empapados de frío . . . mi boca estaba quemada por los recuerdos . . . mi sangre estaba fresca y luciente" [my hands were funereal with silence . . . my bones were soaked with cold . . . my mouth was burned by the memories . . . my blood was fresh and luminous]. The sensations of the I converge in the text, expressions of survivor's syndrome frequently seen among victims of massive tragedies: rage, desperation, guilt, and fear. In addition, the motifs from the poems examined above are repeated here: the afternoon, the breakdown of the light, the funereal silence, and so on. *Nine Years Later* proves that the trauma of Tlatelolco has persisted fitfully in Huerta's poetry, as a hounding pain, as an etherial germinator of metaphor.

This is a quick note on *Incurable*, a very long poem of nearly 400 pages. It could be said that the primary unity of this poem is its continuous meditation on writing, although throughout its long itinerary the poem digresses endlessly with every step, curling up, losing itself in its own labyrinths, exiting, making observations on banal details, and so forth. The book is divided into nine chapters, recalling the period of human gestation. Curiously, however, the poem is conceived as incurable; it is like a sick, suffering human being who—Huerta says—knows it will die. The final chapter is entitled "Rayas" (Lines), as if indicating a kind of annulment of language. In the first chapter, the massacre of Tlatelolco makes an allegorical appearance through the word "October" and through images connected to this wound. We should note in passing that Huerta himself was born in October (on the eighth day). "October" could therefore be an emblem of an ominous coalescence of subject and event in a single voice. To cite examples: "Octubre es como un signo de afuera, engranado/ a la numerosa virtud del pensar" [October is like a sign from outside, meshed/ with the numerous virtue of thought] (1987, 37). "Octubre se afila contra los bruñidos corpúsculos de la ventana como una designación: está en la nieve de la escritura/ como una cuchillada brumosa en la mañana de la tranquilidad" [October hones itself against the polished corpuscles of the window like a designation: it is there in the snow of writing/ like a brumous slash in the morning of tranquility] (1987, 38–39); "el corazón de octubre suena desértico/ en la escena, convida a la postura filosófica a convertirse en un desorden de nomadismo y ebriedad. El pensamiento brilla en la carne de la mano, las letras pasan por el río de luz que conduce octubre" [the heart of October resounds desertlike/ in the scene, compels the philosophical posture into a disorder of nomadism and inebriation. Thought shines in the flesh of the hand, the letters pass by with the river of light that leads October] (1987, 39). The massacre has lost its specific historical connotation and become an emblem of loss, as an atmosphere, almost a mental landscape, which surrounds the I and its reflections. "El mundo es una mancha en el espejo" [the world is a stain in the mirror], says the first verse of *Incurable*. The stain, far from light and transparency, is the suffering of the letter and the ink on the white of the paper; at the same time, however, it is the blood of the bodies of an October fixed motionless in the memory of the poet.

In the prologue to his anthology, *Poetas de una generación: 1950–1959*, Evodio Escalante fittingly characterizes a generation of Mexican poets born between 1950 and 1959 (among whom we could include David Huerta) as sharing a "skeptical reticence" in the face of history, an incredulity coupled with a certain disenchantment. The reading of Huerta's poetry I am presenting here indirectly confirms Escalante's suggestion. The events at Tlatelolco persist in Huerta's poetry; they are fixed beneath the images of this poetry; they give sense to the continual devastation of language; they presuppose a criticism, a rebellion, an agony. The vectors of historical circumstance are widened, through obliqueness, disguise, and latency, rather than reduced or eliminated. As if Huerta had ingurgitated the tragedy and now its traces, residues, and wastes were surfacing in his verses. Tlatelolco is also allegorized there, designated with a single marker of speech: "October." Given that the references to it are veiled, readers may have the impression that the ominous moment appears on the very surface of language itself.

A few final clarifications. This reading is a response to a poetic tone as traced through a series of books: *Cuaderno de noviembre, Huellas del civilizado, Versión,* and *Incurable;* other vectors in Huerta's poetry displace themselves into other directions and spaces: *El jardín de la luz* itself, *El espejo del cuerpo* (1980), *Historia* (1990a), and *Los objetos están más cerca de lo que aparentan* (1990b). It must be pointed out, however, that although 1968 substantially motivates the specific coupling of disenchantment and melancholic humor in Huerta's poetry, it is not the only motivation in his poetry. A more complete account of these motivations would need to examine, among others, themes of alcoholism, frustrated loves, political disappointments, and their connections with the protest movements of the 1970s. Notwithstanding, the poems explored here demonstrate that even if Huerta's poetry can be characterized as "metalinguistic" (as Maureen Ahern [1983] asserts) it is also true that historical circumstance subtly and obliquely permeates his work.[12]

NOTES

1. Even during the economic crisis of the late 1980s, the Mexican government continued to establish funds to provide incentives for creativity: the Sistema Nacional de Creadores offers three-year, renewable fellowships for writers and artists. Prominent Latin American intellectuals (such as Octavio Paz, Carlos Fuentes, Alvaro Mutis, and Gabriel García Márquez) also have been awarded lifetime funds to support their work. Additionally, there are many jobs available in the world of cultural promotion, including positions with literary journals, poetry workshops in schools, and government agencies such as the Departament of Literature of the INBA (Fine Arts Institute), or the cultural programming offices of Mexico City's many delegaciones (municipal boroughs), and so on.

2. David Huerta (Mexico, b. 1949) has published the following volumes of poetry: *El jardín de la luz* (Mexico City: UNAM, 1972), *Cuaderno de noviembre* (Mexico City: Era, 1976), *Huellas del civilizado* (Mexico City: La Máquina de Escribir, 1977), *Versión* (Mexico City: Fondo de Cultura Económica, 1978), *El espejo del cuerpo* (Mexico City: UNAM, 1980), *Lluvias de noviembre* (in collaboration with painter Vicente Rojo, Mexico City: Multiarte, 1984), *Incurable* (Mexico City: Era, 1987), *Historia* (Mexico City: Ediciones Toledo, 1990), *Los objetos están más cerca de lo que aparentan* (in collaboration with painter Miguel Castro Leñero, Mexico City: Galería López Quiroga, 1990), *La sombra de los perros* (Mexico City: Editorial Aldus, 1996), and *La música de lo que pasa* (Mexico City: Consejo Nacional para la Cultura y las Artes, 1997). In 1982, his first book of essays appeared, *Las intimidades colectivas* (Mexico City: Secretaría de Educación Pública). Huerta is the compiler of two anthologies of José Lezama Lima's poetry and two anthologies of romantic stories. He has received fellowships from the Centro Mexicano de Escritores (1971–1972), the Guggenheim Foundation (1978–1979), and the Consejo Nacional para la Cultura y las Artes (1989–1990). He has also been a professor, led writing workshops, written prologues, and served as cultural collaborator in innumerable periodical publications.

3. Evodio Escalante (1992) uses the phrase "white avant-garde" to characterize the poetry of Gerardo Deniz (b. 1934), Alberto Blanco (b. 1951), Coral Bracho (b. 1951), and David Huerta. He identifies an avant-garde subversion of language that, at the same time, relinquishes the "totalizing pretensions" and the

"publicizing gestures" of earlier avant-gardists. As part of a "white avant-garde," these writers' work is characterized by an "introversion" that "empties inward toward a solitude of language." Although conscious of the tradition that underlies their work, they "isolate their linguistic materials in the construction of a crystal fortress immune to social change and resistant to the calls of scandal" (1992, 31). With this affirmation, Escalante returns to the notion of the "ivory tower" in which, ostensibly, writers distance themselves from society. Although the theme of 1968 is neither explicit nor dominant in Huerta's poetry, it does animate that poetry in a very fundamental way. Furthermore, it would not be an exaggeration to say that poststructural questionings of power have a great deal to do with the theoretical presuppositions of Huerta's poetry.

4. Paz, of course, incorporated a wide diversity of philosophical ideas into his poetry: cyclical time from ancient Mexicans, the Buddhist notion of nothing, the silence of music from John Cage, white space from readings of Mallarmé, and so on. In almost all cases, a canticle to transparency underlies the aspirations of his poetry, although history, irony, and critical consciousness never cease to corrode and abrade the condition of peace that is longed for.

5. As far as can be seen, Huerta's "testimony" is not among those included in Poniatowska's book.

6. From 1972 to 1977, Huerta worked with *La Cultura en México*, the cultural supplement of *Siempre!* magazine, directed by Carlos Monsiváis. During those years, he learned a great deal about being a cultural journalist and initiated friendships with Jorge Aguilar Mora and Héctor Manjarrez, which could also be traced in a literary dimension. Evodio Escalante has noted the close relation between Aguilar Mora and Huerta: Aguilar Mora's doctoral dissertation on Paz (later published as *La divina pareja: Historia y mito en Octavio Paz* [Mexico City: Era, 1978]) appeared the same year *Cuaderno de noviembre* was published. Aguilar Mora's essay is permeated with citations and epigraphs from Deleuze, along with evidence of other readings of French theory. During these years Huerta was also associated with Vicente Rojo, an acquaintance that would later result in collaborative projects.

7. Huerta's two anthologies of Lezama Lima's poetry are: *Breve antología* (Mexico City: UNAM, 1977); and *Muerte de Narciso: Antología poética*, with selection and prologue by David Huerta (Mexico City: Era, 1988; Madrid: Alianza Editorial, 1988).

8. Becerra's complete works appear in *El otoño recorre las islas*, edited by José Emilio Pacheco and Gabriel Zaid (Mexico: Era, 1973). According to Escalante, *Cuaderno* also owes a great deal to Eduardo Lizalde's *Cada cosa es Babel* (Mexico City: 1966).

9. Huerta has used the word "hangover" ("cruda") to refer to the years following 1968: "I preferred to study the career of philosophy and not letters. But I did it in the years which I have called 'the hangover of the student movement' for those of us who participated in and survived that movement" [Palma, 3].

10. The demonstration began—according to Poniatowska's work—at 5:30 P.M. The gun shots broke out at 6 P.M. and lasted approximately 29 minutes. Poniatowska entitled her volume, *The Night of Tlatelolco* (1971), perhaps because of

the event's effect of darkness, confusion, and death. In David Huerta's poetry the event is identified with the "afternoon," perhaps because the participating subject escaped during the first shots and his memory remained fixed at the moment in which the massacre was carried out (from 6:00 to 6:29 P.M.). Since the "afternoon" also symbolizes the darkness of the day, it is easily associated with melancholy.

11. In his interview with Silvia Palma, Huerta stated, "I could write a text entitled 'Nine Years Later,' of 1977; that's why it's called that. It was only nine years later that I recapitulated some of the things I felt, which occurred to me immediately following the massacre" (Palma 1992, 3).

12. Various poets of Huerta's generation have also written about 1968 (see number 58 of the magazine *Memoria* [Sept. 1993] and the volume *Poemas y narraciones sobre el Movimiento Estudiantil de 1968*, compiled by Marco Antonio Campos and Alejandro Toledo [1996]). Among these poets is Alberto Blanco (Mexico, b. 1951), whom Escalante includes among the "white avant-garde." Blanco's poem is focused on the "Manifestación silenciosa" [*Silent Manifestation*] (which is also its title) of September 13; the text plays with the association of silence (primordially mystical) in Blanco's poetry. Again, this is a case of the political topic drawing close to the poet's theoretical coordinates. In the Latin American context, we would have to see the effects of political circumstances on the work of poets of David Huerta's generation. Publications of two such poets are important points of reference in this sense: Raúl Zurita's *Purgatorio* (Santiago, Chile: Editorial Universitaria, 1979), inscribed in the context of the Chilean coup de état of 1973 and the ensuing dictatorship (1973–1989); and *Alambres* (Buenos Aires: Ultimo Reino, 1987) and *Hule* (Buenos Aires: Ultimo Reino, 1989) by Néstor Perlongher, written in the face of the Argentine "dirty war" of 1976–1983 and the disappearance of political victims in that country.

WORKS CITED

Ahern, Maureen. 1983. "La poesía de David Huerta: inscripción metalingüística." *Eco* 42, no. 3 (January): 248–269.

Campos, Marco Antonio, and Alejandro Toledo. 1996. *Poemas y narraciones sobre el Movimiento Estudiantil de 1968*. Mexico: Universidad Nacional Autónoma de México.

Escalante, Evodio. 1988. "Prólogo." In *Poetas de una generación 1950–1959*, 7–17, Evodio Escalante, ed. Mexico City: Premiá, UNAM, 1988.

———. 1992. "De la vanguardia militante a la vanguardia blanca (los nuevos trastornos de la poesía mexicana de nuestros días: David Huerta, Gerardo Deniz, Alberto Blanco y Coral Bracho)." In *Perfiles: Ensayos sobre literatura mexicana reciente*, ed. Francisco Patán, 27–45. Boulder, CO: Society of Spanish and Spanish American Studies.

Hinostroza, Rodolfo. 1971. *Contranatura*. Barcelona: Barral Editores.

Huerta, David. 1972. *El jardín de la luz*. Mexico City: UNAM.

———. 1976. *Cuaderno de noviembre*. Mexico City: Era.

————. 1977. *Huellas del civilizado.* Mexico City: La Máquina de Escribir.

————. 1978. *Versión.* Mexico City: Fondo de Cultura Económica.

————. 1980. *El espejo del cuerpo.* Mexico: UNAM.

————. 1987. *Incurable.* Mexico City: Era.

————. 1990a. *Historia.* Mexico City: Ediciones Toledo.

————. 1990b. *Los objetos están más cerca de lo que aparentan* (in collaboration with painter Miguel Castro Leñero), Mexico City: Galería López Quiroga.

Palma, Silvia. 1992. "La condición incurable: Entrevista con David Huerta." *Mapa de Piratas* (Toluca, Mexico) 10 (June 9): 1–7.

Paz, Octavio. 1990. *La otra voz. Poesía y fin de siglo.* Barcelona: Seix Barral.

Poniatowska, Elena. 1971. *La noche de Tlatelolco: Testímonios de Historia oral.* Mexico City: Ediciones Era.

6

Aesthetic Criteria and the Literary Market in Mexico

The Changing Shape of Quality, 1982–1994

Danny J. Anderson

n the late 1980s, a disparaging label began to circulate in the Mexican cultural press: *literatura light* (light literature). Diet Coke, decaffeinated coffee, nonfat sugar-free ice-cream and even Marlboro Lights are all marketed in terms of their "lightness" as attractive alternatives for the body- or health-conscious consumer. Such products promise to tease the tongue and satisfy one's taste, but without (or at least with less of) the problematic ingredients: calories, sugar, caffeine, saturated fats, and nicotine. But we do not consume literature the same way and there is no avoiding the negative connotations of the phrase *literatura light*. Associated with the category "literature," the marketing label "light" suggests a consumer who is willing to settle for less, an unwise reader who invests money and time in a book with lower quality, in short, a reader with bad or undiscriminating taste. Even if the "light" option is respectable with food, drink, and smoke, where there really is no disputing taste, according to the logic of literary discourse *de gustibus sempre est disputandum*.

In Mexican critical debates, the term "light" polarizes rhetorical positions and implicitly defends a more orthodox definition of "literature" as quality, even if such quality is not described explicitly. The phrase reworks dietary folk wisdom to propose that "You are what you read"; according to this line of reasoning, only intellectual lightweights would bother with *literatura light*. To the consternation of many, however, so-called *literatura light* has been largely successful, both commercially and, some would argue, aesthetically. From the start, the terms in this debate are loaded, so tracking their genealogy is like walking through a minefield. At stake in the debate is cultural power and the competition for legitimacy within the larger field of cultural production.

In a recent study, Aralia López González begins an overview of Mexican narrative in the 1970s and 1980s by emphasizing the struggle to define cultural legitimacy: the problem of "la vacilación de los criterios, la dificultad para definir lo que es o no es literatura," 'the vacillation of criteria, the difficulty of defining what is or is not literature' (1993, 659). More than distinguishing between the literary and the nonliterary, these vacillating criteria pose the question of quality understood as the degree of excellence recognized within certain literary works and the lower caliber or even lack of such merit in other texts. Such an attribution of excellence is neither neutral nor disinterested; it is an evaluative act situated within a broader cultural field characterized by relationality among all participants and by competition for the authority to decide what counts as quality. Barbara Herrnstein Smith has emphasized the "radically contingent" nature of literary value because it is "neither an inherent property of objects nor an arbitrary projection of subjects but, rather, the product of the dynamics of an economic system" (1983, 15). Terry Eagleton states this radical contingency in an even starker manner: "Literature, in the sense of a set of works of assured and unalterable value, distinguished by certain shared inherent properties, does not exist." Instead, "literature" is a "highly valued kind of writing" whose definition depends on notoriously variable value judgments. Thus, Eagleton concludes, "the so-called 'literary canon,' the unquestioned 'great tradition' of the 'national literature,' has to be recognized as a *construct*, fashioned by particular people for particular reasons at a certain time" (1983, 10–11).

Pierre Bourdieu's conceptualization of the field of cultural production captures both the dynamics of the system identified by Smith and the actions of "particular" people with context-specific motivations suggested by Eagleton. More exactly, Bourdieu characterizes the field of cultural production as a game in which the various social actors compete to accumulate symbolic capital and cultural legitimacy. In this game, literary creation, publishing selection, and critical evaluation all constitute self-characterizing acts of position-taking, investments in a specific kind of "quality" that "classifies the classifier" as much as the texts (1984, 6). Description of the contemporary cultural conversation about literature and quality in Mexico is difficult; the various mechanisms of the literary field operate to mask the social and economic relations that enmesh literary texts, cultural value, commercial value, and market pressures. The masked nature of these relations often makes descriptive statements appear heretical because all the terms are loaded. In addition, description of a conversation often is mistaken for endorsement of a particular argument, much like the motivations a listener suspects when one repeats juicy gossip. Given these difficulties, I will first try to eavesdrop on the conversation before I get dragged in myself and pressed to define my position. I will attempt to overhear the conversation by shifting my analytical focus from the novels contentiously classified in this debate to the study of publishing and the competition for critical legitimacy in the literary field during the period 1982–1994.

The study of cultural and commercial institutions such as a publishing houses has two principal advantages as an entry to this period. First, rather than plunging immediately into the competing discourses that describe and define textual traits and force one almost immediately to take up a position among them, the study of publishing houses keeps the focus on the larger dynamics of the cultural field and the struggle to accumulate symbolic capital and cultural authority. Second, because one of the issues under contention is the degree to which the "market" affects literary quality and determines the commercial success of *literatura light*, the study of publishing houses makes more evident the combined goals of establishing cultural authority as a legitimate consecrating agent and, at the same time, successfully selling literature. To situate these various cultural antagonisms over quality and the definition of literature, I first outline the contours of Mexican literary publishing in 1982–1994. Then I trace the emergence of a simmering debate over aesthetic criteria that centers upon the polarized terms *literatura difícil* (difficult literature) and *literatura light*. Throughout these considerations I will maintain that quality is not an intrinsic aspect of texts but instead a contingent aspect of context.

In 1982, in the midst of currency devaluations, disruptions in the international oil market, and the nationalization of the Mexican banking system, the publishing industry went through a major crisis. Devaluations radically affected publishing because of Mexican dependency upon paper imports. The dramatic increase in production costs immediately resulted in an equivalent increase in the cost to potential buyers. These consumers, already a small group, were similarly experiencing the effects of the devaluation in other aspects of their daily lives.[1] The case of Editorial Joaquín Mortiz, Mexico's preeminent literary publisher, and its negotiation of these dramatic economic tensions both exemplifies how publishing houses experienced these crises and dramatizes the profound transitions that began in Mexican publishing in 1982.

Since its founding in 1962 by Joaquín Díez-Canedo, a Spanish immigrant and refugee from the Spanish Civil War, Editorial Joaquín Mortiz has stood out as the sole Mexican publisher to stake its reputation on literary quality, especially quality in contemporary Mexican literature. Although other important publishing houses such as the Fondo de Cultura Económica, Era, Siglo XXI, Grijalbo, and Diana have published Mexican literature, these companies structure their catalogue around a more diversified offering. In contrast, Editorial Joaquín Mortiz emerged primarily as a meeting place where novels and short stories by consecrated authors such as Agustín Yáñez, Rosario Castellanos, Juan José Arreola, and Carlos Fuentes appeared alongside the new trends of self-conscious *escritura* texts by Salvador Elizondo, José Emilio Pacheco, and Julieta Campos and *onda* novels by Gustavo Sainz and José Agustín. Besides promoting narrative during the period of the "Boom" in Latin American fiction, throughout the 1960s and 1970s Joaquín Mortiz also published translations and important lines of poetry and essays. In brief, between 1962 and 1982, Editorial Joaquín Mortiz emerged as a culturally and commercially successful publishing house associated with lasting markers of prestige: quality, openness to innovation, international high culture, cosmopolitanism, and a steadfast concern for contemporary Mexican literature.[2]

Whereas other publishers folded, radically cut back their activity, or reorganized in response to the economic crisis, Joaquín Mortiz received offers for mergers from companies like Diana and Grijalbo but decided to become a part of the transnational Spanish corporation Grupo Editorial Planeta in 1983. In a recent interview Díez-Canedo expressed disenchantment with his decision. Through the merger he had hoped to gain access to the book market in Spain. Now he says: "me confundí porque creí que Planeta estaba interesada en Mortiz y lo que querían era simplemente un pie de venta para entrar en México," 'I was mistaken because I thought Planeta was interested in Mortiz and what they wanted was simply a point of sales to enter Mexico' (Vega 1992). I would also suggest that Grupo Editorial Planeta strategically selected Joaquín Mortiz, not simply as a Mexican beachhead but also as the most prestigious available entry into the Mexican book market.[3]

In January 1987 Díez-Canedo turned over the direction of Joaquín Mortiz to his son, Joaquín Díez-Canedo Flores (*gerente*) and from 1988 to 1993 "Joaquín hijo" was accompanied by his sister Aurora Díez-Canedo Flores (*asistente editorial*). This was a period of intense readjustment not only internally, as Joaquín Mortiz negotiated its relation and position within the Grupo Editorial Planeta, but also in the general field of cultural production in Mexico. Even a superficial review reveals how the various Mexican publishing houses each promoted a certain kind of literature in the struggle both to gain a niche in the market for literary goods and to assert a claim for cultural legitimacy. During the 1970s, for example, Era emerged as the main promoter of the testimonial novel in Mexico, a literary trend that has gained increasing recognition throughout the 1980s in terms of a growing readership and consecration by academic criticism. The journal *Vuelta* began its own literary publishing house in the late 1980s to promote a cosmopolitan aesthetic. In contrast, Cal y Arena, associated with the journal *Nexos*, and Planeta often competed for the best-sellers associated with *literatura light*. Although attention to specific texts and authors reveals some surprising crossovers or contradictions, in rough terms the profiles of the different publishing houses map a social world that relates textual trends to institutions and to competing positions in a contested field of cultural production.

In this context, Joaquín Díez-Canedo Flores has drawn upon and made visible the quality established in the company's early years to reassert Joaquín Mortiz's bid for cultural authority and symbolic capital. For example, much as the midcentury writer Juan José Arreola was consecrated as a Joaquín Mortiz author by the line "Obras de Juan José Arreola," in 1989 the company began "Obras de Jorge Ibargüengoitia"; this new line gathered previously uncollected pieces by Ibargüengoitia and reprinted his classic titles published by Joaquín Mortiz. Similarly, in 1992 Díez-Canedo Flores began planning another line, "Serie Laurel," that would reprint other classics of Mexican narrative first published by Joaquín Mortiz in the 1960s and 1970s. Most of these works first appeared as inexpensive pocket-sized editions in the "Serie del

Volador" and have recently been released with a new design in a larger and more refined format. Díez-Canedo Flores initially conceptualized this series to include titles such as Vicente Leñero's *Estudio Q* (1965), José Agustín's *De perfil* (1966) and *Se está haciendo tarde* (1973), José Emilio Pacheco's *Morirás lejos* (1967) and *El principio del placer* (1972), Carlos Fuentes's *Cambio de piel* (1967), and María Luisa Mendoza's *De ausencia* (1974), to name just a few. Both of these lines—"Obras de Jorge Ibargüengoitia" and "Serie Laurel"—rely on the recognition of Joaquín Mortiz's past quality and seek to place back in public circulation this older symbolic capital.

Alongside these new lines, Joaquín Mortiz continued to publish titles in the important "Novelistas Contemporáneos" and the "Serie del Volador." However, "Nueva Narrativa Hispánica" was reconceptualized. The "Boom" had calmed and the term *nueva narrativa* (new narrative) was part of standard critical discourse. For this reason, in 1990 Díez-Canedo Flores launched the series "Cuarto Creciente" to emphasize the emergent literary values of the present rather than the "nueva narrativa" of the past.

Finally, their divergent cultural profiles notwithstanding, Joaquín Mortiz and Planeta pooled their resources in 1992 to promote the new "Premio Planeta/Joaquín Mortiz." Modeled after the long-standing "Premio Planeta," which successfully publicizes contemporary literature each year in Spain, the first "Premio Planeta/Joaquín Mortiz" was awarded to Paco Ignacio Taibo, II, for his historical novel, *La lejanía del tesoro* (1992). The following year the Uruguayan-born Daniel Chavarría won the prize with the first installment of a historical trilogy about fifth-century Athens, *El ojo Dindymenio* (1993). The writer and publisher Sealtiel Alatriste then won the prize with *Verdad de amor* (1994), his novel about the search for an erotic film starring a famous Mexican actress, obviously María Félix, under the direction of the French director Jean Renoir. In the following year, *La corte de los ilusos* (1995), Rosa Beltrán's historical novel about the early nineteenth-century Independence leader and later emperor, Agustín de Iturbide, received this distinction. The prize aims for public visibility and strategically proclaims the publishing house's cultural authority as an arbiter of value.

In spite of these strategies for maintaining the symbolic capital of Joaquín Mortiz and insuring the ongoing return of economic capital, published interviews with Joaquín Díez-Canedo Flores suggest a sense of frustration in the 1990s as fundamental changes in the cultural field become increasingly manifest. Noting such changes, Díez-Canedo Flores commented that "el apego rígido a la tradición de la letra impresa puede no ser muy favorable a la nueva situación que se vive en el mundo. Insisto, hay contenidos específicos para el libro, por eso a mí no me interesa la literatura 'light,' los libros de reportaje y similares," 'the rigid attachment to the tradition of the printed word may not be very favorable for the new situation in which we live today. I insist there are contents specifically for books, and for this reason I am not interested in *literatura light*, in journalistic books, and others along these lines' (Leyva 1993, 10). In another interview, Díez-Canedo Flores discusses marketing information provided by Planeta and explains how "la actual imagen del producto, lo que la gente está buscando, no coincide con la gráfica tradicional de Joaquín Mortiz," 'the current product image, what people are looking for, does not coincide with Joaquín Mortiz's traditional profile' (Estrada 1993, 3). Finally, in a third interview, Díez-Canedo Flores outlines in greater detail the disparity between the firm's "traditional profile" and current literary production. On the one hand, he describes a more "difficult" literature that experimented with narrative techniques and held "globalizing pretensions" in its social interpretations and thematic content; on the other hand, he notes a current preference for the "nineteenth-century precepts for the novel and short story"—a return to "realism"—and an interest in personal themes ("ámbitos íntimos"), biography, the *Bildungsroman*, and historical episodes with "ready-made stories and characters" (Díez-Canedo Flores 1993, 59).

These observations by Díez-Canedo Flores situate the publishing house in relation to the entire field of cultural production. On the one hand, Díez-Canedo Flores's comments point toward the editor's "feel for the game" and sense of "the action." On the other hand, they constitute a resistance to the trend known as *literatura light*. The question is whether the innovative, experimental, and cosmopolitan literary production fostered by Joaquín Mortiz in the past will continue to be valued, to accrue symbolic capital. From this perspective, what has changed by the 1990s is the configuration of the field of literary production in Mexico and hence Joaquín Mortiz's position according to the firm's "traditional profile."

In one interview Josefina Estrada asked Joaquín Díez-Canedo Flores about Joaquín Mortiz's loss of "el antiguo prestigio," 'the old prestige,' after the merger with Grupo Editorial Planeta. In response, he emphasized that "nada de lo que le ha pasado a [Joaquín] Mortiz puede ser imputable a Planeta," 'nothing of what has happened to [Joaquín] Mortiz can be blamed on Planeta.' Instead, he attributes the change to a broader series of factors: "Considero que la pérdida de prestigio es producto del escepticismo general, de un cuestionamiento general de todo tipo de autoridad; no sólo [Joaquín] Mortiz ha perdido prestigio, muchos escritores nacionales que siguen siendo los mejores que tenemos también lo han perdido," 'I consider the loss of prestige to be the product of general skepticism, a general questioning of all kinds of authority; not only has [Joaquín] Mortiz lost prestige, many national writers who continue to be the best we have have also lost it' (Estrada 1993, 3). Díez-Canedo Flores points to the questioning of cultural authority as a fundamental contemporary phenomenon. This questioning appeared in critical discourse beginning in the mid-1980s and principally relates to three areas: (1) the perceived changes in market pressures upon literature; (2) a related change in the opposition between cultural prestige and the commercial success of a best-seller; and (3) the articulation of aesthetic criteria around the emergent and competing definitions of quality.

First, the central factor lamented by Díez-Canedo Flores and identified by critics as the basis for this dramatic change in the field of cultural production is a new market sensitivity in literary publishing (Alatriste 1990, 1991a, 1991b, 1991c; López González 1993, 665; Prada 1991, 56). The extreme closure of "high" literary culture in the 1960s and 1970s— when a community of writers producers created for an audience generally composed of other writers, including an even smaller group of influential writers often referred to as the "Mafia"—allowed for the large accumulation of symbolic capital in Joaquín Mortiz and made possible the economic return on "classics" of contemporary Mexican literature as best-sellers in the long run.[4] In contrast, the economic crisis of the early 1980s hastened the movement toward publishing conglomerations, such as the transnational debut of Planeta in Mexico, and, concomitantly, ushered in an increasing concern for the economic bottom line and the search for a wider audience and larger market. Whereas in the 1960s Joaquín Mortiz could justify holding in warehouse an inventory of published books for up to three years, Díez-Canedo Flores points out that in the 1990s "un inventario de más de seis meses es desaconsejable, si no es que peligroso. La vida promedio real de un libro en exhibición es de 45 días, de dos meses: antes eran años," 'an inventory over six-months old is inadvisable, if not simply dangerous. The average real life of a book in promotion is about forty-five days, two months: before it was years' (Leyva 1993, 9).

Second, concurrent with this change on the part of publishers is a change in both the writers and the potential audience of readers. Díez-Canedo Flores's comments point toward the current "game" for legitimacy occurring in the field of Mexican literary production, a game in which publishers, writers, and readers, especially in their role as purchasers of books, are all taking positions. Aralia López González underscores the best-seller status of Angeles Mastretta's *Arráncame la vida* (1985) and Laura Esquivel's *Como agua para chocolate* (1989) and the ensuing debates over their status as either "una literatura comercial" (commercial literature) or as "obras 'buenas' y respetables desde el enfoque de la 'alta' cultura," '"good" and respectable works from the perspective of "high" culture'.[5] Because of this debate, López González concludes that "el *mercado* es ya un elemento determinante en el campo intelectual," 'the *market* is already a determining factor in the intellectual field.' She goes on to emphasize the necessity of defining new criteria for judging literary production and for critically evaluating the pertinence of categories such as "high," "consumer," "mass," or "popular" culture (1993, 665).[6] In a 1994 issue of *Fiction International* dedicated to contemporary Mexican narrative, Gabriel Trujillo Muñoz's introduction argues that Mexican publishing is thoroughly market driven, responding to the "mass-mediated values" of fragmented groups of readers. To survive, publishers and writers have to carve out specific niches: "Each work has a specific public. Therefore, fiction writers now choose as their site the spirit of the readers with whom they wish to have a dialogue and the cultural level on which they wish to do so. . . . This is the option—and also the predicament—of current fiction" (1994, 5).

Others note the phenomenon of market awareness not only in Mexico but in a larger international context. Responding to the problem of labels and categories, Sealtiel Alatriste notes the worldwide success of Umberto Eco's *The Name of the Rose* (1980), Gabriel García Márquez's *Chronicle of a Death Foretold* (1981), and Milan Kundera's *The Unbearable Lightness of Being* (1984)—books originally published in Italian, Spanish, and Czech as *Il nome della rosa*, *La crónica de una muerte anunciada*, and *Nesnesitelna lehkost byti*, and immediately translated into numerous languages—to suggest the emergence of "el nuevo *best-seller* de calidad," 'the new quality best-seller,' a category that goes beyond the conventional division between "high" and "low." According to Alatriste, these works combine "dos aspectos aparentemente irreconciliables: el producto editorial de éxito [comercial] con el producto literario de calidad," 'two apparently irreconcilable aspects: the editorial product of (commercial) success with the literary product of quality' (1990, 89). In other words, in the 1960s and 1970s the publishing industry, writers, and the reading public implicitly cooperated to support the symbolic capital of "high" culture, cosmopolitanism, and formal experimentation. By the late 1980s, economic pressures grew alongside an expanding reading public with higher hopes for social affluence and a stronger educational background; this reconfigured group of social actors began renegotiating the terms of legitimacy, a phenomenon that modified Joaquín Mortiz's position in the field and required the formulation of new strategies for the ongoing maintenance of prestige as accumulated symbolic capital and economic viability.

The growing awareness of market pressure and changing perception of the relation between quality and commercial success becomes most apparent in a third area: the antagonistic competition to define the cultural connotations of "quality" and "literature." Cynthia Steele's *Politics, Gender, and the Mexican Novel, 1968–1988* (1992) identifies a wider context for the debates of the late 1980s. She addresses the broad question of whether changes in Mexican fiction after the 1968 sociopolitical turning point are symptomatic of a decline in literary quality or indicative of democratization in the literary field. Citing the increasing number of published novels, the growing popularity of cocktail parties to launch new titles, and the flourishing interest in writing workshops, Steele notes that with this democratization "writers are frequently publishing works before they are ready; the quality of new novels has varied widely" (1992, 10). Additionally, she emphasizes that the evaluation of quality is problematic because "critics often limit their judgments to a very narrow definition of the novel, failing to take into account new innovative discourses which draw on other traditional literary genres, as well as on oral history, the chronicle, and the essay" (1992, 11). The debates over *literatura light* appeared in the second half of the 1980s as a particular manifestation of the larger realignments in the literary field that Steele has discussed.

At the center of statements debating the value of *literatura light* reside two issues that easily lead to confusion. On the one hand, the debates about *literatura light* emerge parallel to a resurgence in the "realist" technique, or what John S. Brushwood describes as a more accessible narrative style in which many novelists have "gone back to telling stories" (1989, 83; see also Anderson 1995). On the other hand, there is potential confusion between accessibility for readers (books that are less "difficult" to read) and literary "lightness." This second factor is problematic because regardless of one's position in the debate, there is near universal agreement that difficult reading is not automatically equivalent to literary quality and, inversely, that ease in reading is not necessarily a *differentia specifica* of *literatura light*. The question, then, is what is *literatura light?* Is it an aesthetic category or a rhetorical label used to discredit certain writers?

In *México: País de ideas, país de novelas* (1987), Sara Sefchovich became one of the first critics to address this confusing issue in aesthetic terms. Sefchovich acknowledges the existence of a narrative trend that extends cosmopolitan concerns with linguistic and technical experimentation, a tendency that has antecedents in the *vanguardista* writing of the 1920s and 1930s; she describes these works as "extrañas en nuestro horizonte cultural, difíciles y cultas," 'strange on our cultural horizon, difficult and refined' (1987, 215). In contrast, Sefchovich sees a more dominant trend in the 1980s in a turn toward two kinds of realism. Rather than include all of these new "realist" novels in a single category, Sefchovich distinguishes between a *realismo mimético* (mimetic realism) designed to satisfy market demand and readers' entertainment and a *realismo crítico* (critical realism) created to explore present conditions in the committed struggle to change society (1987, 226–232).

Taken all together, then, Sefchovich's comments map out three competing positions. First, a cosmopolitan aesthetic defends what could be called an "art for art's sake" position that values linguistic innovation and formal experimentation, regardless of whether it makes reading more difficult. Second, a critical aesthetic, associated by Sefchovich with realist style, holds a socially committed position and values literature's ability to make evident the mechanisms of oppression in national life. Finally, an escapist aesthetic, also associated with a realist style, rests upon a commercial position; it values a literature that poses no problems to readers and that interests them in its story.

In spite of Sefchovich's nuanced articulation of the differences among these positions, by 1992 the debate rapidly had escalated, polarized, and reduced these three positions to two: a minority cosmopolitan aesthetic versus a populist realist aesthetic that collapses Sefchovich's critical and mimetic strands together because of their shared realism. Furthermore, the terms of this debate directly relate aesthetic positions to political positions in the broader field of Mexican society. Although significant exceptions and crossover figures can be identified, as a general rule the group associated with the journal *Vuelta* defended the cosmopolitan aesthetic and the group associated with the journal *Nexos* supported the realist aesthetic variously labeled democratic, populist, or "light." Nobel laureate Octavio Paz and historian Enrique Krauze headed the *Vuelta* group, whereas historian and novelist Héctor Aguilar Camín stood as the figurehead for *Nexos*. Both *Vuelta* and *Nexos* attempted to exert influence on public life through analyses of national politics and the future of the dominant Partido Revolucionario Institucional (PRI). After the elections and economic crisis of 1982, the future of the PRI increasingly became contested, leading to the highly contentious 1988 elections in which presidential candidate Cuautémoc Cárdenas separated from the PRI, rallied massive popular support, and effectively questioned the nature of political legitimacy in Mexico. PRI candidate Carlos Salinas de Gortari won the elections and opposition groups immediately claimed that the PRI had resorted to the old tricks of electoral fraud.

During the period 1988–1994, under the Salinas administration, dramatic shifts in Mexican society became evident. First, market pressures, which had assumed a new importance in the literary field, also became dominant in the political field; popular political faith grew and prosperity appeared to return with the privatization of state-owned corporations and the implementation of a neoliberal economic policy. Second, the relation between the state and intellectuals changed. The tragic massacre of students and protesters on 2 October 1968 at the Plaza de Tlatelolco displayed the Mexican state's repressive, authoritarian powers; intellectuals, distrustful of politics and politicians, distanced themselves (Camp 1985, 208–222). However, during the Salinas administration intellectuals accepted a new public role: They began to make clear their alliances and to benefit from such political relationships. During this period, Héctor Aguilar Camín strongly supported neoliberal policies and from the pages of *Nexos* emerged as the intellectual ideologue of the Salinas administration.[7] The uprising of the Ejército Zapatista de Liberación Nacional in 1994, numerous currency devaluations attendant upon the beginning of the North American Free Trade Agreement, the revelation of corruption at high governmental levels, scandalous political assassinations, and the ongoing accusation of intrigue and deceit associated with now-exiled former president Carlos Salinas de Gortari make it retrospectively easy to discredit, or at least question the judgment of, many prominent figures from the previous administration, including Héctor Aguilar Camín. However, during the Salinas administration there was a widespread hope for a better national future. At this juncture and amid the wide-ranging questions about the best path to national prosperity, the debate over *literatura light* began to simmer.

The 26 March 1992 issue of *Macrópolis*, a weekly guide to cultural events, entertainment, and leisure activities, published a series of interviews by María Ximena and Alejandro Toledo entitled, "Por una literatura fácil," 'For an easy literature.' Rafael Pérez Gay, director of Cal y Arena, and Jaime Aljure, director of Planeta, speak positively of *literatura light* and characterize its direct language, eschewal of experimentation, and accessibility to readers. In the same series of interviews, however, novelists Hernán Lara Zavala and David Martín del Campo (both authors published by Joaquín Mortiz), who were selected for the interview because of their own connections to journalism and because of a proposed link between journalistic writing and *literatura light*, respectfully dodged the closure of the category and defended a writer's freedom to experiment.

In the May 1992 issue of *Vuelta*, the "secretario de redacción" Aurelio Asiain responded to the *Macrópolis* interviews. The response, "Lo que hay que ver: El populismo literario y los nuevos científicos," 'What One Must See: Literary Populism and the New *científicos*,' explicitly claims an analogy between the present situation and the attacks on the avant-garde group of writers who converged in the short-lived yet influential journal *Contemporáneos* (1928–1931).[8] Asiain describes "los Contemporáneos" as "víctimas de una campaña de hostigamiento que, desde la prensa del gobierno, se expresaba como vocera de la opinión pública y obedecía a los intereses de un grupo en lucha por el poder político," 'victims of a harassment campaign that, through the government press, spoke as the voice of public opinion and obeyed the interests of a group struggling for political power.' He cites the *Macrópolis* article and the rejection of "las excentricidades formales de autores de los años 60 y 70, como Salvador Elizondo," 'the formal eccentricities of authors from the 1960s and 1970s, such as Salvador Elizondo,' as aspects of an attack on *Vuelta*. Unlike the attacks against *Contemporáneos*, however, "el reproche no apela hoy a la virilidad y las buenas costumbres. Pero en ambos casos se acude al voto de la mayoría para acallar la voz de la minoría," 'today's reproach does not base its claim on virility and good manners. But both instances rely on the majority vote to silence the minority voice' (1992, 10). In contrast to a *literatura light* defined by the ease of reading, Asiain promotes "la literatura que aspira a crear sus propios lectores y exigir de ellos un gusto riguroso," 'literature that aspires to create its own readers and to demand from them a rigorous taste' (1992, 10–11). Although he underscores textual and stylistic preferences, Asiain's comments evidence the blurring of the debate between aesthetic criteria and groups in competition for legitimacy.

In spite of the lack of a response from the supposed interlocutors at *Nexos*, the July 1992 issue of *Vuelta*, a special issue dedicated to a "Defensa de la literatura difícil," 'Defense of Difficult Literature,' drew out the debate even further. The issue includes a chapter from Octavio Paz's *La otra voz: poesía y fin de siglo* (1990), the translation of presentations from the December 1991 symposium of the Swedish Academy on "La literatura difícil," 'Difficult literature,' and literary critic Fabienne Bradu's interview with French novelist Michel Butor on the question of *literatura light*. Although the papers presented before the Swedish Academy examine a variety of concerns, especially the challenge of defining difficulty and the tension between referential (that is, realist) and nonreferential writing, a brief editorial by Aurelio Asiain casts this special issue in terms of the struggle in Mexico between "un grupo de periodistas doblados de escritores" in favor of "literatura democrática," 'a group of journalists who double as writers in favor of a 'democratic literature' (also known as the *Nexos* group) and others who support a "literatura de minorías, que no se define políticamente ni considera numéricamente a sus lectores y es difícil si le resulta necesario," 'a literature for the minority of readers that is not defined politically and does not consider its readers numerically and that is difficult whenever difficulty is necessary' (1992, 11). The opening selection from Octavio Paz's *La otra voz* frames the *Vuelta* position in slightly different terms:

> La industria editorial contemporánea tiende a disolver la diversidad de públicos en una mayoría impersonal. . . . El comercio literario hoy está movido por una consideración meramente económica: el valor supremo es el número de compradores de un libro. Ganar dinero es legítimo; también lo es producir libros para el "gran público," pero una literatura se muere y una sociedad se degrada si el propósito central es la publicación de *best-sellers* y de obras de entretenimiento y de consumo popular. (1992, 14)

[The contemporary publishing industry tends to dissolve the diversity of audiences into an impersonal majority. . . . Literary commerce today is motivated by a merely economic consideration: The supreme value is the number of buyers of a book. Earning money is legitimate; it is also legitimate to produce books for the "large audience," but a literature dies and a society is degraded if the central purpose is the publication of best-sellers and works for entertainment and popular consumption.]

Although someone writing from the position that Sefchovich described as *realismo crítico* could easily agree with Paz's affirmation, the polarization of the debate between *light* and *difficult*, between a realist aesthetic and an openness to experimental options, forecloses this possibility and reduces the debate to a manifestation of the political struggle between *Vuelta* and *Nexos*. Equally important, the polarized rhetoric of this debate monopolizes public discourse and limits the possible terms for understanding and explaining literature. For example, in an April 1993 interview with Angeles Mastretta in *Nexos* and a January 1994 interview with Laura Esquivel in *Proceso*, both writers attempted to reject the connotations of difficulty and lightness in current circulation, yet their language and views are confined to the polarized terms of this opposition.[9]

In addition to sparking a debate that gradually became more polarized and politicized, the interviews in *Macrópolis* also made evident an important gender polarization associated with *literatura light*. Although María Ximena and Alejandro Toledo interviewed two male editors and three male novelists, two of the novelists kept their distance from full identification with *literatura light* and the editors spoke mainly about the women writers associated with "easy literature": Angeles Mastretta, Laura Esquivel, Guadalupe Loaeza, and Margo Su. Similarly, mention of the enormous commercial success of Angeles Mastretta's *Arráncame la vida* (1985) and Laura Esquivel's *Como agua para chocolate* (1989) always begins the discussion of *literatura light*, which implies a link between this category and contemporary women's writing. In Esquivel's words, "El otro día leía una entrevista que me dio mucha ternura, porque decía que los que venden mucho, Humberto [*sic*] Eco, Gabriel García Márquez, no son *light*, las *light* nada más somos las mujeres. Hay esa diferenciación," 'The other day I was reading an interview that I found really precious, because it said that the men who sell a lot, Humberto [*sic*] Eco, Gabriel García Márquez, aren't light, the light ones are only us women. There's that differentiation' (Rivera 1994, 51). Indeed, Mastretta's novel appears in Cal y Arena and Esquivel's in Planeta, the two publishing houses that pride themselves on their promotion of *literatura light* in the *Macrópolis* interviews. Planeta has even launched a special series, "Colección Fábula," which mainly consists of contemporary women's writing, including *Demasiado amor* (1990) and *La señora de los sueños* (1993) by Sara Sefchovich, *Novia que te vea* (1992) by Rosa Nissán, *Los colores del principio* (1992) by Alicia Trueba, *La insólita historia de la Santa de Cabora* (1990) by Brianda Domecq, *La muerte alquila un cuarto* (1991) by Gabriela Rábago Palafox, and *Amora* (1989) by Rosamaría Roffiel, in addition to Laura Esquivel's international best-seller.

All of these details—the popularity of women's writing, the association of some women with *literatura light*, and the concentration of women writers in certain publishing houses and collections—unfortunately have led to a conflation mistakenly suggesting that all contemporary women's writing is *literatura light*. To the contrary, contemporary Mexican women writers explore a large range of aesthetic positions in their works, and current reader interest in women's writing points to a social phenomenon larger and more profound than the commercial success of "light" or "easy" literature. To deal first with the issue of aesthetic variety, Sefchovich's novels, for example, address popular romance novels and women's reading in a self-conscious and strategic way, aiming to modify the genre and to promote an empowering political awareness. *La señora de los sueños* follows a patterned regularity of structure that facilitates reading, much like formula or popular literature, but it also thematically explores the empowering ability to imagine the world differently when a depressed middle-class homemaker, wife, and mother becomes an avid reader and sets out to change her lot in life. Although Sefchovich strives for accessibility, for stylistic "lightness" as it were, and readers interested in a certain kind of complexity may reject this style, the political motivations evident in these texts cannot be dismissed as "light." Similarly, Brianda Domecq's *La insólita historia de la Santa de Cabora* is structurally sophisticated, historically complex, and commitedly feminist—a far cry from the typical description of *literatura light*. In this novel a contemporary female researcher explores the social significance of Teresa de Urrea, a peasant woman, faith healer, and social organizer who was perceived as a threat to national security by president Porfirio Díaz in the late nineteenth century. And to include two other influential women writers in this brief discussion of aesthetic variety, Elena Poniatowska's novels blend journalism, (auto)biography, and history to challenge the conventional limits on genre in recent titles such as *La "Flor de*

Lis" (1988) and *Tinísima* (1992), whereas Carmen Boullosa's literary experimentation in *Mejor desaparece* (1987) and *Antes* (1989) gives an entirely new meaning to the concept of family life and domestic space. Moreover, whereas Poniatowska's novels are published by Era, Boullosa's novels demonstrate the complex institutional alliances of an author who crosses over my lines of analytical generalization: *Mejor desaparece* first appeared in Océano, which soon became Cal y Arena, whereas *Antes* was released only two years later by Editorial Vuelta.

As a phenomenon parallel to the variety among women writers, the current popularity of women's writing in general derives from more than the commercial success of *literatura light*. A more accurate assessment of contemporary writing by women in Mexico might follow Toril Moi's reasoning. According to Moi (1991) and her interpretation of Bourdieu's sociological theories, the "symbolic capital" associated with gender changes in different historical and cultural contexts. At present, female gender in Mexico represents a higher symbolic capital than in previous periods, an increase that perhaps results from a combination of factors: feminist initiatives in recent decades; academic attention to women writers and the consecration of figures such as Rosario Castellanos, Elena Garro, and Elena Poniatowska; and, of course, the current preferences of a contemporary reading public, a public that now includes more- and better-educated women than the readership of the past, as well as men with changing interests and evolving perceptions of gender. In this context of heightened gender value, feminist writers have a particularly effective position from which they can exploit the crisis of authority in the field of cultural production to question the terms of patriarchal legitimacy. Aralia López González directly relates the way contemporary women's writing challenges canonical definitions of literature to the current "situación vacilante en cuanto a las interpretaciones del hecho literario," 'vacillating situation with respect to interpretations of the literary phenomenon' (1993, 665). In this perspective, if *Vuelta* has been the victim of a repetition of the attacks on *Contemporáneos*, there is an important inversion. In 1924–1925, *literatura afeminada* was the "literatura de minorías" (literature of a minority) associated with the elite avant-garde and *literatura viril* was the populist realism found in the novels of the Mexican Revolution. In the 1990s, although the terms have reversed—now the "populist" (or more popular) literature has been described as *afeminada*—they paradoxically remain the same. In the current debate the "feminine," like *literatura afeminada*, appears on the disqualified side of the comparison: *Literatura light*, mistaken for women's writing, is assumed by many to be not quite literature and lacking in quality.

Throughout this study I have characterized the notion of quality traditionally associated with Editorial Joaquín Mortiz, examined the fate of this quality in the period 1982–1994 when the literary field underwent radical changes, and finally I have related these changes in the literary field to the debates around *literatura light*. My circuitous approach to the debate—covering first the historical moment and the dynamics of publishing—slowed my approach to the confusing web of statements about *literatura light* that began appearing in the late 1980s, but this indirect approach does not resolve or simplify the problematic nature of the statements themselves. Since the field of cultural production is characterized by relationality and competition, each statement is a starting point that leads outward to the other positions in the field. At stake in this competition is the accumulation of cultural authority and the power to decide what counts as quality and literature. Beyond this characterization of the cultural field and the contemporary debates, I believe that my approach suggests four implications for the study of Mexican literature.

First, considerations of the contested corpus called "the canon" often fail to take into full account processes of cultural selection that occur outside of and precede decisions made in the academy. Thus the study of publishing houses as cultural institutions gives a broader basis for understanding why and how certain "texts" become important works of "literature." A canon is only the tip of an iceberg. Beneath it lies a social world of differentiated groups that compete and configure networks. The competition for cultural authority and accumulated symbolic capital suggests that such groupings radically affect and determine selection processes, functioning as a sorting mechanism that remains hidden from view when literary studies attend only to the close reading of published texts. Aralia López González proposes that beginning in the 1980s, as market forces exert a new and stronger role, groups are less able to achieve the hegemony of a particular discourse, and, at the same time, public culture becomes more divided, entropic, and multifaceted (1993, 682–684). Moreover, the situation that López González describes reaches its culmination in the 1990s and perhaps fulfills the older rumors surrounding the "Boom" in the 1960s, that literary success and popularity were the result of aggressive commercialization, marketing, and publicity on the part of publishing houses.

Second, my attention to the broader field of cultural production attempts to carry to an extreme the implications of what Edward Said calls the "worldliness" of texts: "The point is that texts have ways of existing that even in their most rarefied forms are always enmeshed in circumstance, time, place, and society—in short, they are in the world, and hence worldly" (1983, 35). Said emphasizes this worldliness as a point of departure for the interpretation of textual representations and their manner of existing and circulating in society. I have attempted to carry this concern a step further by tracing the connection between such representations and the factors that affect their material existence and circulation as commodities within a market of cultural goods.

Third, the polarized rhetoric of public discourse creates a smoke screen and masks fundamental issues from view. In fact, my attention to the debates over *literatura light* turns the focus away from a central group of social actors constantly mentioned yet seldom studied: the behavior of readers and their actual reception of literary texts, whether they be light or heavy, easy or difficult. Janice Radway's ground-breaking study, *Reading the Romance: Women, Patriarchy, and Popular Literature* (1984), cogently demonstrates the sophisticated and discriminating reception of popular romances by everyday women readers in a Midwestern city in the United States. In a later article, she goes on to argue that the dietary metaphor of "consuming books" is highly mistaken in its implications that readers passively or complacently accept the illusions promoted by mass-produced literature (Radway 1986). In a similar manner, the debates about *literatura light* suggest docile readers who naïvely accept the world constructed by such texts and, similarly, *literatura difícil* would automatically insure an active reader who perspicaciously critiques textual realities. A more attentive and less *manichean* questioning of reading needs to explore with greater flexibility the role of reading in everyday life. Attention to the questions of who reads, what they read, under what circumstances, and for what purpose, will move beyond the debate over "lightness" and "heaviness" to reveal the complex behavior associated with reading and responding to a book. Reading is a unique phenomenon, partly public and collective because it is an acquired skill requiring education and shared codes of knowledge, but also partly private because it is practiced individually and frequently in isolation. Reading, in this perspective, is an activity limited to certain groups in which it functions as a strategy for producing, maintaining, differentiating, or even changing their sense of identity.

And finally, although I have attempted to separate description of the debate from an endorsement of certain values, my own position is not innocent, neutral, or disinterested. Given the tradition of studying Mexico from within U.S. universities—a tradition that Sefchovich (1990) has examined in much detail because of its often damaging insinuations and allegations about Mexican life—I believe that it is important to situate this study of contemporary Mexican aesthetic criteria in relation to my cultural context both in the academy and the United States. The crises over cultural and political legitimacy that I have studied here are quite similar to crises experienced at the same time not only in the United States but also throughout the world. Within the U.S. academy, in particular, debates over "the Western canon," discussion of what can or should be included in "American" literature, and considerations about "quality" that include or exclude women's writing, Chicano literature, or Native American literature from "serious," critical attention all bear strong parallels to debates over cultural legitimacy in Mexico. Outside the academy, the public struggle to redefine the cultural connotations of "liberal" or "conservative" politics in the United States follows a rhetorical practice of polarization and discrediting similar in dynamics to the struggle between charged terms such as *literatura light* and *literatura difícil*. In brief, although there are historical and institutional differences between Mexico and the United States that bear serious consideration when comparing literature, politics, and public discourse—the traditional taboo against public "attacks" on presidential power in Mexico in contrast to widespread public critiques and ridicule of both the office and person of presidents in the United States, to name only one example—in both countries we are living through an acrimonious period that questions all forms of legitimacy and authority. Although polarization of public discourse impoverishes our creative ability to seek new solutions and imagine alternatives, the crisis of values and authority is also an important opportunity for change and innovation if we can find a language for constructive dialogue.

NOTES

1. The dynamics of this crisis were discussed widely throughout the Mexican press in the last quarter of 1982 and throughout 1983. The publishing industry in this period owes its visibility and viability to the concerted efforts of the "group of the ten" ("el grupo de las 10"), ten publishers who united to propose restructur-

ings necessary for the economic viability of the Mexican publishing industry. These publishers were Siglo XXI, Nueva Imagen, Era, Joaquín Mortiz, Prensa Médica, Martín Casillas, Nuestro Tiempo, CIDE, El Colegio de México, and Fondo de Cultura Económica. Special issues of *Diálogos* (1984) and *Casa del Tiempo* (1983b) provide overviews of the publishing crisis. *Casa del Tiempo* (1983a) focuses more broadly on the general sense of social crisis. See also Greaves 1988, 365–368.

2. This study draws in part upon my history of Joaquín Mortiz; see Anderson 1996.

3. Leyva (1990) describes the organization of Grupo Planeta and Leyva (1993) discusses Joaquín Mortiz's thirtieth anniversary and merger with Grupo Planeta.

4. Whereas a strictly commercial publisher promotes titles that provide short-term returns and publishes numerous new titles (*novedades*) each year in the search for a best-seller, a cultural publisher strives for an accumulation of symbolic capital that produces the symbolic return of prestigious quality in the short run and later, through reprintings, will guarantee the economic return of "*classics*, best-sellers over the long run" (Bourdieu 1993, 100).

5. Not coincidentally, both of these works were rapidly translated into English. Esquivel's *Like Water for Chocolate* enjoyed months on best-seller lists in the United States and an internationally successful film version; Mastretta's *Mexican Bolero*, however, did not meet with such dramatic acceptance.

6. This shift has a paradoxical relation to Bourdieu's characterization of cultural production. Bourdieu distinguishes between the "field of restricted production," which refers to "high" literature, and the "field of large-scale production," which refers to commercial literature. According to Bourdieu, the economic logic of the two fields is opposed. In the field of restricted production, commercial success is not as important as symbolic success or prestige, and the commercial success of a book can even have a negative effect in terms of prestige. In the other field, however, commercial success means everything. See "The Field of Cultural Production, or: The Economic World Reversed" (29–73), "The Production of Belief: Contribution to an Economy of Symbolic Goods" (74–111), and "The Market of Symbolic Goods" (112–141) in Bourdieu 1993. The current Mexican debates confirm this characterization to the degree that commercial success is taken de facto as an indicator of light literature. The situation differs, however, to the degree that the debate attempts to change the criteria for determining literary success within the field of restricted production; in other words, at least one position within this debate attributes aesthetic value to a literary work that succeeds in attracting a large readership in the short run.

7. Jaime Sánchez Susarrey's *El debate político e intelectual en México: Desde la represión de 1968 hasta nuestros días de Encuentros vs. Coloquios* (1993) provides a detailed if partisan coverage of the rivalry between *Vuelta* and *Nexos* in a broad social context.

8. Asiain's rhetoric heavily sediments various terms from previous cultural debates. The term *científicos* in his title, literally "scientists," harks back to the team of "liberal" advisors during the presidency of Porfirio Díaz, 1876–1911; the control of the *científicos* on economic policy contributed to and exacerbated the conditions that gave rise to the Mexican Revolution of 1910. The gendered language

of *viril* and *afeminado* derives from a debate begun in December 1924 in which critic and writer Julio Jiménez Rueda decried the effeminacy of refined Mexican literature written under foreign literary influences; the critic and writer Francisco Monterde responded by affirming that Mariano Azuela's novel, *Los de abajo* (published serially in October–November 1915) already proved the existence of a virile Mexican literature. Díaz Arciniega (1989) provides the most detailed coverage of this debate. Finally, the terms of this gendered language continued into the late 1920s and early 1930s, when the journal *Contemporáneos* came under attack and met its demise. This attack involved competing views of how to place the nation in the world (nationalist versus internationalist) and also attempted to wrest power from the *Contemporáneos* group, whose members held successful bureaucratic careers, by homophobically maligning the "virility" of a group that included several gay writers.

9. For Mastretta's interview see de Beer 1993, and for Esquivel see Rivera J. 1994. In a December 1993 editorial published in the cultural supplement *Sábado*, "Vejamen de la narrativa difícil," 'The Abuse of Difficult Literature,' the novelist Enrique Serna is perhaps the most effective in underscoring the "falsa polarización entre narrativa fácil y narrativa para entendidos," 'false polarization between easy narrative and narrative for insiders.' Serna rejects the dichotomized debate and offers a different set of terms for understanding the contemporary literary dilemma: "La disyuntiva no es hacer literatura ligera o pesada. El reto es cautivar sin complacer, vencer con astucia la pereza de los lectores y llevarlos adonde no quieren ir. . . . Para esto debemos tener bien claro que la narrativa está muerta si le da la espalda a la diversión. El novelista del futuro que aspire a tener un auditorio más o menos amplio sin renunciar a su búsqueda personal, habrá de ser un consumado encantador de serpientes y entremezclar distintos niveles de significación en el mismo texto . . . para seducir también al lector avisado que aprecia la ambigüedad y sabe leer entre líneas" (1993, 3), 'The alternative is not to create light or heavy literature. The challenge is to captivate without having to accommodate, to astutely claim victory over readers' laziness and take them where they do not want to go. . . . To do this, we must clearly understand that narrative is dead when it turns its back on entertainment. The novelist of the future who aspires to a more or less broad audience, without giving up a personal search, must become a consummate snake charmer and must mix together different levels of meaning in the same text . . . to also seduce the informed reader who values ambiguity and knows how to read between the lines.' In other words, the future of literature does not rest on whether it is light or heavy, easy or difficult, but on its ability to engage readers. And if readers have different preferences—some like an easier read whereas others enjoy a complex challenge—Serna proposes that a writer can try to reach both kinds of readers at the same time.

WORKS CITED

Alatriste, Sealtiel. 1990. "El negocio de los libros." *Nexos* 156: 89–91.

———. 1991a. "El negocio de los libros." *Nexos* 161: 111–112.

————. 1991b. "El negocio de los libros." *Nexos* 163: 99–100.

————. 1991c. "El negocio de los libros." *Nexos* 167: 91–92.

Anderson, Danny J. 1995. "Difficult Relations, Compromising Positions: Telling Involvement in Recent Mexican Narrative." *Chasqui* 24, no. 1: 16–29.

————. 1996. "Creating Cultural Prestige: The Case of Editorial Joaquín Mortiz." *Latin American Research Review* 31, no. 2: 3–41.

Asiain, Aurelio. 1992. "Lo que hay que ver: El populismo literario y los nuevos científicos." *Vuelta* 186: 10–12.

Bourdieu, Pierre. 1984. *Distinction: A Social Critique of the Judgment of Taste*, trans. Richard Nice. Cambridge, MA: Harvard University Press.

————. 1993. *The Field of Cultural Production: Essays on Art and Literature*, ed. Randal Johnson. New York: Columbia University Press.

Brushwood, John. 1989. *Narrative Innovation and Political Change in Mexico*. University of Texas Series in Contemporary Spanish-American Fiction. New York: Peter Lang.

Camp, Roderic A. 1985. *Intellectuals and the State in Twentieth-Century Mexico*. Austin: University of Texas Press.

Casa del Tiempo. 1983a. Special issue, "Cultura y Crisis." No. 27.

————. 1983b. Special issue, "Presente, Pasado y Futuro del Libro en México." No. 33.

de Beer, Gabriela. 1993. "Una entrevista con Angeles Mastretta: Entre la aventura y el ligitio." *Nexos* 184: 33–39.

Diálogos. 1984. Special issue, "La industria editorial." 20, no. 2.

Díaz Arciniega, Víctor. 1989. *Querella por la cultura "revolucionaria" (1925)*. Mexico: Fondo de Cultura Económica.

Díez-Canedo Flores, Joaquín. 1993. "Los editores en *Vice Versa*: Entrevista a Joaquín Díez Canedo." *Vice Versa* 3: 58–60.

————. 1994. "Las razones de J. Díez-Canedo Flores." *El Búho* (2 January): 2.

Eagleton, Terry. 1983. *Literary Theory: An Introduction*. Minneapolis: University of Minnesota Press.

Estrada, Josefina. 1993. "Un artífice del matiz: Entrevista a Joaquín Díez-Canedo Flores." *Sábado* (20 May): 3.

Greaves, Cecilia. 1988. "La Secretaría de Educación Pública y la lectura, 1960–1985." In *Historia de la lectura en México*. Seminario de Historia de la Educación, Colegio de México. Mexico: El Colegio de México.

Leyva, José Angel. 1990. "Por la órbita editorial de Planeta." *Libros de México* 18: 5–9.

————. 1993. "Joaquín Mortiz, las grandes transfiguraciones editoriales." *Libros de México* 31: 7–12.

López González, Aralia. 1993. "Quebrantos, búsquedas y azares de una pasión nacional (Dos décadas de narrativa mexicana: 1970–1980)." *Revista Iberoamericana* 164–165: 659–685.

Moi, Toril. 1991. "Appropriating Bourdieu: Feminist Theory and Pierre Bourdieu's Sociology of Culture." *New Literary History* 22: 1017–1049.

Paz, Octavio. 1990. *La otra voz: Poesía y fin de siglo*. Barcelona: Seix Barral.

————. 1992. "Cuantía y Valía." *Vuelta* 188: 11–15.

Prada, Javier. 1991. "Las decisiones editoriales." *La Gaceta del Fondo de Cultura Económica* 245: 56–57.

Radway, Janice. 1984. *Reading the Romance: Women, Patriarchy, and Popular Literature.* Chapel Hill: University of North Carolina Press.

———. 1986. "Reading Is Not Eating: Mass-Produced Literature and the Theoretical, Methodological, and Political Consequences of a Metaphor." *Book Research Quarterly* 2, no. 3: 7–29.

Rivera J., Héctor. 1994. "Refuta Laura Esquivel los ataques a *Como agua para chocolate.*" *Proceso* (3 January): 48–51.

Said, Edward W. 1983. *The World, the Text, and the Critic.* Cambridge, MA: Harvard University Press.

Sánchez Susarrey, Jaime. 1993. *El debate político e intelectual en México: Desde la represión de 1968 hasta nuestros días de Encuentros vs. Coloquios.* Mexico: Grijalbo.

Sefchovich, Sara. 1987. *México: país de ideas, país de novelas. Una sociología de la literatura mexicana.* Mexico: Grijalbo.

———. 1990. "La mirada sobre nosotros: Los norteamericanos y México." *Plural* 221: 30–40.

Serna, Enrique. 1993. "Vejamen de la narrativa difícil." *Sábado* (18 December): 1–3.

Smith, Barbara Herrnstein. 1983. "Contingencies of Value." In *Canons,* ed. Robert von Hallberg, 5–40. Chicago: University of Chicago Press.

Steele, Cynthia. 1992. *Politics, Gender, and the Mexican Novel, 1968–1988: Beyond the Pyramid.* Austin: University of Texas Press.

Trujillo Muñoz, Gabriel. 1994. "Mexican Narrative at the End of the Century: A Tourist Guide." *Fiction International* 25: 1–11.

Vega, Patricia. 1992. "Joaquín Mortiz: Pieza fundamental para la literatura mexicana." *La Jornada* (9 December): 23.

Vuelta. 1992. Special issue, "Defensa de la Literatura Difícil." No. 188.

Ximena, María, and Alejandro Toledo. 1992. "Por una literatura fácil." *Macrópolis* (26 March): 32–37.

1

Un hogar insólito

Elena Garro and Mexican Literary Culture

Rebecca E. Biron

idely considered one of Mexico's most important writers after the publication of her first novel, *Los recuerdos del porvenir* (1963), Elena Garro is also one of its more contentious public figures. Her personal and authorial identities have haunted national cultural politics and literary history since she went into voluntary exile in the early 1970s. Her life and writing occur simultaneously in absence from the Mexican cultural center and in extreme interdependence with it. She challenges the status of Mexican cultural critics who claim to speak from within national borders and imagined communities. She violates the private/public divide by writing about negative personal experiences with Mexican cultural elites such as Octavio Paz, and yet she claims her own space as a canonical Mexican author. Garro's uncanny presence in national cultural debate reveals the determining power of dichotomies such as Mexican/foreign, inside/outside, hero/traitor, and life/work in public reception of her. How readers struggle to reconcile her roles as provocative writer, conflictive political actor, and enigmatic public personality reflects larger currents in contemporary Mexico's intellectual and artistic production.

Dramatizing the disjunction between Elena Garro's importance in print and her marginalization in person, more reporters than mourners attended her funeral after she died in Cuernavaca, Mexico, on 22 August 1998 (*La Jornada* 23

August 1998). Major Mexican newspapers published respectful if brief professional biographies. They quoted Rafael Tovar y de Teresa, Director of the Consejo Nacional para la Cultura y las Artes (Nacional Council for Culture and the Arts), linking Mexico's loss of Garro to the national mourning for her former husband Octavio Paz, who had died just four months earlier: "Las letras mágicas de México están de luto nuevamente, ayer por Octavio Paz y hoy por Elena Garro, dos grandes del siglo XX," 'Magical Mexican letters mourn anew, yesterday for Octavio Paz and today for Elena Garro, two giants of the twentieth century.' In spite of this association between the two writers, the quiet observance of Garro's funeral offered stark contrast to Octavio Paz's funeral service in the Palacio de Bellas Artes of Mexico City. Almost every major Mexican intellectual as well as President Zedillo and other high-level government officials attended Paz's funeral; newspapers, magazines, journals, and television and film companies rushed to produce a flurry of commentary on his work as poet, cultural analyst, and ambassador for Mexico. Even among his critics, Paz's death elicited positive declarations regarding his extraordinary role in both producing and interpreting Mexico's cultural identity in the context of international debates on modernity and postmodernity. When Elena Garro died that same summer, however, national as well as international reactions confirmed the enigmatic and phantasmatic role her public *persona* continues to play in the collective imaginary of the Mexican literary world.

It may seem inappropriate to compare public response to the passing of these two writers, divorced for more than thirty years, and further separated by geography, aesthetic practices, political investments, social circles, and personal histories. Perhaps a greater tribute to Elena Garro's literary achievement would be to read her work in isolation from her complicated personal and public association with Paz and the ideological role for Mexican intellectuals that he embodied. Such a reading, though, would miss the intricate nature of the Mexican reception of Garro's writing. It would also deny her the right to talk back in her own way.

As if she were one of Juan Rulfo's characters, Garro can only be heard along with the multiple voices behind her publications, behind her public declarations, and behind what is said about her. Of course, the first of those voices belongs to Paz. The historical Octavio Paz was an early promoter of Garro's work. The Paz she later imagined served as a model for characters and situations in her fictional texts. The Paz she finally remembered fused with the poet-critic's international fame to form the principal antagonist in Garro's personal narrative.[1] Either through his own actions or through Garro's continual reconstructions or projections of his power over her, Octavio Paz subtends much of her literary output and her public self-representation. The intermingling of the personal and the literary in this complicated relationship is not limited, however, to Garro's perspective. Rafael Tovar y de Teresa's rhetorical marriage of the two as fellow giants of Mexican letters reflects the conflict between a desire to ensure Garro's legitimate place in the national canon and the difficulty of valuing her accomplishments independently of her association with Octavio Paz.

More importantly, and yet not fully distinguishable from Paz's role, another collective voice echoes both in Garro's work and in criticism written about it. Curiously, Mexican literary critics, feminists as well as antifeminists, and journalists covering art and culture tend to conflate Garro's life and work in their respective modes of reception. Perhaps they do so because, whether used in reference to a woman, a writer, or a political or historical actor, the very name *Elena Garro* signifies conflict in the most fundamental categories of national identity construction: the public/private dichotomy, political history, gender relations, marginalized social sectors, authority (whether literary or governmental), authenticity, and representativity. Debates regarding national identity in Mexico turn with particular insistence to class differences, the indigenous past and present, the paradoxical celebration of death, the gradual disintegration of the governing political party (the Institutional Revolutionary Party, or the PRI) since 1968, external and internal exile, feminism, and the role of writers/intellectuals in addressing these themes. Garro's position in the pantheon of Mexican writers remains vexed because these are precisely the most evident themes in both her life and her work; she consistently blends sociocultural commentary with her individual history, thereby complicating the Mexican reception of her writing, her politics, and her personal choices.

Garro's prodigious output includes eight novels, more than twenty theater pieces, five short story collections, an autobiographical memoir (*Memorias de España*), and a collection of essays on Mexican revolutionaries. She was married to Octavio Paz in 1937.[2] They divorced in the late 1950s. Reacting to government and intellectuals' accusations against her amid the ideological turmoil of the student movement and the violence of 1968, Garro lived in what she considered a state of exile in the United States, Spain, and France from 1971 to 1993. In 1993 she returned to Mexico and remained there for the rest of her life.

Elena Garro is an enigma, intriguing in multiple ways. Beyond this brief biographical sketch, concrete information about her private life and loves, her friendships and professional relationships, and her political/cultural values is elusive, yet informal knowledge about these aspects of her life explicitly shapes much criticism on her literary work.[3] Much of Garro's work published since her departure from Mexico treats themes of sadism, persecution, manipulation, and power games among cultural elites. In Mexican literary and cultural criticism, the most typical response to her treatment of those themes reflects a strong tendency to conflate the writer's personal experience or supposed psychological makeup with her literary subjects. Such approaches usually lead to her depiction as either a helpless victim of Paz's mammoth influence on the Mexican literary world or as a mentally ill former wife/political agitator whose writing gradually became infected with resentment and slander. In the 1970s and 1980s, for example, a series of radio interviews with Garro's and Paz's early colleagues Emmanuel Carballo and Huberto Batis was titled "Elena Garro: ¿Perseguidora o perseguida?" ('Elena Garro: Persecutor or Persecuted?').[4] Such a title indicates that reciprocal victimization is the only possible frame for understanding Garro's real relationships and literary accomplishments. In the 1990s, the literary community's anxiety about Garro's return to Mexico results from a complex web consisting primarily of three issues: her unique status as a public figure who also happens to be Octavio Paz's former wife, the obscure and confused (according to most accounts) reasons for her exile, and the lack of consensus concerning the amount and the truth of autobiographical reference in her published prose since 1980.

Garro's 1993 homecoming occasioned a flurry of news reports, interviews, homages, and the redistribution of her most widely known plays, short stories, and novels. It also spurred the publication of a number of manuscripts she brought back from Paris.[5] Public reference to Garro and her work, however, displays collective anxiety over her presence in Mexico through an ambiguous denial of her complicated past. She is referred to affectionately and possessively as "nuestra Doña Elena," 'our Doña Elena'; respectfully and epically as "La Gran Dama de la escritura contemporánea mexicana," 'the grand mistress of contemporary Mexican writing'; and dismissively or sympathetically as "la pobre loca, ex-esposa del gran poeta mexicano," 'the poor crazy woman, ex-wife of the great Mexican poet.'

The methodological problem I confront in attempting to address the literary community's reception of Garro and her work hinges on issues that Amy Kaminsky begins to work through in her essay "Residual Authority and Gendered Resistance." Kaminsky explains residual authority as the dynamics of power at play in the production *and* reception of texts:

> [The] willingness to give credence to a narrative that reinforces traditional power relationships and retells a familiar story about women's lives is attributable to residual authority. . . . I refer to that authority which is still brought to bear on the production and reception of texts, despite oppositional feminist literary acts such as writing, narrating, and reading that call into question the authoritative discourses of male domination, as well as those of, for example, class hierarchy and European rationalism. Residual authority is not a quality of any particular text, author, or reader but, rather, is an effect that floats among them in the literary process. (1993, 104)

When Kaminsky refers here to the "familiar retelling of women's lives," she is addressing those reading practices that often misrecognize "feminist literary acts," compulsively reencoding them so that they will conform to traditionally accepted roles for women. To illustrate her point, she critiques specific readings, looking for traces of residual authority in statements about three texts written by women: Garro's *Los recuerdos del porvenir*, Rosario Ferré's *Maldito amor*, and Luisa Valenzuela's *Aquí pasan cosas raras*. My project extends this discussion of residual authority's effects on textual interpretation to address the intersection of Garro's public/political life, the authorial persona that she projects for herself through her publications, and the authorial persona that the reading public constructs for her (whether based on her writing, on her life, or on both at once). As we will see, collective desire for the "retelling" of Elena Garro involves what she tells as well as what is told about her. In Kaminsky's terms, the retelling is "familiar" insofar as it privileges the personal over the political and the emotional over the critical. It is "oppositional" insofar as it registers the author's own political and critical intentions.

In Elena Garro's case, the remarkable affinity between the stories people tell about her as author, agitator, or Paz's former wife and the literature she herself has produced blurs the line between biography and fiction. It also challenges any profound distinction between "familiar" and "oppositional" narratives of a woman's life. To begin to chart some key elements of this dynamic, I look to three moments in the contemporary reception of Elena Garro: her final return to Mexico in 1993, the reactions to her death, and recent debate among feminist literary critics regarding her life and work. My task here is to inquire into the production and erasure of Garro's voice in contemporary Mexico, without reducing her writing to mere autobiography, and without constructing a biography of the author that ignores her writing.

A brief analysis of one typical newspaper report of Garro's return to Mexico, combined with a reading of a televised interview with her one year later, indicate common elements in the literary community's uneasy reception of this author. In her 1981 novel, *Testimonios sobre Mariana,*[6] Garro already had offered her own literary description of the intelligentsia's reaction to an enigmatic woman. Through that novel's representation of its protagonist, Garro reveals some of the machinations and microlevel power plays within the social groups poised to shape midcentury expressions of Mexico's cultural identity for international forums. Her literary critique of the mechanisms by which dichotomies such as inside/outside, active/passive, sane/insane, come to structure cultural power still makes many of her fellow writers uncomfortable, as evidenced by the curious mixture of hyperbolic praise and pitying condescension displayed in current reception of her and her work.

The *Excelsior* account of her arrival in Mexico in 1993, penned by Arturo Alcantar Flores (11 June 1993), reveals respect for Garro's political and cultural role twenty-five years earlier as well as an inability—or refusal—to register the strong criticisms of contemporary public life, which she offers in her characteristically soft-spoken way. At the press conference, still in the airport after her flight from Paris, reporters ask, "¿Cómo encuentra a México ahora?" 'How does Mexico seem to you now?' The reply is vintage Elena Garro: "No lo he visto al pobrecito," 'I haven't seen the poor thing yet.' Personification infuses her statements with a sense of the concrete, of lived experience, and of a critical eye, even though the reporters read her speech as vague and confused.

The perceptive reader will recognize in Garro's combinations of topics a heavy dose of social commentary and hidden sarcasm. One example from this press conference is her answer to the question, "¿Trató en París de ser reconocida como escritora?" 'In Paris did you seek recognition as a writer?' Garro responds by seeming to be self-critical, but her words reveal that, even though she is not a member of the Mexican cultural center, she knows exactly how it works and why she was never to be included in it: "No, soy anónima. Porque yo no me he movido para nada. Para ser reconocida hay que ser importante y tener amigos importantes. Octavio Paz me dijo hace como dos meses: 'Oye por qué no te haces publicidad,' le dije que yo no sé hacerme publicidad," 'No, I'm anonymous. Because I haven't promoted myself at all. To be recognized you have to be important and have important friends. Octavio Paz said to me about two months ago, "Listen, why don't you publicize yourself?" and I told him that I don't know how to publicize myself.' This statement is loaded with potential meaning. Octavio Paz's name follows "hay que ser importante y tener amigos importantes." By having offered her some good-willed advice, Paz had shown that he was Garro's friend. And he was obviously an important contact for any Mexican writer to have. Garro, however, embeds this reference in a larger point, which is that she is not important and does not have important friends. Therefore, she is both appealing to and dismissing Paz's importance, either as a helper in her own publicity or as a friend. Either way, her refusal to engage in any publicity campaign cannot be attributed to the ignorance she claims. She clearly recognizes the requirements of successful public life and with this answer implies that she defines importance and friendship differently from the "amigos importantes" to whom she refers.

After recounting all of her problems with citizenship—from passport difficulties after 1968 to the fact that even in 1993 she had trouble entering Mexico because she had not been aware that her passport had expired—she deftly points out the ironic nature of such documentation requirements: "Qué cosa rara, que uno tenga que tener un papel para existir. Me parece monstruoso. Y los gangsters tienen 70 papeles y van y vienen y nadie dice nada. En cambio una pinche señora de setenta años tiene que estar bien documentada," 'How strange, that one would need a paper in order to exist. It seems monstrous to me. Gangsters have 70 papers and come and go and no one says anything. And then a goddamned seventy-year-old woman has to be totally documented.' Identification, documentation, and registration are all signs of state legitimacy, and Garro's protest against the inhumanity of such requirements upon her attempt to return home echoes the problems she has had with such "official recognition" throughout her life.[7]

The *Excelsior* writer notes a combination of emotional elements in her bearing, but ultimately concludes that she is more childlike than keenly perceptive: "A veces parece que va a llorar, pero se ríe. Escucha con atención cada pregunta. Y las contesta amablemente. Con cierta dulzura infantil," 'Sometimes she seems on the verge of tears, but she laughs. She listens attentively to every question. And she answers kindly, with a certain childlike sweetness.' This assessment, although more about her way of speaking than about the content of her answers, complements the general line of questioning directed to Garro. There are no follow-up questions to her most provocative answers, and the topic of questions shifts most dramatically each time her answers include less than sweet, childlike vocabulary, such as "goddamn" or "pissing."

Almost one year after Garro's return to Mexico, the Channel 11 television network aired a half-hour interview with the author, which was divided into three segments and shown on three different nights. Unlike the *Excelsior* coverage of the 1993 press conference, this interview features a visual text along with the verbal exchanges between Garro and Sari Bermúdez of *Hoy en la cultura* (*Today in Culture*). The actual interview features Garro sitting in the small living room of her apartment in Cuernavaca, facing Sari Bermúdez. In the last half of the second segment the camera angle widens to include Helena Paz, who apparently has been sitting silently beside her mother throughout the taping. Each of the three segments opens with a short introduction with voice-over by Bermúdez and a collage of photos matched with three themes: (A) childhood, courtship, and wedding; (B) travel with Paz to the Second International Congress of Anti-Fascist Writers and her involvement in the performance group "Poesía en voz alta" (for which Garro wrote "Un hogar sólido"); and (C) her first novel (*Los recuerdos del porvenir*, 1963), her lack of publication from 1968 to 1980, and her current plans.

All three segments begin with a long shot of a black-and-white photo of Paz in his twenties. There are several photos of Garro and Paz, taken in the year after their wedding. As an introduction to the third segment, Helena Paz is shown in a few photos from her life in Europe. In the total time allotted to still photos, however, Paz is featured longest. Not until the last segment does the narrator mention Garro's literary prizes, the Premio Villaurrutia in 1963, and the Premio Grijalbo in 1981. Only then does Bermúdez list the author's total publications.

As in the 1993 press conference, whenever Garro's answers reveal an attempt at discretion, or when her answers are witty critiques of the questions, the interviewer immediately changes the subject, moving to issues of the author's age, her courtship with Paz, or her current living conditions. The interview includes nine questions concerning Octavio

Paz and eleven questions related only to Garro or to their daughter Helena Paz. Only four of those eleven questions deal with Garro's writing. The rest are biographical. There is no discussion of the events of 1968 or of Garro's politics, even though Garro brings up these topics in answer to the question, "Y dejó de publicar entre 1968 y 1980—¿por qué?" 'And you stopped publishing between 1968 and 1980—why?' There are no follow-up questions to Garro's response, "Porque después de lo ocurrido en '68, estaba en la lista negra. No me publicaban. . . . Mucha gente me dijo que era prohibido que me publicaran," 'Because after what happened in 1968, I was blacklisted. They didn't publish me. . . . Many people told me that they were prohibited from publishing me.' In fact, an immediate deflection from the question of politics and cultural politics in Mexico shifts toward the specifics of Garro's individual experience: "Cuéntenos de su época fuera de México," 'Tell us about your period away from Mexico.' Garro's brief reply suggests many possible directions for more profound questions: "Muy dura, la época. No sé cómo lo hicimos. Escribía y escribía, pero no me publicaban," 'Very hard, that period. I don't know how we did it. I wrote and wrote, but no one published me.' The interviewer abruptly skips ahead to the present, asking "Y qué está haciendo ahora? ¿Está escribiendo?" 'And what are you doing now? Are you writing?' When Garro answers, speaking more emphatically than at any other point in the interview, "No, desde venir, no he hecho nada," 'No, since I've been here I haven't done anything.' A full face shot of Bermúdez shows the interviewer smiling, as if she were reacting to some other reply. The concluding questions concern Garro's living arrangements, and there is no further discussion of her work.

Garro had stated earlier in the interview that she returned from Paris because her daughter wanted to live in Mexico, but neither Bermúdez nor any reporter at the 1993 press conference ever asked the writer to elaborate on her feelings about the conflict between her own history and Helena Paz's needs. This Garro interview is conducted like an installment in a superficial women's magazine. Given that the program avoids serious inquiry into the author's work, political opinions, or personal situation beyond her youthful feelings for Paz, it is difficult to understand Channel 11's motivations for producing the interview at all. The program's almost exclusive focus on the author's personal relationship to a major male Mexican intellectual not only trivializes the literary import of Garro's career, but it also effectively erases her relevance as a political actor in national events. The silences and the smiles gloss the problematic implications of Garro's exile from Mexico, forcing her into the simplistic role of happy and grateful prodigal daughter returned to the fold. Regardless of the producers' motivations, the interview effectively defuses the potential political and literary significance of Garro's return, constructing an image of this author that invites benevolent curiosity about her love for Paz and unexamined respect for her identity as aging writer, if not for her actual work.

The problem is that the Mexican "family" to which Garro might have returned does not have any name or social category for someone like her. Even those who value her writing find her public *persona* troubling. Whether it was for her apparently contradictory involvement in the events of 1968—attending student protests and yet also providing the government with names of supposed intellectual instigators of the movement—or for accusing Octavio Paz of economic abandonment, many writers and prominent cultural figures simply opted to remain silent regarding Elena Garro rather than openly criticize her during her period in exile. After her return, and in response to her publication of a number of new works, some intellectuals still blame her for endangering them and betraying the student movement through her accusations in 1968. They consider her to be a sexist manipulator who at one moment complains about male abuses of power and the next begs to be forgiven for her girlish innocence regarding political intrigue. For example, in *Comala*, an electronic forum for cultural debate, cultural and literary critic Evodio Escalante calls her reactionary:

> Si ella tuvo que abandonar el país no fue porque aquí nadie la comprendiera; fue porque en el 68 hizo declaraciones realmente siniestras involucrando y *denunciando* a decenas de intelectuales, y haciéndole con esto el juego sucio al régimen de Díaz Ordaz. . . . A Elena Garro no le queda el papel del ángel inocente pero tampoco el de la genio incomprendida. (26 de agosto 1998)
>
> [If she had to leave the country, it wasn't because no one here understood her; it was because in 1968 she made truly vicious declarations, involving and *denouncing* dozens of intellectuals. She played dirty with the Díaz Ordaz regime. . . . Elena Garro is no innocent angel, but neither is she a misunderstood genius.]

Although this is a fairly common interpretation of Garro's role in 1968, those who publish interviews with the author typically limit their treatment of it to superficial questions or they defer to Garro's own control over the representation of events, which she maintained by repeating a single, focused narrative (in interviews or letters exchanged with

Ramírez [1994], Landeros [1980], or Carballo [1982], for example). Elena Garro always held that she had been manipulated by both the government and the aforementioned intellectuals into playing the role of scapegoat for each side. According to her accounts of the period between 1968 and 1971, as included in a variety of interviews, she was hounded by police, rejected by former friends, and threatened with physical harm by anonymous callers. Any more penetrating, historically detailed accounts of her life in the period have yet to be written.

The general refusal to engage in profound investigation and debate regarding Garro's political positions in part reflects her readers' respect for her as author. Few wish to renew antagonisms, revive debates, or throw salt on wounds from an extremely conflictive moment in Mexican history, and especially not in mass media such as Channel 11 or journalistic rather than literary interviews. On the other hand, though, it is clear that those same wounds motivate and shape Mexican interpretation and valorization of Garro's literary works. Similar to so many of her main characters, about whom are woven elaborate accounts that cannot be confirmed within the novels (Julia and Isabel of *Los recuerdos del porvenir*, Mariana of *Testimonios sobre Mariana*, Verónica of *Reencuentro de personajes*, *Inés*, and so on), Garro does not cooperate with the collective desire to place her in a well-defined, "familiar" role as either only persecuted or only persecuting.

Even feminist literary critics have had trouble overcoming the analytical problems posed by Garro's historical role in combination with her status as a literary genius. Luz Elena Gutiérrez de Velazco has argued, for example, that *Testimonios sobre Mariana* is a conscious act of social critique and personal liberation at the same time:

> Mariana representa el producto que los otros rememoran y configuran. Es una muestra de la mujer que, en la civilización patriarcal, debe coincidir con los presupuestos que la sociedad le impone, sin escapatoria posible. Sin embargo, en el texto se urde una salida, en tanto que la escritura nos muestra el rastro de la escritora que se construye a sí misma en su oficio. Por esa instancia, más allá del relato que gobierna la estructuración de las partes y, por ese movimiento, se afirma en la vida. (1992, 25)

> [Mariana represents the product that others recall and configure. She is an example of the woman who, in patriarchal civilization, must adapt to the suppositions that society imposes on her, without possible escape. However, an exit is devised in the text, insofar as the writing shows us the trace of the female writer who constructs herself in her work. By this means, beyond the narration that governs the structuring of the parts, and by this movement, she is affirmed in life.]

Fabienne Bradu, on the other hand, warns against the tendency to limit readings of *Testimonios sobre Mariana* to searches for correspondence between characters and real people from Garro's life.[8] However, Bradu ends her essay on Garro by criticizing the author for including personal details in her novel:

> El acercamiento a la ficción autobiográfica provoca en Elena Garro una excesiva atención narrativa a los hechos, a las situaciones, en detrimento de una visión más global del mundo donde más se ensanchan sus extraordinarias posibilidades creativas. Su voluntad de seducción se vuelve así más tensa, más desesperada, y sus recursos literarios recuerdan los trucos del prestidigitador que ya no halla cómo competir con el gran mago que fue antaño. (1987, 27–28)
>
> [The movement toward autobiographical fiction in Elena Garro provokes excessive narrative attention to the facts, to situations, to the detriment of a more global vision of the world where her extraordinary creative powers unfold the most clearly. Her will to seduction in this way becomes more tense, more desperate, and her literary resources recall the tricks of the conjurer who now finds no way to compete with the great magician he used to be.]

This comment shifts focus away from readings of the novel and toward a demand for the way it ought to have been written. Martha Robles echoes this approach when she comments that *Testimonios sobre Mariana* is "un recorrido infernal que, por su contenido anecdótico, resulta tendencioso y más próximo al libelo a que al propósito novelístico" (1989, 134), 'an infernal repetition that, because of its anecdotal content, becomes tendentious and closer to libel than to its novelistic purpose.' It seems that much Mexican literary criticism on Garro is deeply affected by the Garro/Paz split, leading to this kind of prescriptive attitude about acceptable topics for Garro to treat in her work.

Another aspect of the problem of confusing life and work in feminist reception of Elena Garro appears most clearly after her death. The lack of mourners from the literary world at her funeral caused much commentary in newspapers as well as in the electronic forum *Comala*. With the exception of a brief note written by Carlos Monsiváis in *La Jornada* the day after she died, there was little immediate public response to the news of Garro's passing. Some feminist critics such as Monique Le Maitre and María Dolores Bolívar compared that relative silence with the national mourning for Paz, concluding that a widespread sexism in literary circles produced a collective decision to *ningunear* (reduce to a non-person) one of Mexico's most important female writers.[9] The immediate response to their analysis (in editorials by Escalante and others) insisted that there is a huge difference between, on the one hand, appreciating the importance for Mexico of Garro's work (specifically of *Los recuerdos del porvenir*, her short story "La culpa es de los tlaxcaltecas," and the majority of her theater pieces) and on the other hand of accepting Elena Garro the woman as a figure of national relevance. Both positions in this debate evidence a similar conceptual problem: For opposite motives, all of the participants in the discussion establish a rigid distinction between life and work when it is convenient to their argument, but they later deconstruct that distinction to advance literary and sociopolitical interpretations. Whereas some feminists read all negative criticism of Garro's work as a result of sexism and Octavio Paz's influence on Mexican literary culture, many conservative critics as well as some leftist intellectuals deny the possibility that Garro might contribute serious observations on Mexican culture after 1968. For leftist intellectuals, she proved her allegiances against them that year. For some critics (e.g., Bradu, Robles, Jorge Volpi) or for those variously associated with Paz, the inclusion of personal experience or commentary or both on *el poeta* in her work since then disqualifies her as a legitimate voice in contemporary Mexican literature.

As we have seen, reading *Testimonios sobre Mariana* is an especially delicate operation, given that the principal male character in the novel is named Augusto (which happens to be the name taken by César Octavio upon becoming emperor of Rome) and other obvious references to Octavio Paz abound. The story traverses a decade in postwar France, interspersed with trips to New York. The main group of characters features wealthy South American intellectuals (from unspecified countries) who claim to support socialist revolution and whose topics for dinner party conversation typically focus on Sartre or the Marquis de Sade. It is relevant to the contextualization of this group that Elena Garro joined Octavio Paz in Paris in 1946, where he was sent to reopen the Mexican embassy after World War II. This period is described in the "Chronology of Elena Garro as Told to Michele Muncy by the Author" (Stoll, 1990), which recalls that Paz and Garro "knew all the intellectuals in the arts and in the theater in the French capital, especially the surrealist group. . . . This whole period appears in great detail in *Testimonios sobre Mariana*" (1990, 34). The novel depicts Garro's relationship with the international cultural circles within which Paz became famous. Her literary representation of the treatment of women who refuse to play by the accepted rules of such company is instructive for understanding Mexico's current ambivalent reception of her.

In the novel, Mariana is kept economically dependent by her husband Augusto, analyzed and defined by his friends as if she were no more than an object to be studied, and usually relegated to silence in their company. The narrative structure silences her as well by offering three testimonial texts about her, each provided by a different character-narrator whose *testimonio* is in turn traversed by a variety of secondary and tertiary characters who introject their own brief *testimonios.* These partial narrations of Mariana add new bits of information that sometimes contradict other versions and sometimes seem wholly unrelated to them. Each of the three narrators of her "story" takes a particular stance in regard to her possible insanity and her definite victimization by Augusto. Although they are more complex than I have space to acknowledge fully here,[10] each narrator has a principle interest in Mariana: Vicente, who wants her as a lover, describes Mariana in a cinematographic eternal present; Gabrielle, who uses her as a weak friend to shore up the older woman's ego, emphasizes Mariana's condition as an exile; André, who wants to become a hero by saving Mariana, underscores her irrationality and unpredictability. No matter what their individual focus, they all record their own conviction that Mariana does not fit into their systems of representation.

Although neither Augusto nor Mariana ever speaks in the novel without having their words framed by the narrators' interpretations of what they say, Augusto is still the controlling subject par excellence in *Testimonios sobre Mariana.* He supports the narrators' comfort within masculinist discourse about a woman. Each of the narrators in the novel demonstrates vulnerability to his accounts of his relationship to Mariana, even when they have evidence that contradicts him. They take Augusto's words at face value while at the same remaining suspicious of anything Mariana says. Wealthy, educated, and the "head" of his "household," Augusto is accepted and respected by government officials, influential members of the intellectual community, leading postwar leftists, and sectors of the Parisian art world. Augusto controls Mariana through his language, through his orchestration of social scenes, and through his threats to take their daughter from her. His influence on the narrators' (de-re)constructions of her image, although not total, grants him power over Mariana in the realm of the aesthetic as well. Even though all three narrators admit in different ways that they respect Augusto's laws of order and representation, Mariana continues to be their strongest obsession. Ironically, in this, too, they follow

Augusto. They take on the desire to represent her through *testimonio* just as he seeks to control her on the level of plot through depriving her of money and a passport or by manipulating her friends and lovers. The particularity of each narrator's desire, however, interferes with Augusto's machinations. Although he is certainly able to distort others' images of her, he cannot completely erase their individual memories and impressions of Mariana.

Although Mariana never offers her own *testimonio* (or, more to the point, *because* she never narrates her own story), her ineffability gives her power over her fellow characters. As the conclusion of each *testimonio* indicates, her indeterminacy haunts them as even her physical disappearance is never satisfactorily explained: She may have gone mad and become a beggar in the streets of Paris, or she may have become a ballerina in the Soviet Union; she may have committed suicide, or she may have been murdered by Augusto. She eludes the narrators' understanding, but the intense present that she imposes on the text assures that Mariana transcends the narrators' and readers' misperceptions and self-absorption. When they recognize their own inability to capture her in narrative, she successfully escapes representation and appropriation by remaining both dead and alive, by forcing the simultaneous recognition of contradictory outcomes. She remains radically other to the text and yet also its central preoccupation, serving as both the borderline of its power and the condition of possibility of its representations.

One particularly effective scene that illustrates Mariana's ability to transcend the narrators' assessments of her by silently demonstrating the deconstruction of their own positions occurs early in the novel in Vicente's *testimonio*. At one of the many dinner parties hosted by Augusto, his lover Eugenia asks why he does not divorce Mariana. Augusto answers: "Desgraciadamente soy como Sartre y creo en la responsabilidad. Mariana es tan pobre que si me divorcio terminaría pidiendo limosna," (1981, 33) 'Unfortunately I'm like Sartre and I believe in responsibility. Mariana is so poor that if I divorced her she'd end up begging.' Vicente's private reaction to this exchange is to wonder indignantly why Mariana tolerates discussion about her as if she were not present, and he angrily asserts that she would be better off as his lover.

Although Mariana's response to Augusto's insults is narrated by Vicente, his misrecognition of his own controlling desire foregrounds her as a woman free of the group's representations of her as passive victim or as dangerous witch:

Los mendigos son los únicos que confían en la bondad del hombre y yo los amo—dijo. Nos volvimos a verla, bajo la luz de los candiles, contemplando el fondo de su copa de vino y con los cabellos rubios sobre los hombros me pareció una hermosa bruja salida del corazón del fuego para leernos su propio destino y el nuestro, pues parecía conocernos mejor a todos de lo que nos conocíamos nosotros mismos. Apoyó los codos sobre la mesa y puso la barbilla sobre los dedos cruzados, en esa postura nos miró.
　　Sigamos hablando de la revolución y de la igualdad de clases—dijo.
(1981, 33)
　　[Beggars are the only ones who trust in man's good will and I love them—she said. We turned to look at her, contemplating the bottom of her wine glass in the candlelight; with her blond hair resting on her shoulders she seemed to me a beautiful witch who had emerged from the heart of fire to read us her own destiny and ours, because she seemed to know each of us better than we knew ourselves. Resting her elbows on the table and putting her chin on her crossed fingers, she gazed at us in this posture.
　　Let's continue talking about the revolution and class equality—she said.]

In spite of Vicente's attempt to relegate her to the realm of the magical witch, or mythical muse for her dinner companions, Mariana's comment deflects attention away from that portrait and toward the group's hypocritical, pseudorevolutionary discourse. Although Vicente seems unaware of the disjunction between his description and Mariana's words, she forces reader awareness of the disruptive effects of that which the narrators' discourse cannot represent. Mariana does not directly confront misinterpretations of her or cruelty directed to her. Her refusal to be subordinated to others' conceptions of her (here, those forged from a blatant masculinist manipulation of existential philosophy and Marxism) requires them to accept her silences. No matter what aspect of Mariana's experience is being described—her affair with Vicente, her friendship with Gabrielle, her supernatural contact with André, or her death—the narrators' reliability and consensus are in question. Readers are left to construe a story based on their own projections while always depending on the narrators' prior projections, which are in turn dependent on Augusto's games.
　　All of the *testimonios* respond to this lack of consensus by highlighting the notion that Mariana's life is in some sense a literary game. For readers aware of Elena Garro's own estrangement from Mexico, from her former circle of friends, and from Paz, the different narrators' relationships to the game in *Testimonios sobre Mariana* represent an uncannily familiar range of approaches to analyzing a literary woman. Vicente calls Mariana "diabolical" for accepting this situation:

> En un sentido más profundo que Mariana, también yo pensaba que la vida sólo era un juego literario. Ella no había superado la idea infantil del juego y esta cualidad la convertía a veces en un ser profundamente diabólico. (1981, 53)
>
> [In a way more profound than Mariana, I also thought that life was only a literary game. She hadn't outgrown the infantile idea of the game, and this quality sometimes converted her into a profoundly diabolical being.]

The contradictions evident in this short passage, however, reveal Vicente's own immaturity: He is more profoundly literary, but she is more profoundly diabolical. The repetition of "profundo" unites the two "players" linguistically—literarily—in spite of Vicente's claim of having a higher degree of sophistication and self-knowledge than Mariana. If, in their respective literariness and devilishness they are equally profound, then Vicente's phrasing makes them profoundly equal.

Gabrielle, too, contradicts herself when drawing a relationship between Mariana and writing. She plans to write a novel to avoid thinking about Augusto's abuse of Mariana, but the novel will be about Mariana:

> A partir de esa noche me prohibí a mí misma recordar a Mariana. Fue entonces cuando se me ocurrió escribir una novela sobre su vida, recordé que la naturaleza imita al arte y decidí darle un final feliz, que cambiaría su destino. . . . Era lo menos que podía hacer por la pobre Mariana: un conjunto, una obra mágica, una pieza maestra. Escribí muchas cuartillas, modifiqué algunas de las situaciones que había vivido con ella para poder llegar al final feliz que me proponía. Y así, rebosante de felicidad reapareció Mariana en la puerta de mi vivienda. (1981, 210)
>
> [From that night on, I didn't let myself think about Mariana. That was when it occurred to me to write a novel about her life. I remembered that nature imitates art, and I decided to give her a happy ending, one that would change her destiny. . . . That was the least I could do for poor Mariana: a mixture, a magical work, a masterpiece. I wrote a lot of pages, changed some of the situations that I had experienced with her in order to get to the happy ending I wanted. And that's how, exuding happiness, Mariana reappeared at my door.]

In a single paragraph Gabrielle shifts from a dreaded reality to a pure fiction, and then ends with an improved reality. After Mariana's "real" appearance, however, the illusion wears off, and, ironically, Gabrielle muses that her friend is "incapaz de enfrentarse con la dura realidad cotidiana," 'incapable of facing the harsh realities of everyday life.' It is Gabrielle, however, who has just confessed that it was too difficult to think about Mariana's reality as victim, and that she herself would prefer to escape into idealized fictions. Readers must question here which of Gabrielle's fictions (her *testimonio* as a whole, or the novel mentioned within it) is meant to give Mariana a happy ending and which is meant to serve the narrator's own needs for social validation.

André enters the literary game when he steals a piece of writing from Mariana. After having rented a hotel room for her because she would have needed a passport to register alone, he sees Mariana on the bed, writing something. He later steals the paper to read it in secret:

> Nervioso, busqué en el bolsillo de mi americana el papel que le había robado a mi amiga en el que estaba escribiendo algo, lo leí: "Augusto es perverso," "Augusto es perverso," la misma frase estaba repetida hasta cubrir la página entera. La acusación lanzada contra su marido me dejó atónito y me dio la respuesta que buscaba: Mariana había ido al hotel a suicidarse. (1981, 299)
>
> [Nervous, I looked in my jacket pocket for the paper that I had stolen from my friend and on which she had been writing something. I read it: "Augusto is perverse," "Augusto is perverse," the same phrase was repeated, covering the whole page. The accusation directed against her husband left me shocked and gave me the explanation I was looking for: Mariana had gone to the hotel to kill herself.]

André chooses to respond as if Mariana were asking for him to save her from herself, rather than as if Mariana were expressing a problem that had nothing to do with André. He steals her own text, a strong statement of judgment against Augusto, and then he interprets it as proof that Mariana needs his help, not in dealing with Augusto, but in dealing with herself.

After Elena Garro's return to Mexico, public representation of her reflected the same refusal or inability to listen to her as that evidenced by the narrators she portrayed in *Testimonios sobre Mariana.* Through her fiction, Elena Garro already had "gone public" with her understanding of her own place in international literary culture. She explored the effects of different readers' investments in capturing, through interpretation or through "retelling," someone living her own multiple forms of exile and presence, living the past, present, and future as coterminous categories, and living out what many observers consider scenes of irrationality or insanity. Clearly, newspapers and television show none of the spite and vindictiveness attributed to Augusto and his friends in Garro's novel. However, when they see her as *either* inaccessible or all too present, *either* silent or all too revealing, and *either* irrational or all too powerful in an idealized mythical sense, they do impose their own desire on their representations of her. Each of these readings limited to an either/or conclusion requires Elena Garro to fit prescribed models of extreme passivity or extreme aggression, and are always partly determined by readers' investments in her status as Octavio Paz's former wife.

Garro certainly incorporates various implications of that status into her writing and interviews, but she often appropriates it to point out larger patterns in Mexican cultural politics.[11] Her public life and literary production, when read in counterpoint to Paz's public life and writings, radically critique and undermine what Raymond L. Williams (1993) has called "the Octavio Paz Industry's" tendency toward self-legitimization as both voice and analyst of Mexican culture. Whereas historians and social theorists observe the breakdown of even the illusion of centralized authority under neoliberal policies in Mexico at the end of this century, literary criticism recognizes the revolution in canon formation caused by the proliferation of women's writing, the selling power of ethnic identity in authorship, and increasingly decentralized publishing and distribution practices. However, Elena Garro's work still has not been studied adequately in relation to contemporary Mexican cultural/political debates, perhaps because she occupied such a curious position amid these changes. She belonged to Paz's generation of cultural elites, and she never claimed to write from a subaltern position (understood in terms of ethnic or economic class). In contrast to Paz and his followers, though, she never granted her writing any particular status in the construction of an imaginary national edifice. She consistently wrote about Mexico and Mexicans, observing, critiquing, and celebrating their particularity.[12] Yet, in writing from her own life history and from the surrealist roots of her early associations in Europe, she shows the popular image of self-styled analysts such as Octavio Paz to be the fictional result of their own narratives of the nation; she denies them the position of some knowledgeable elite speaking from outside their own desire, or from outside the messy intersubjective reality of the so-called private sphere. Garro develops her more modest observations concerning the social fabric through her pointed and imaginative fictions. Her political effectiveness as well as her vulnerability reside in the delicate relationship she constructs between her texts and her life: "Hay obras y vidas que se funden. Elena podría ser, como lo es, uno de sus personajes" (Robles 1989, 133), 'There are works and lives that merge. Elena could be, indeed she is, one of her own characters.'

Literary interpretation of Garro's work is changing, particularly among the relatively small (and often foreign) groups of scholars that try to admit openly their investments in studying this author's problematic position in Mexican literary history. But there is much exploration still to be done. As the conversation regarding Garro's legacy evolves from an intimate, magical, feminine (in the limited sense) and individualist approach toward a more critical consideration of how larger Mexican social structures inform her work, we begin to see more clearly the tight link between Garro's writing and Mexican cultural politics in each major period of her literary production, including her years in exile. Elena Garro the writer, woman, and the public figure can be read adequately only through a combination of analytical perspectives simultaneously addressing her aesthetics (both personal and literary), her biography (both documented and imagined), and her politics (both practiced by her and attributed to her). This writer, public yet private, historical yet magical, prolific yet silent, still has much to teach us about Mexican(s) reading.

NOTES

1. Paz was instrumental in encouraging Garro to write from the beginning. Not only did he ask her to contribute an early play,"Un hogar sólido," to their theater group Poesía en voz alta, but he was also the most enthusiastic supporter of her first novel, *Los recuerdos del porvenir* (Garro, "A mí me ha ocurrido todo al revés"). Even after their separation and after he ceased mentioning her or her work in public, Octavio Paz continued to affect Garro's career. She based characters on her own construction of him, and her published memoirs highlight the history of her relationship with him. In addition, and in direct contrast to Paz's relative silence regarding their failed marriage, Garro never hesitated to answer when questioned about it in interviews. She never stopped claiming her right to a share of his income after their separation. Even after his death she continued to argue that their marriage was never legally dissolved and that she was entitled to a share of his estate (María Luisa López and Arturo Mendoza Mocino, 1998).

2. During their marriage, Garro and Paz traveled to the United States, Europe, and Japan in diplomatic roles. Together, they spent time with surrealists Breton, Peret, and Picabia as well as with Latin American writers who were living or traveling abroad: Borges, Bioy Casares, and Vallejo. In the late 1950s, and again after her return to Mexico in 1963, Garro publicly defended the *campesino* struggle for land redistribution laws. See "Chronology of Elena Garro as Told to Michele Muncy by the Author" in *A Different Reality*, 1990).

3. In a footnote to her essay, "Residual Authority and Gendered Resistance," Amy Kaminsky addresses the question of how to read and acknowledge the importance of "discredited discourses" such as gossip, anecdote, or memoir: "How do we make room for 'what everybody knows' about Garro's marriage and subse-

quent relationship with Octavio Paz? Among the rituals of disempowerment and divestiture at play is the fall from literary grace Elena Garro suffered, according to literary gossip, at the hands of her famous ex-husband. But gossip is another form of discourse, and Paz is still powerful enough to make it sound foolish, even if it is as likely to be true as not. (There is, somewhere, a resonance between the conventional reading of Garro's text and the subsequent censorship of her work at the hands of a powerful ex-husband)" (119).

4. Transcribed for *Sábado* (2 September 1989) by Fernando García Ramírez.

5. Recent publications include *Inés* (Inés), *Un traje rojo para un duelo* (A Red Outfit for Mourning), *Busca mi esquela y Primer amor* (Look for My Note and First Love), *Un corazón en un bote de basura* (A Heart in a Trash Bin), *Revolucionarios mexicanos* (Mexican Revolutionaries) and *Mi hermanita Magdalena* (My Little Sister Magadalena).

6. The novel was written in 1964, and Luis Spota published a section of it in the journal *Espejo* in 1965. It won the Premio Novela Juan Grijalbo in 1980. For a complete listing of Elena Garro's works to 1992, see *Elena Garro: Reflexiones en torno a su obra* (México: INBA/Centro Nacional de Investigación y Documentación Teatral Rodolfo Usigli, 1992), 11–14.

7. See her autobiographical essay from 1979, "A mí me ha ocurrido todo al revés." Garro's comments on passports in this 1979 interview as well as at the 1993 press conference resonate with the fact that the victimization of many of her fictional characters is figured in the loss of control over their own passports: Mariana (*Testimonios sobre Mariana*), Verónica (*Reencuentro de personajes*), and Inés (*Inés*).

8. "Sería inoportuno y por lo demás inexacto afirmar que Mariana es únicamente un reflejo de la vida pasada de Elena Garro. Algunos quisieron leer *Testimonios* como una novela en clave donde se tratara de descifrar nombres y situaciones de la vida real. En la relación que se establece entre la escritora y su personaje femenino, lo más elocuente ha de buscarse en la manera en que Elena Garro construye a Mariana como una representación de sí y no tanto en el desciframiento de ciertos episodios puntuales de su vida privada" (Bradu 1987, 20), 'It would be inopportune and also inexact to say that Mariana is only the reflection of Elena Garro's past life. Some have tried to read *Testimonios* as a cryptic novel in which names and situations from real life must be deciphered. In the relation established between the writer and her feminine character, the greatest eloquence must be sought in the way in which Garro constructs Mariana as a representation of herself and not in the deciphering of certain key episodes of her private life.'

9. For a summary of online debates in *Comala* from 23–30 August 1998 go to comala@humnet.ucla.edu.

10. For a more detailed structural analysis of the novel, see my article "*Testimonios sobre Mariana*: representación y la otra mujer."

11. Lady Rojas-Trempe (1991) offers a compelling semiotic analysis of Garro's self-portrait as developed in her journalistic essays, interviews, letters, and memoirs from the 1960s through the 1980s.

12. At a conference in homage to Garro held in Cuernavaca in 1997, for example, Patricia Rosas-Reed spoke of the author's condemnation of PRI racism; Luz Elena Gutiérrez de Velasco treated the themes of censorship and self-censor-

ship in Garro's work; Lady Rojas-Trempe analyzed her pre-Foucaultian representation of madness; Javier Durán examined her denunciation of the hypocritical Left; and Alessandra Luisella signaled the contrast between Garro's anticlassism and the ethnocentrism of the film conventions that were applied in the translation of "El árbol" from print to screen. A collection of selected presentations from that conference is forthcoming from the Programa Interdisciplinario de Estudios de la Mujer of the Colegio de México.

WORKS CITED

Biron, Rebecca E. 1995. "*Testimonios sobre Mariana:* representación y la otra mujer." *Sin imágenes falsas, sin falsos espejos: Narradoras mexicanas del siglo XX.* México: Programa interdisciplinario de estudios de la mujer, El Colegio de México.

Bradu, Fabienne. 1987. *Señas particulares: Escritora.* México: Fondo de Cultura Económica.

Carballo, Emmanuel. 1982. "La vida y la obra de Elena Garro rescatadas por Emmanuel Carballo." *Unomásuno* 24 January 1982, *Sábado,* 2–5.

Escalante, Evodio. 1998. "Re: La ninguneada" 26 August. Online Posting. *Comala.* Comala@humnet.ucla.edu.

Garro, Elena. 1981. *Testimonios sobre Mariana.* Mexico: Editorial Grijalbo.

———. "A mí me ha ocurrido todo al revés." *Cuadernos hispánicos,* April 1979, 39.

———. 1989. Interview by Fernando García Ramírez. *Sábado* (2 September).

Gutiérrez de Velazco, Luz Elena. 1992. "Elena Garro, maga de la palabra." In *Elena Garro: Reflexiones en torno a su obra.* México: INBA/Centro Nacional de Investigación.

Kaminsky, Amy. 1993. "Residual Authority and Gendered Resistance." In *Critical Theory, Cultural Politics, and Latin American Narrative,* ed. Steven M. Bell, Albert H. LeMay, and Leonard Orr, 103–121. Notre Dame, IN, and London: University of Notre Dame Press.

Landeros, Carlos. 1980. "La Garro y la Paz." *Siempre* 1414: 40–74.

López, María Luisa, and Arturo Mendoza Mocino. 1998. "Nos mueve la lucha justa." *Milenio* 42 (15 June): 46–47.

Monsiváis, Carlos. 1998. "Elena Garro." *La Jornada,* 23 August.

Muncy, Michele. 1990. "Chronology of Elena Garro as Told to Michele Muncy by the Author." In *A Different Reality,* ed. Anita Stoll. Toronto: Associated University Presses.

Ramírez, Luis Enrique. 1994. "Elena Garro: El destino errante." In *La muela del juicio,* 201–236. México: Consejo Nacional para la Cultura y las Artes.

Robles, Martha. 1989. *La sombra fugitiva: Escritoras en la cultura nacional.* Vol. II. México: Editorial Diana.

Rojas-Trempe, Lady. 1991. "El autorretrato de Elena Garro." *Alba de América* 9: 163–180.

Stoll, Anita, ed. 1990. *A Different Reality.* Toronto: Associated University Presses.

Williams, Raymond. L. 1993. "The Octavio Paz Industry" [Review of Helen Lane, *The Other Voice: Essays on Modern Poetry*]. *American Book Review* 14 (August–September): 1–10.

8

René Derouin
Dialogues with Mexico

Montserrat Galí Boadella

Translated by John V. Waldron

Dans mon identité culturelle, le métissage est la seule façon de me regenerer. Je n'ai pas peur des autres. . . . Les cultures des autres me métissent en enrichissant mes mémoires, mon identité.

René Derouin, *L'Espace et la densité*

Mexico has long been open to dialogue with foreigners. The nineteenth-century *artistas viajeros,* or "traveling artists," for example, exerted considerable influence on many aspects of the nascent republican art of the time, so much so that they have become fixtures of Mexican cultural history. More recent versions of these traveling artists have likewise played an important role in twentieth-century Mexican art. The story of this influence is reciprocal, with the artists' contact with Mexican culture having a transformative effect on them as well. Mexico has looked at itself in their work as if in a mirror, while the traveling artists frequently have seen in Mexico not only a new source of inspiration but also a romantic alternative to their own disenchantment with their cultures of origin.

The term "romanticism," of course, covers complex and even contradictory concepts. Nonetheless, it is useful to summarize its complexity in two aspects, one chronological, the other transhistorical. Understood chronologically, "romanticism" refers to the cultural—artistic and ideological—movement roughly coinciding with the final decades of the eighteenth century and the first half of the nineteenth. Viewed transhistorically, romanticism goes beyond this chronological framework to refer to certain attitudes, sensibilities, and ways of expressing aesthetic emotions that we identify as romantic. In the latter sense, many artistic and literary movements of the second half of the nineteenth century and, in particular, the avant-gardes of the twentieth century can be seen as a continuation of the romantic sensibility. At the very least, these movements held key affinities with the concepts and attitudes of historical romanticism. Thus, we could see commonalities between the work of traveling artists in Mexico associated with historical romanticism—such as the painters Baron Gros, Thomas Eggerton, and Moritz Rugendas—and those associated with the early twentieth-century avant-garde, including Antonin Artaud, Sergei Eisenstein, or Edward Weston, to name a few of the most prominent examples. Despite important differences, both groups share similarities beyond the phenomena of the journey to Mexico itself. For example, all of these artists could be seen as searching for what they considered a more pure and genuine stimulus for their creation, a process that sometimes is associated with their fascination with the exotic. The two groups of artists also demonstrate disenchantment with their own culture. In fact, according to many historians of romanticism, an attitude of nonconformity with respect to the values of Western modernity served as a detonator that sparked the explosion of romanticism.

The affinities among the traveling artists in Mexico over the last two centuries are continued in the work of a contemporary Quebecois artist, René Derouin, who could be seen as sharing three key elements of transhistorical romanticism with his forebears. The first element would be the journey itself as a mechanism that stimulates the artist vitally and aesthetically. The second is the artist's immersion in cultures that are, to him, exotic and primitive. The third derives from the previous two and relates to the artist's own sense of self: the putting into play of a distancing from what is proper to one's self by means of contact with the other. Despite these affinities, however, Derouin demonstrates some crucial differences from his traveling predecessors. Of fundamental importance in his work is that for him Mexico is, above all, the developing fluid that has permitted the best of his art to flourish. Among other possible differences, the important point of distinction is that Derouin considers himself a migrant and not a traveler. That is, he does not merely pass through Mexico at a distance, but commits himself to his surroundings, creating *mestizaje* and biculturalism in himself and in his work. These two categories of *mestizaje* and biculturality might appear to be characteristics only of artists of foreign extraction who reside permanently in Mexico, such as, for example, Arnold Belkin, Gunther Gerszo, Marta Palau, Roger von Gunten, and Mariana Yampolski. Of interest in Derouin's case is that he does not become a Mexican artist of foreign origin, but rather he becomes a Quebecois fertilized by Mexico, through engaging in an ongoing process and dialogue. Then, too, like the romantics, Derouin is a critic of his epoch, but, unlike them, he is neither disenchanted with nor is he a fugitive from a reality that he finds displeasing.

Born in Montreal in 1936, René Derouin has become a central artistic figure in his own country. In 1955 he left the Ecole des Beaux-Arts of Montreal to travel to Mexico. Upon his first contact with Mexican art he became acquainted with the muralist movement and studied at the La Esmeralda school (a subsidiary of the school of Bellas Artes) and the old Academy of San Carlos. Later he traveled through the United States reaffirming his intention to make an art of American scope. Starting with these travels, the concept of territory quickly became a theme of constant reflection for Derouin, as well as the strongest and most original aspect of his artistic theory and practice.

The 1970s saw Derouin engaged in intense activity in his work as an engraver and as cultural promoter in the founding of the publishing agency Editions Formart. Through Formart he produced approximately ten books on art and a wide range of artistic and cultural projects. His work as a cultural promoter continues to the present day, as Derouin has been responsible for various cultural and artistic exchange projects between Mexico and Quebec. For example, the René Derouin Foundation organizes symposia and other activities in Val-David, where Derouin resides, in which artists from Mexico, Quebec, and other American countries are invited to participate.

Derouin's thought as well as his work consistently has tended toward synthesis and inclusion. He works in nearly every contemporary artistic medium, from engraving to animated film as well as painting and installation art. He learns from all the media at his disposal, at times creating an audacious synthesis of all of them. He is not intimidated by new techniques or by the most advanced technology. At the same time, he does not fall into a Futurist enthusiasm for technology per se, or into a romantic rejection of it, but rather recognizes its advantages, explores its possibilities, and puts it at the service of an art that would speak for its epoch.

Reflecting his eclectic production, Derouin's work is also quite extensive. The critical thought generated around his artistic process and his relationship with Mexico are of a richness and complexity that the topics touched upon by the present study represent only a small portion of his work. A fundamental axiom of his artistic thought (both theoretical and practical) is the concept of territory, which unites the two anthropological coordinates of space and time. A territory is not simply a place but is also an inhabited place, traversed, apprehended, and conceived by humans. French ethnologist André Leroi-Gourhan theorizes that prior to the invention of tools and language, humans had to create a human space and time. Such a phenomenon is basic to understanding the process involved in all aesthetic creation, as Leroi-Gourhan himself demonstrates in his analysis of prehistoric art.

In his most autobiographical text, *L'Espace et la densité* (1993), Derouin uses the concept of space and density to summarize what Mexico and Quebec have contributed to his life and his work. The concepts distill as his relationship with Mexico deepens. In the process, *mestizaje*—another conceptual axiom for Derouin—is produced. *Mestizaje* should not be understood as an aleatory mixture of Mexican and Quebecois cultural elements but rather a real transformation of the artist. Derouin identifies on the one hand an interior territory that is the state of the "soul," and on the other an exterior territory that composes the space where the artist lives and works. These territories are in communication. The soul, or the interior territory, places itself in contact with certain places, as if these evoked memories and uncovered affinities. "This interior place," writes Derouin in his *Ressac: De Migrations au Largage*, "has always been present in me much more strongly than the ethnic or national dimensions. In this way there is a part of the South in me that I have sensed to be original ever since I made my first trip to Mexico in the fifties" (1996, 22). The process of creation of these two spaces is accompanied by that of a third, that of *mestizaje:* a new territory composed of interfertilization and mixing. This does not mean that the North is rejected in favor of the South, or vice versa, but rather that in the territory of *mestizaje* the artist finds equilibrium and synthesis.

In *L'Espace et la densité*, Derouin describes his first trip to Mexico, his return to Québec, and the construction of his house-workshop as well as the works he produced up to the end of the 1970s. In this account, Mexico does not always appear, or at least is not always evident. On the contrary, the artist seems more preoccupied with resolving problems presented by a technological civilization. His trips to the United States had awakened him to geography, factories, and the machine. Then, as the South entered his horizon, technology, which had preoccupied him at first, began to take a backseat and Derouin began to reflect on the concept of territory.

In Quebec large areas of the landscape are unpopulated, a phenomenon that permits contact with an almost pristine nature. Derouin opposes the great, unpopulated areas (emptiness, space) of the Canadian north to the human and cultural density of the South. The North is still a land to be conquered, it presents nature untouched by humanity, and it is also the future, what is still to be done. The South, with its millenary culture, represents the cultural roots of America, its past, its history, and its memory; that is, the South is density. In the North, space predominates, in the South it is time. The North is the horizontal, with its vast forests and lakes; the South is vertical, the architecture millenary, particularly the pyramid, the sign of culture.

In Derouin's first works up to *Suite Baskatong* (1977) there is no human presence. But starting with the latter work some calligraphic signs appear that Derouin interprets "as if an ancient civilization had wanted to leave traces on my landscape" (1993, 55). *Mestizaje* begins to appear. From this point onward, Derouin created a distinctive series of landscapes in which topography and geological accidents are seen from a bird's eye view. But these signs that represent accidents are, according to Derouin, like ancient signs of Mexican civilization that suddenly arose in his memory in the midst of the great Canadian countryside, from its forests, its lakes, and its tundra.

Derouin's works are created on an ever-larger scale. His engravings are conceived modularly, forming larger and larger groupings of objects. In relation to this aspect of his work, Patricia Ainsle observes that "challenging the traditions of printmaking, he has expanded its scope and possibilities in scale, three-dimensional form, and concept" (1998, 6). However, this is not merely a technical exercise or simply an aesthetic recourse; rather, an exploration in the field of engraving responds to a necessity to express his ideas concerning territory. The vastness of empty space in the North is now connected with the enormity of colossal structures such as the pyramids in the South. In the size of his engravings and in the distinct, syntactic solutions offered, the novelty of installation art and environmental art are clearly evident, but so too are influences of the Mexican School (muralism and engravings) and, as Ainsle has observed, of artists such as Rauschenberg or Christo (1998, 19).

Derouin's *Suite nordique* showed in Mexico City in 1985 in the Museo Universitario del Chopo. The day of the show's opening coincided with the devastating earthquake of September 19, a telluric commotion that postponed the inauguration but also had the effect of identifying the artist even more with Mexico. The *Suite nordique* series is composed of enormous wood engravings conceived modularly, with forms and textures that allude to the altitude curves on topographical maps but also give the impression of flying over a particular territory, with its topographical accidents, its earth tones, and its panoramic perspective. The relief is such that at times the engravings become virtual scale models. The idea of working with modules resulted from Derouin's trips through the American continent, during which he became intrigued with the use of maps. From his first trip to the United States in 1969 he was fascinated with highway maps: By following its signs he felt he could "inhabit" rapidly and globally a given territory, despite its extension. This period of Derouin's life culminated in a trip to Europe, where he definitively integrated the notion of time that his experience in Mexico had begun to awaken. Derouin's particular notion of time in this sense has to do with the decisive presence of humans in territory, in particular the traces of human creativity imprinted on territory by monuments. He sees the work of the artist, likewise, as a mark and an expression of human time, a time that exceeds the life of a single person and is therefore no longer physical time (chronological) but becomes a cultural time (biological). "In Sienna" writes Derouin, "I admired the work of the early Siennans. One artist had labored forty-five years on a single work and later his children continued it" (1993, 8).

By this time, everything was in place for Derouin to begin a series of works that would be monumental in size, effort, and depth. The *mestizaje* between North and South, between Mexico and Quebec, had reached a high level of concretion in his work. As a result of his journeys and his experience of *mestizaje*, the artist had created his own concept of space and time and had synthesized it in a particular notion of territory (a natural, cultural, and plastic territory, as we shall see). He understood his work as a vital and total experience in which beginning and end were not important, but coherence with life was; that is, his was truly a work in progress. His more and more frequent trips to Mexico with periodic returns to Quebec turned him into a permanent migrant. In an interview with Patricia Ainsle, Derouin expressed his absolute need for traveling as an act of survival. It is a journey that always has as its referents North and South: "In the North, I live with solitude, space, physical means, as if I am on a temporarily protected little island. In the South, I live on the move and in austerity, exposed to the driving force of life" (1998, 8).

Derouin has continued to take other trips to places such as Japan and California, among others. However, his stays in Mexico have become more and more frequent, becoming a way of life for him. Nonetheless, he does not go on these trips as if on a romantic flight from the homeland, nor does he simply go in search of folklore or primitivism. Rather, on these trips Derouin establishes what will be a form of work; a permanent dialogue between his interior and exterior territory, between North and South, between nature and culture, between space and time. In the series *Between* (1984) and the later *Equinoxe* (1990), Derouin synthesizes his major ideas: duality, contrast, the passage from one space to another, the bicultural experience.

The five works that I will comment on in continuation form a whole, as a mature synthesis of a life of work and reflection. Mexico is the thread that connects all of these particular works: its art, culture, and above all its people, the masses in constant movement, the density of the human, both cultural and temporal. Derouin produced these five works—*Migraciones, Plaza Pública, Largage, Fleuve-Mémoire,* and *Paraíso*—in only eight years. They are held together by a formal and conceptual link. *Migraciones* and *Plaza Pública* are installations; *Largage* could qualify as performance; *Fleuve-Mémoire* a testimony in exhibition, while *Paraíso* represents a return to muralism, a more traditional artistic language. These five works are the product of many years of formal investigation, an accumulation of experiences and considerable reflection. There is no other explanation for how the artist could have completed a work of this magnitude with such a degree of coherence between its parts in such a short period of time.

Migraciones (1992) was conceived for the Tamayo Museum in Mexico City with the objective, in the words of the artist, of "transposing my vision of the great Nordic space to Mexico." The work consists of a strip of wood more than fifty meters long—a true engraved wooden plate on a grand scale—on which twenty thousand ceramic figures form a line (Illustrations 8.1 and 8.2). The figures show the stream of human-

Illustration 8.1. René Derouin, *Migraciones*. Museo Tamayo: Mexico City.
(Photo: René Derouin. Reproduced by permission of the artist.)

Illustration 8.2. René Derouin, *Migraciones* (fragment). Museo Tamayo: Mexico City. (Photo: Arturo Zurita. Reproduced by permission of René Derouin and Arturo Zurita.)

ity that has populated the continent, each carrying a bundle or a back-pack. Each piece is unique, made by hand with artisan techniques in Oaxaca (San Bartolo Coyotepec) and Quebec. The colossal work represented by this installation in the Tamayo Museum had barely begun: At the end of 1992 the installation was presented in the Québec Museum, where it was adapted to its new spatial and cultural context. Finally, in 1993, using the same material and the same concepts on a slightly larger scale, Derouin's performance, *Largage*, took place, along with the exposition *Fleuve-Mémoire:* two events tied to the process originally set in motion by *Migraciones.*

Place-Publique (Illustration 8.3) was produced almost in parallel with,

Illustration 8.3. René Derouin, *Place-Publique*. Fragment of the installation located in Baie-Saint-Paul for the exposition *Fleuve-Mémoire:* In the background are the boxes containing the clay figures from *Migraciones* and the photomural functioning as a memory of its migrants. (Photo: Lucien Lisabelle. Reproduced by permission of René Derouin.)

and in close relation to, *Migraciones*. It was composed of twenty-five-hundred figures taken from the latter work. Both the installation itself as well as the title refer to Mexico City's famous Zócalo, the main plaza built on top of the ancient site of Tenochtitlan. Twenty years after his first contact with Mexico, Derouin reminds us in this work of the brutal consequences of development politics and neoliberalism: disordered growth, demographic explosion, social inequality, pollution. The Zócalo is the central point for this mixture, the place where celebrations and protests are held and the site of political repression and cultural expansion. For Derouin the multitudinous concentrations of people and culture in the Zócalo create a thread that runs through history. On this same site the main Aztec temple, the *Templo Mayor*, and the market of Tenochtitlan once stood; here also is where the viceroys and archbishops of New Spain entered the city. Today, separated by only a few hours, one can witness lively patriotic celebrations and angry protests here. In *Place-Publique* René Derouin pays homage to the heart of the city and laments that his Nordic cities lack this plaza of collective memory and history. This is the density, the time of Mexican history.

The conceptual allusions of *Place-Publique* return us to the concepts and the fruit of the earlier work, *Migraciones*. Derouin claims to have acquired his notion of territory in Mexico, where he feels that the people are more American than are Canadians and people from the United States. This observation could come as a surprise to Mexicans accustomed to a deeply rooted discourse of national identity that portrays them as permanently forsaken, unsure of themselves, and lacking identity. For Derouin what ties Mexicans to territory is their cultural density, understood as memory, and memory is what creates the possibility for the conjunction of space and time.

In 1993 Derouin stored away the twenty thousand figures of *Migraciones* and departed for Iceland, where he would complete a series of engravings on a Nordic theme. Meanwhile, he received an invitation to show his work in Baie-Saint-Paul, Quebec, at the mouth of the Saint Lawrence River. The framework for the exposition was a symposium on the theme of memory, a topic that led him logically, almost naturally, to *Largage*. The river was the territory of his childhood and personal memory: His father and his brother had drowned in the Saint Lawrence River when René Derouin was very young. He began to prepare the exposition in silence:

> . . . in the way of ritual, in order to put an end to my sorrow and to be able to understand my long absence from the banks of that river. Working on the

Illustration 8.4. René Derouin, *Largage*. 7 July 1994 in the Saint Lawrence River, Quebec. (Photo: Jeanne Molleur. Reproduced by permission of René Derouin.)

concept of the exposition, the idea of *largage* [release, or letting go] appeared as a central point. The thought that I had found an exit, a road, the passage that permitted me to open the boxes and to carry on with the migration filled me with happiness. The release (*largage*) reconstructed a bridge between various types of memories. . . . This exposition, which is crucial for me, will be a reconciliation with my past. . . . This time the river would not be only a place of passage, a road for migration, but it also is a place of recognition, for me, of its point of departure. It was necessary to encounter this place of origin for me to be able to continue forging ahead in my searches and understand their meaning. (1996, 59–64)

The *Fleuve-Mémoire* exhibition, presented in the Baie-Saint Paul Symposium (1994), is the continuation of *Migraciones* but more than anything is constituted in the memory of the performance of *Largage*, in which Derouin threw thousands of clay figures to the depths of the Saint Lawrence River (Illustration 8.4). A circle was closed—although the image of a spiral would be more accurate: With his act of renunciation Derouin created an end point but at the same time an opening toward a new, vital period of creativity. The character of the installation piece *Fleuve-Mémoire* reinforces this idea of the ephemeral or transitory.

Illustration 8.5. The artist finishing the photomural in the exposition called *Fleuve-Mémoire* in Baie-Saint-Paul, Quebec. (Photo: Lucien Lisabelle. Reproduced by permission of René Derouin.)

The photomural that presides over the exposition (1,152 photographs of the clay figures, mounted on a surface measuring 2.77 × 7.22 meters) is the memory of *Migraciones*, but it is also an autonomous work in its own right (Illustration 8.5). A series of engravings he made while in Iceland also accompany the photomural.

In the inaugural moment of the *Fleuve-Mémoire* exposition, the ritual of release or *Largage* was carried out in silence and in the most absolute intimacy. The only people present were Derouin and his wife Jeanne and the boat's pilot. The Saint Lawrence River thus became the "marine cemetery" to more than nineteen thousand works of art. The river, metaphor for the flow of life but also of life's fragility and precarious nature, is the perfect allegory of temporality, the synthesis of the idea of place (space) and time (memory).

The exposition included a series of photos as a testimony registering the act of *Largage*. Although all of this is seemingly distant from the South, it found inspiration from another lesson learned in Mexico: that of death. However, before hearing the artist's testimony in this regard it is worthwhile to reflect on *Largage* as an artistic act to better understand what it accomplished. With the destruction of nearly twenty thousand clay figures, Derouin demonstrates, with a degree of valor and risk, a way to understand performance. He also widens the scope of conceptual art by taking it to its limits; and, most importantly, he suspends the world of art commerce as well as the phenomenon of museum conservation as a form of alienation. And in the final analysis, Derouin uncovers the original meaning of art, which, like all forms of religion, is identified with sacrifice.

Derouin did save some of the figures, in a positive gesture and as a protest against this other form of alienation. Two-hundred-twenty of them are now permanently on display, donated to the Tamayo Museum in Mexico City. Another 250 were sent to friends and persons involved in culture and who were in some way linked to his activities, in a demonstration of his friendship and solidarity with his supporters. That said, however, the principal point of *Largage* continues to revolve around the notion of total release, that is, death.

In a personal interview following *Largage*, Derouin reflected:

> After *Migraciones* the weight of so much work, of so much effort, was crushing me. The fear of death as a general rule provokes gestures of conservation. . . . Mexican culture has taught me to not fear death. To learn how to die, to disappear in order to be reborn in something else. That's part of my apprenticeship in Mexico. It's difficult to understand it, but when you achieve it it's beneficial. (Unpublished interview with author)

The result of this intense period in his life was another book, *Ressac: De Migrations au Largage*, a diary of the path Derouin took from the inception of the idea for *Migraciones* to the final release of the figures into the Saint Lawrence River. Included in this book are testimonies (letters, texts, poems) from the people who received a clay figure from *Migraciones*. It could thus be called a collective book in which the artist continues dialoguing with his friends, with collaborators on projects, and with cultural personalities that participated in this process.

From January to May of 1998 a retrospective of Derouin's work took place at the Glenbow Museum in Calgary, Alberta, with a special focus on Derouin's relationship with Mexico. Part of the exhibit featured a mural titled *Paraíso* (Illustration 8.6), which later went on display in the Musée de la Civilisation in Quebec. Along with the mural he created a logbook called *Paraíso, la dualité du baroque*, about his navigation through Mexican baroque art and culture. Here, as in other works, Der-

Illustration 8.6. René Derouin and his assistant making the ceramic reliefs for the mural *Paraíso* in his workshop in Quebec. (Photo: Jeanne Molleur. Reproduced by permission of René Derouin.)

ouin speaks of duality. The result is also dual: a mural and a book, both of which explore the graphic function of signs, creating images that "are written in a language between drawing and writing" (1998, 10). In both media, impressed by the Franciscan temple of Santa María Tonantzintla in Cholula, Puebla, Derouin initiates a dialogue with Mexico's baroque. His journey through popular baroque is fascinating because he does not undertake it as an art historian but rather as an artist who perceives the secrets of a language with which he feels a kinship. Derouin sees in the Mexican baroque, particularly in its most popular articulations, an expression of freedom; in the world of baroque forms he discovers a way to arrive at the hidden symbols of a collective memory.

For Derouin, the exuberant language of the baroque creates the possibility for feelings and repressed desires to express themselves. In the baroque emptiness and density are at play, two of the most important elements in the work and thought of the artist himself. He writes:

> In the baroque there is multiplication. We are in the epoch of the baroque
> .... To travel through Mexico, to lose oneself in the multitude of people,
> the objects, the centuries, the smells. The baroque is everywhere. It
> manifests its difference with the Protestant world. . . . The baroque is the
> magic of quantity, of the superfluous, of abundance and disproportion in the
> belief of paradises beyond the bounds of reason. (1998, 57)

His study of the baroque and his preparation of the mural, *Paraíso*, led Derouin once again to Cholula, Puebla, and to Santa María Tonantzintla. He returned to wander through Mexico City, its baroque churches, and its cathedral. He traveled through Oaxaca, where he stopped in the capital to take notes on the convent of Santo Domingo and the Rosario chapel. With these trips came a period of isolation and reflection on the Pacific Coast covering almost an entire year, from February to November 1997. On March 7, from his refuge on the coast of Oaxaca, he wrote:

> *Entre Fleuve-Mémoire and Between.* The task consists in realizing a work of
> contrasts, leaving darkness toward light and color: a duality of black with
> opposing reliefs that present the rich, luminous colors of the baroque. . . . I
> construct this work with a mixture of acquired knowledge of techniques and
> materials that I am already acquainted with. I try to realize a work of art! Is
> this possible in 1997? Is it possible to create a work of art that will mean
> something in fifty years? (1998, 87)

On the eighth day he notes, "At last I've found the adequate motifs: series of people who multiply from the bottom to the top and spirals that interweave around them. These motifs are inspired by the relief models in the church of Tonantzintla" (1998, 92). Later he would add fruits and vegetables (the memory of the markets), water and fish (the Oaxacan fishermen returning from fishing, but also the Saint Lawrence River, the familiar origin, the act of *Largage*). Here we see the motif of the tree of life, that of *Migraciones;* in an evocation of memory, every-one returns. The work has barely begun but Derouin here records something that is extraordinary at first sight: These drawings, conceived on the coast of Oaxaca and inspired by the baroque church of Tonant-zintla, bear astonishing similarities to the art of the Inuit Indians of Canada. *Mestizaje*, paraphrasing an idea of Jocelyn Connolly's (1995), would form a third territory, that of the artist and his creative gesture. A gesture whose foundation is memory.

Derouin finished the mural on the first day of November 1997 in Quebec. The work is filled with thoughts of the significance of that par-ticular date for Mexican culture. The first of November is the celebra-tion of the dead, a central date in the Mexican calendar. But it is superimposed, for Derouin, with the day commemorating a national Quebecois poet and great friend of the artist, Gaston Miron. On the first of November Derouin wrote in his diary:

> Month of the dead: an important celebration in Mexican culture. I imagine today the temple of Tonantzintla covered in flowers in rich and exuberant colors, in symbolic abundance and the multitude. These are the rituals that have always impressed me. To bring to life the quotidian by means of excessive rituals, to construct passages between life and death, to make of the celebration an instant of eternity. (1998, 134)

Paraíso, a work Derouin considers of great importance in his artistic development, expresses a desire to share the vast spaces of the Ameri-can continent and the richness of Mexico's cultural patrimony, which nourish his work.

In *Paraíso*, Derouin has achieved the type of graphic representation that ethnologist André Leroi-Gourhan (1971) calls mythogram, in opposition to the linear and narrative discourse that dominates the pic-togram. In the mythogram mythic space and time are condensed simul-taneously with the creation of a system of relations and ramifications that approximates a constellation. There is no exclusion as occurs in lin-ear language, but rather association, addition, and multiplication. His deep understanding and empathy for Mexican art and culture has led this Montreal-born artist to seek what all romantics desperately sought: the secret of the art of ancient peoples, whether Zapotecs or Inuits. René Derouin may rightfully affirm that "my work is a wake in the human memory of Amerindian Indians" (1998, 3).

The relationship between René Derouin and Mexico is a new one between artist and country. It is unlike that of the majority of foreign artists who have visited Mexico and been inspired by its art. Derouin is neither tourist nor hunter of the exotic. In his work and in his reflections, we can measure what makes up his dialogue with Mexico and on what bases his *mestizaje* is established. Derouin consciously elaborates his concepts and meditates on his experiences in Mexico, in contrast to the romantic tradition based on emotive resonances. Derouin tries to understand Mexican culture and way of life by analysis and above all by placing in constant dialogue his Nordic and Mexican experiences. He does not discard either one, but rather he integrates them to create the new territory of creation. The *mestizaje* that is produced is thus not the product of superficial references provoked by the tourist's surprise with the exotic. Nor is it in the tradition of the work of avant-garde artists, who by the combination of diverse materials or ideas (collage) create another reality and another meaning. Much less than a mixture, an eclecticism or a syncretic process in which some of the parts disappear, the dialogue between René Derouin and Mexico is polyphonic; in his work all voices are important, even indispensable. This dialogue has allowed him to produce a body of work of international proportions that opens pathways to new generations of American artists.

NOTE

Epigraph: [In my cultural identity, mestizaje is the only way to regenerate myself. I have no fear of others. . . . The cultures of others recombine me by enriching my memories, my identity.]

WORKS CITED

Ainsle, Patricia. 1998. *Frontiers, Frontières, Fronteras.* Calgary, Glenbow Museum.

Connolly, Jocelyn. 1995. "Baie-Saint-Paul: Dessaisissement et délocalisation." *ETC, Revue de l'art actuel* 29: 43–48.

Derouin, René. 1993. *L'Espace et la Densité: Entretiens avec Michel-Pierre Sarrazin.* Montreal: Editions de l'Hexagone.

———. 1996. *Ressac: De Migrations au Largage.* Montreal: Editions de l'Hexagone.

———. 1998. *Paraíso: La dualité du baroque.* Montreal: Editions de l'Hexagone.

Leroi-Gourhan, André. 1971. *El gesto y la palabra.* Caracas: Universidad Central de Venezuela.

Unhomely Feminine
Rosina Conde

Debra A. Castillo

few years ago Carlos Monsiváis published an article in a volume on the North American Free Trade Agreement in which he underlines the political, social, and cultural cost of the traditional division between Mexico City and the rest of the country: "Se sanctificó el juego de los opuestos: civilización y barbarie, capital y provincia, cultura y desolación. Desde principios de siglo . . . cunde una idea: la provincia es 'irredimible,' quedarse es condenarse," 'A play of opposites was sanctified: civilization and barbarism, capital and provinces, culture and desolation. Since the beginning of the century . . . the idea has been propagated that the province is "unredeemable," that to stay is to be condemned' (1994, 197). From Mexico City's point of view, the northern border is imagined as perhaps the most "unredeemable" of all the provincial representations. It is from a centrist perspective the region most affected by the cultural, linguistic, and moral corruption of Mexico's unfortunately proximate and powerful neighbor, the United States.

Rosina Conde, a product and chronicler of the Californian border, has been, I suspect, one of the victims of this centrist snobbery about the northern border region of the country. Her numerous volumes of fiction and poetry[1] have been published by a variety of small, provincial presses, have received very little attention from the Mexico City mainstream cultural critics, and unfortunately have not been well studied either in Hispanist circles in the United States. As María-Socorro Tabuenca Córdoba, a culture critic working in Juárez, reminds us, both Chicano and mainstream Mexican writers have tended to ignore contributions of Mexican border writers such as Conde, who do not fit well into either group's cultural agenda: "for Chicano/a literature the border is a topic, an inexhaustible utopia. . . . In Mexican border literature the topic of the border occupies an ordinary space, a place which is infrequently represented in writing" (1995–1996, 161–162).

Reading Conde's works requires a shift of attention. She asks us to move away from a world imagined in terms of Mexico City versus the provinces or Mexico versus the United States; likewise, her works also demand that we rethink a notion of human motivations based on gender stereotypes of passive women and aggressive men (compare with Octavio Paz's influential dichotomy of men and women in Mexico according to the *Chingón/Chingada* binary in his *Labyrinth of Solitude* [1961]). For this border writer, the consciousness of liminality extends itself to all realms of experience, and with it an effort to imagine/produce the subject of writing as more complex. She often focuses on what Trujillo Muñoz describes as a region "beyond taboos" in his brief note on this author. Trujillo Muñoz continues with a lapidary phrase that has become the most quoted comment on Conde's work: "Rosina Conde fue la primera escritora bajacaliforniana en explorar, sin ninguna clase de cortapisas, la relación amorosa en un mundo de dominados y dominadores," 'Rosina Conde was the first Baja Californian writer to explore, without any restraints, the amorous relationship in a world of dominators and dominateds' (1990, 181). I would go somewhat farther than Trujillo Muñoz in this characterization and say that Conde's work directly addresses the traditional dichotomies of Mexican fiction and inscribes the border existence as a particularly privileged location— simultaneously strange and familiar—to explore the gender bound and regionally bound nature of discursive constructions of Mexicanness itself. Her explorations of the intimate spaces of daily lives of border dwellers offer themselves at the same time as a political release from erasure on the national cultural scene as they also effect a rejection of sexually marked repression in relationships both ordinary (portraits of stress lines in working-class and middle-class families) and liminal (her delicate explorations of the insistently border-inflected worlds of assembly plants, prostitution, and striptease).

This is most strikingly true when Conde brings her reader, as she often does, into the liminal world of abusive relationships, or of female sexuality bought and sold in Tijuana's many nightclubs. In these stories Conde's interrogation of the tight imbrication of (provincial) identity and (deviant) female sexuality is particularly pronounced. In a manuscript on female prostitution in Tijuana, Gudelia Rangel Gómez writes a concise summary of the working of this stereotype:

> Como puede observarse en el proceso histórico de Tijuana, tanto su crecimiento poblacional como su desarrollo económico han ido de la mano de actividades estigmatizadas o consideradas prohibidas en otros lugares, esto ha provocado que la concepción generalizada de la ciudad haya sido un proceso de feminización de Tijuana; identificada primero con una "dama generosa" que permitió mejores niveles de vida a su población, posteriormente una "joven coqueta" que atraía hombres para "perderlos" y finalmente la visión que se tuvo de una "prostituta decadente y grotesca" que utilizaban aquellos que pasaban por Tijuana. (1996, 30)
>
> [As one may observe in the historical process of Tijuana, its population growth as well as its economic development have gone hand-in-hand with activities that are stigmatized or prohibited in other places. This has resulted in a generalized conception of the city in terms of a process of feminization of Tijuana; identified first as a "generous lady" who allowed a better standard of living to her inhabitants, later as a "frivolous young woman" who attracted men who "got lost" and finally, the vision of a "decadent and grotesque prostitute" who used those who passed through Tijuana.]

Rangel Gómez's reading of Tijuana's infamous international image as a meat market for the United States—U.S. men cross the border to purchase sex from Mexican women while Mexican men cross the border to sell their labor in U.S. fields—is a potent one, suggesting that from both central Mexico as well as the United States there arises a tendency to feminize Tijuana in a particularly marginalizing and stigmatized manner. Tijuana, in this respect, confirms the primacy of centrist notions about the provinces by antinomy. By setting Tijuana and its inhabitants outside the traditional construction of the motherland (*madre patria*) as a domestic space writ large, those Tijuanan generous ladies, frivolous women, and decayed prostitutes help define the normalized space, holding up a distorting mirror to central Mexico's sense of itself as a nation of decent women and hardworking men. Even more curiously, in view of Tijuana's notorious representation through an image of undomestic femininity, until very recently, whether because of or despite the stereotype, writers and social scientists have tended to avoid analysis of the actual women who work in the nightclubs as waitresses, dancers for pay, stripteasers, and prostitutes. As Patricia Barrón Salido acutely comments, even in respected studies of marginal figures from Tijuana, "parecería que la prostitución queda entre puntos suspensivos," 'it seems that prostitution remains in the ellipsis' (1995, 9).[2] It is this slipperiness of a term that is both essential and elided that Conde explores, and that requires further analysis.

This slipperiness is patent in one of Conde's recent stories, narrated from the point of view of a suicidal former prostitute called Sonatina currently involved in an intermittently oppressive relationship with Pilar, the lesbian lover who took her out of the life on the streets. "Nunca se esperan que una reaccione," 'They never expect one to react,' says the lover to Sonatina at one point when two men threaten them silently and Pilar responds with an aggressive gesture. Sonatina tells the reader that Pilar specifically emphasizes the feminine form of the word "one": "porque siempre se refirió a sí misma como *una*, recalcando la *a* para reafirmar su condición femenina. Pilar es ingeniera agrónoma, y estudió en la UNAM porque, dice, es la única universidad en América Latina que te da el título en femenino," 'because she always referred to herself as *one* [feminine gender marker], stressing the *a* in order to reaffirm her female condition. Pilar is an agricultural engineer, and she says she studied in the UNAM because it is the only university in Latin America that gives you a degree in feminine' (1994b, 25). Pilar's gesture and her insistence upon finding an equal space for the feminine in language is an important one. Likewise, her consistent ideological stand on the issue of all degrees and levels of gender oppression is admirable, ranging from her attention to biases built into the language to a concern for women's right to hold fulfilling professional careers. For Sonatina, however, her lover's familiar response is at the same time appropriate and excessive. The former prostitute initially applauds her lover's liberating feminist gesture, while later she comes to believe that men need such mostly harmless displays of potential violence to reaffirm their oft-threatened and insecure masculinity. Extrapolating from Sonatina's perspective, the reader is led to understand that the aggressively butch attitude of the lover only inverts an unjust gender-based hierarchy without seriously questioning it.

Thus, the most nuanced commentary on gender performativity in this story comes from an unexpected source, as filtered through an insistently female-gendered perspective, but one that is referred to the readers through the counterpointed perceptions of that most unreliable of storytellers, a prostitute, and the most marginalized of women: a butch lesbian defiantly out of the closet. Conde's overall project in this story offers a point of view similar to that espoused by Monique Wittig. In her 1985 essay, "The Mark of Gender," Wittig reminds us that in French (as in Spanish, and unlike English), "Sex, under the name of gender, permeates the whole body of language and forces every locutor, if she belongs to the oppressed sex, to proclaim it in her speech, that is, to appear in language under her proper physical form and not under the abstract form, which every male locutor has unquestioned right to use. The abstract form, the general, the universal, this is what the so-called masculine gender means" (1985, 6). What Conde does in her story is to disturb this assumed universality of the masculine gender in foregrounding gender itself as a problematic social and ontological category. "Sonatina" privileges the point of view of a feminine "they," who provide its basic narrative grounding. Yet there is no attempt to counterpose *ellas* to *ellos* in a universalizing gesture, but rather to open up the discourse to a multiplicity of distinctly positioned *ellas* whose streams of voice combine to create the narrative point of view. It is this technique, more than any other, that marks Conde's literary practice and makes it an important addition to modern Mexican literature. It is this same estranging technique that makes her stories seem so unfamiliar, difficult to read, and so ineluctably part of a border reality.

This same edgy quality, it seems to me, is exactly what will make Conde's stories attractive to the U.S. literary establishment, which has a long, if largely untheorized, connection to borderness. María Rosa Menocal points to the significance of the community of exile scholars in the United States in shaping the discipline of comparative literature, which she argues is structured along the lines set out by "the legacy of exilic Romance philology . . . [having] no set languages or texts, no necessary borders, no temporal constraints or narrative shape" (1994, 137). Likewise, Emily Apter also picks up on the importance of remembering the degree to which the personal experience of displacement has come to shape the theoretical concerns of literary study: "From Spitzer to Bhabha (despite their being worlds apart) one discerns a recalcitrant homelessness of critical voice." Apter goes on to characterize "this unhomely voice,[3] together with the restless, migratory thought patterns of the discipline's theory and methods" as the grounding of comparative literature, concluding, "I would tend to frame the issue as a border war, an academic version of the legal battles and political disputes over the status of 'undocumented workers,' 'illegal aliens,' and 'permanent residents' " (1995, 94). Apter's description of elite theory in terms of a metaphorical border crosser may make some border scholars uneasy, yet her point about the freshness of this emerging, unhomely theory is well taken. According to this argument, U.S. elite literary theory returns to the shock of recognition born from these cultural displacements; thus, crossing the border offers an occasion for theoretical production precisely because of necessary personal accommodations involving a doubled cultural location.

Conde's contribution to U.S. theoretical discussions may well have something to do with an insistently gendered awareness of these border issues, as well as with sharpening our consciousness of the many regional differences among these writers and of the sometimes-uncomfortable spaces they portray. Her characters, however, often operate in a translational hermeneutic space and consistently tend to function in an implicitly contestatory relationship with the everyday operation of the basic premises that underlie centrist political structures on the one hand and patriarchal authority on the other. In this doubly displaced cultural and social location, Conde's women (her point-of-view characters tend to be female, or marginalized males) engage in activities and exchanges that point out the frame for this limited space while at the same time demonstrating how sexist thinking distorts the relationships of women to one another.

The longest section of *En la tarima* is a series of nine short prose pieces (eight numbered fragments and an epilogue) entitled "Viñetas revolucionarias" ("Revolutionary Scenes") and carrying the dedication: "Para Gilberto, hermano de armas," 'For Gilberto, brother at arms' (1984, 11). Given the traditional obsession of Mexican writers with the 1910 Revolution, the reader new to Conde's work might forgivably expect to find in this section of the book a contribution to that well-nourished subgenre of postrevolutionary fiction. Conde's *En la tarima*, however, is specifically Tijuanan, referring not to the Mexican Revolution, but its namesake: "Revolución," the main avenue in Tijuana, the center of that international city's tourist industry and site of such notorious delights as the world's longest bar and some of Tijuana's toniest striptease and prostitution establishments. Each brief vignette in the sequence of "viñetas revolucionarias" gives the reader a glimpse into this Revolution: either through introduction to a half-dozen of its warriors: initiate stripteaser "Virgen, aún virgen," 'Virgin, still a virgin'

(1984, 15); Lyn, "la reina de la rumba," 'the rumba queen' (1984, 16); Zoraída, immaculate in white (1984, 18); Mariela, the cocaine addict (1984, 20); Darling, the transvestite (1984, 22); and Zarina, who buries her pain in gluttony (1984, 24); or to evoke the sounds of its battles: the songs "Granada" (1984, 17) or "Rumba-rumbera" (1984, 21), and the eager solicitations of sidewalk callers: "¡Camin, sir! ¡Camin, sir! ¡Chou taim nau, sir . . . !" (1984, 29).

In each of these brief sketches, the excessiveness of performance belies a narrative of lack. For example, the poignancy of the first vignette comes from the performative qualities of an unexpected display of virginity poised on the imminence of its loss. A young woman, still technically a virgin, which is also her stage name, performs a masculinist stereotype of virginity as a titillating spectacle in a striptease club. The performative innocence evoked through Virgen's appearance on the stage, however, is framed by two references to her sensuality, which offset it and raise questions about traditional Mexican society's obsession with a bit of hidden female flesh. The first reference to sensuality also involves a performance of sorts and is called into being by (presumably) her boyfriend: "Pablo vendría a verla y habría que ser sensualmente bella, sobre todo después de las flores," 'Pablo would come to see her and she'd have to be sensually beautiful, especially because of the flowers.' The reference indicates a quid pro quo in which the man's gifts require a certain payment of a sensual—if not necessarily sexual—nature on her part. The second of the two men, the master of ceremonies, constructs her along similar grounds and demands a stage and off-stage performance aligned with that image: "A él le gustaba así: *sexy* e ingenua," 'he liked her that way: *sexy* and naïve' (1984, 15). Notably, it is very clear that what the men like in and desire from her is the staging of sexuality rather than the fact of it; as Virgen recalls to herself, her entire performance consists of simultaneously projecting sexuality and convincing the audience of her innocence—a double bind requiring an intense awareness of a denied presence. The central section of the sketch precisely delineates this dilemma: "Habría que bajar lentamente la escalera, apretando las piernas sin ver el público . . . cruzando las rodillas para esconder *aquello* con los muslos," 'She had to come down the stairs slowly, squeezing her legs together without looking at the audience . . . crossing her knees to hide *that thing* with her thighs' (1984, 15). Virgen's performative focus on her physical virginity estranges her sexuality and makes it unhomely: a contortionist's trick. Furthermore, the display of virginity on the stage points to its fungibility; when the narrator tells us that she is "aún virgen," 'still a virgin,' Conde not only signals the appropriateness of the stage name to the physical woman, but also marks a temporal moment, that of the time just before virginity's loss, a moment of transit between physical states and identities.[4]

The focus on something hidden is common to other sketches as well and tends to arise in situations that emphasize the estranging qualities of the stripteasers' lives. Zarina eats potatoes compulsively until they provoke nausea in order to hide from herself her possible pregnancy. Despite her efforts to deny it, her pregnancy is, nevertheless, narratively acknowledged, and makes itself seen and salable in the short run: "subió a la tarima en biquini sacudiendo las nalgas y las chichis aumentadas de tamaño por el posible embarazo," 'she stepped up to the platform in her bikini, shaking her ass and her tits, enlarged by the possible pregnancy' (1984, 25). In the stuttering syntax of this phrase the "possible" pregnancy becomes the proximate cause of the dancer's enlarged breasts, shifting the reader's perception between a fearful potential and a concrete actuality.

Darling, too, has a secret that must be hidden and displayed. A transvestite dancer, Darling's act consists in convincing the audience of her realness, to the point of inciting a sexually aggressive gesture on the part of males eager to "prove" their masculinity (here satisfied when a young man leaps on the stage and kisses her), then revealing the secret that she is really a he: "Darling avienta penacho y lentejuelas y, sonriente, triunfante, muestra de lleno el *flet up* y un pecho plano y brillante ante los ¡ohes! estupefactos de los admiradores. Un hombre vomita," 'Darling throws aside feathers and sequins and smiling, triumphant, shows off *flat top* and smooth, flat chest to the stupefied "Ohs!" of the admirers. A man vomits' (1984, 23). Darling's act is staged as much in the carefully chosen syntax of the sketch, which scrupulously avoids revelatory male gender markers until the reader and the audience are hit with the punchline at the same time. Curiously, both Zarina and the hapless overeager audience member in Darling's performance respond to the unhomely intrusion (the presence of the unwanted fetus, the unwanted—or unacknowledged desire for—the touch of male lips) with an identical gesture of physical rejection: the nausea that symbolically expels the forbidden/undesirable object.

The fifth sketch opens when Mariela applies makeup to her eyes to hide the traces of her disappointment with a man as she prepares for her act. The word choice in the meticulous description, however, once again calls attention to itself by a minute strangeness in the syntax: "Mariela *optó* por abrir el estuche de malaquita," 'Mariela *opted for* opening the malachite box' (1984, 19). The importance of this odd phrasing, with its implication of options not taken, becomes clear only at the end of the sketch in which Mariela hesitates before going onstage and picks up the malachite box again: "y lo abrió por el fondo; tocó con cuidado el talco—ahora blanco—con la yema del anular, lo acercó a la nariz, e inhaló," 'and she opened the bottom, touched the talcum powder—white now—with the tip of the ring finger, held it up to her nose, and inhaled' (1984, 20). Economically, Conde turns the familiar scene of a woman's betrayal by her man into something quite different. The familiar and the estranged touch each other in the two sides of the malachite box, which holds facial powder to cover up bags under the eyes on the one side, and on the other, secret side, hides cocaine. At all times, then, Mariela has two choices when opening the box, and the sinister weight of that unusual verb "optar" becomes clear in retrospect. Here two very different but equally stereotypical performances of the feminine touch in counterpoint. Yet, that very knife-edge of contact between contrasting stereotypes points to the particular issue problematized in this sketch. In the contact between the two sides of the box, Conde once again addresses the counterpunctual force of the edgily marginalized border reality.

The title of Conde's later volume of short stories, *Arrieras somos. . . .* (*Women on the Road. . . .* [1994a]) emphasizes these edgily self-aware displacements once again, in a different key. From the very title of the collection readers know that we are dealing with a moment of transit, and indeed, the book as a whole interrogates the boundaries of contemporary Mexican society through the active forgetting of the stereotypical domestic life. In an article on aporia, Derrida makes an apposite comment in his discussion of what we might call the border trauma induced by such transitional actions: "The crossing of borders always announces itself according to the movement of a certain step [*pas*]—and of the step that crosses a line. . . . There is a *problem* as soon as the edge-line is threatened. . . . There is a *problem* as soon as this intrinsic division divides the relation to itself of the border and therefore divides the being-oneself of anything" (1993, 11). For Derrida, the play on "*pas*," the French word for "step" and for "not," serves to clarify and delimit this problematic defining and dividing of the self. At the same time, the action of "crossing the line" evokes both literal movement across a boundary and the ontological and ethical decision to step outside traditional moral judgments.

Thus, for example, the narrator in the film *Barbarella*, following a trajectory exactly the opposite of—and in implicit dialogue with—actress Jane Fonda's famous roles on film and in life, was once a perfect little lady according to her own self-description, but now wears Madonna-style, aggressively sexy clothes. In this story, then, female self-presentation has everything to do with a nuanced understanding and manipulation of implicit dress codes from at least two cultural contexts: middle-class Mexican and Hollywood American. Each context offers its own stereotypical coding of proper and improper dress, and each offers an implied narrative of the woman's destiny as ciphered in her choice of clothes. In *Barbarella*, the two narratives play off against each other, each opening a space for commentary on the vagaries of female dress and on the shared affinity in both Mexican and U.S. cultural settings for encouraging girls to play with dolls and to play with themselves as if they were just life-size Barbies. Thus, an exaggerated Shirley Temple mode of dress provides the young girl with the rewards of familial approval while allowing her to retain an ironic distance from her own style of presentation. Likewise, the aggressively rebellious implications of rock singer clothing become part of a code tacitly understood by the narrator and the reader and intentionally incomprehensible to the mainstream manifestations of either Mexican or U.S. culture, where Madonna(s) are always blond Barbies and Barbarellas.

In this manner Conde's protagonist demonstrates how an exaggerated performance of femininity—whether through childlike bows or tight bustiers—points to a deplorable internationalization of pop culture bad taste in which the worst of U.S. cultural models serve as visual signs of a Mexican woman's "stepping across the line" in both senses of the phrase, and with all the double charge of negativity and forward action that Derrida uncovers in his discussion. At the same time, and more importantly, Barbarella also reminds us how a performative attitude infuses clothing style with ideological content. She says of her clothes: "They intimidate whoever looks at me and they force him to swallow his thoughts because the sensual intimidates and *attacks*" (1993, 73–74). This perception of an edgily violent dimension of sensuality, one that women can manipulate to attack men rather than the reverse, gives overt form to a conflict that elsewhere in the collection is expressed more often in barbed comments, suggestive silences, and subtle rebellions against the status quo.

Frequently, though, for these women on the road, powerlessness and empowerment equally turn on questions of self-presentation and on the aggressive rereading and reinterpretation of a specific style. One of the most dazzlingly accomplished stories in the collection, "Rice and Chains," utilizes the metaphor of knitting and mimics a woman's thoughts as she knits a sweater for her unborn child. As Sergio Elizondo notes in his introduction to the English translation of the collection, the narrative technique in this story has a deliberate—and deliberative— monotony about it that simulates the placid activity it describes. At the same time, "we come to realize that the stitch that goes 'backwards,' the purling stitch, reveals that the protagonist also takes steps backwards; then, by knitting a few more stitches, she advances" (1994a, 17). Knitting, then, is not just a typically female task, but also serves as a way of silently coming to a greater understanding of the narrative of a human life as well as a concrete embodiment for that activity. It too, then, concerns itself with a metaphorical "stepping across the line." In this complementary and counterpunctual activity of knitting and purling, Conde not only signals the strange shape of an embodied language, but also continually foregrounds its gendered quality. Knitting can stand for gender oppression, and the lulling process of setting stitches smoothes over the unhappy circumstances described, until at last we are pulled up short with a telling metaphor: "Isn't your knitting like your mother's life? Everything's made up of rice stitches and chains; stitches to the right, back stitches, loops, knots. Rice when she got married, chains in her marriage, knots in her throat" (1994a, 28). Rice, chains, and knots symbolize a woman's life and her entrapment in the repressive discourse that harms her. In evoking her mother's story, the narrator, a single mother-to-be, signals the deep spiritual wounding of a Mexican woman living with repressive customs. Trinh T. Minh-ha comments, in words that seem equally applicable to Conde's aesthetic, and also capture the back-and-forth motion of a woman's painful unlearning of institutionalized tropes as she works toward a more liberating language: "In trying to tell something, a woman is told, shredding herself into opaque words while her voice dissolves on the walls of silence. . . . And often [she] cannot *say* it. You try and keep on trying to unsay it, for if you don't, they will not fail to fill in the blanks on your behalf, and you will be said" (1989, 79–80). Conde, however, differs from Trinh, for while she impresses upon us the potent image of the marriage chains and the knotted throat, her work also imagines an alternative to the mother's silencing. Silent herself, the daughter recognizes the fact of her mother's oppression, and through her own coming to terms with her knitting allows us to see in this womanly task an unlikely process for working through a liberating discourse.

In this way, the words that wound and silence women, and that women use to wound and silence themselves, have an ambiguously empowering outlet by which the young woman is able to reevaluate her own life in the light of her mother's and to move toward a more conscious and empowered position. The young woman in this story, thus, imagines herself in the context of a textured, knitted language, and in the projected embodiment of the next child in this knotted text, her own baby. While retaining from her mother's repressed world the silent and seemingly inoffensive practice of knitting, the younger woman uses that occupation as a strategy to situate herself on the borders of a different way of imagining that knitted text of a woman's life.

Still further: through the powerful image of a marriage characterized by "knots in her throat" of a woman who finds refuge in what hurt her, and of another, unmarried mother-to-be who uses the knotting threads as a silent reproach to masculinist constructions of narrative, Conde implicitly questions the Enlightenment heritage of a mind–body split and also outlines the far more radical question about the nature of representation itself. As Butler says of Irigaray, in words roughly applicable to the Mexican border writer, "Irigaray would maintain, however, that the feminine 'sex' is a point of linguistic *absence*, the impossibility of a grammatically denoted substance, and, hence the point of view that exposes that substance as an abiding and foundational illusion of a masculinist discourse" (1990, 10). Substance, in these stories, is an abiding illusion, one ideologically charged by an unexpected performative, just as illusion offers a foundational reality for self-reinvention. Both alternatives involve a conscious self-presentation that may be deeply estranged from the home (as in the sketches from *En la tarima* and in Barbarella's hip rebellion against her family mores), or, in "Rice and Chains," the coming to awareness of a practice of repression from within that repressive structure.

"My Birthday Gift" revolves around a busy husband who leaves his wife a check and a note "in which he wished me a happy birthday and assured me, 'not without a certain perverse pleasure,' that the check was to be used to buy myself 'some lingerie' " (1994a, 43). The wife takes umbrage, seeing the ostensible gift to her as in fact a gift to him, intended for his pleasure. The sister, on the other hand, reinterprets the gift as a way for the husband to show his appreciation of his wife, to enhance *her* pleasure (1994a, 45). Each of these alternative interpretations is plausible, and each fits into a certain, well-traveled domestic economy. Conde once again takes a further step, one that crosses the line. The story ends, not with a resolution of this counterpoint between these two homey alternatives, but with an ambiguity that suggests a third, more "perverse" interpretation. The wife arrives home, strips, and steps into the shower, only to discover her husband already there. Here is the last sentence of the story: "Finally, I threw my stockings on the bed and stepped into the shower naked, surprising Gustavo, who smiled, delighted, with my lace panties in his hands" (1994a, 47). Is Gustavo delighted because his wife is, as he imagines, offering herself for his pleasure? Or is the sister's interpretation more accurate? Or, equally likely, does Conde's delicate initial suggestion of a streak of perversity in the husband hint that his pleasure is found not in his wife, but in his wife's lingerie, which he enjoys as fetish objects or as the core of a transvestite wardrobe? The point, I think, is not to decide among these alternatives—though to my mind the body of Conde's work convincingly demands of its readers unhomely readings of unhomely situations—but rather to open out the ideological spaces by virtue of which dislocation and borderness themselves become interpretative categories.

Other stories also turn on a conscious manipulation of stereotypical expectations about male–female relationships. In "Do You Work or Go to School," both Miguel Angel, the sales manager at the narrator's job, and the narrator's boyfriend, Antonio, manipulate the rhetoric of feminism in the service of ends that support male privilege. Miguel Angel "laid on a line about women's liberation: that I was intelligent, self-confident, and super sexy. . . . He lays it all on me and proposes that I go take modeling classes in San Diego" (1994a, 31). When she tells Antonio about this suggestion, the boyfriend "starts on his women's liberation line, the exact opposite of Miguel Angel's. He started telling me how women become objects, things to be used, and how models are the worst thing about the capitalist system." (1994a, 32). In each case, the men's motive is exploitation; reading one against the other tells us exactly in which mode. Antonio, who tells the narrator that women become objects through modeling, is concerned because he does not want to lose the comfortable woman-object he has been enjoying for his sexual pleasure. Miguel Angel, who tells her that she is sexy and independent, eventually exploits her as the company prostitute to soften up potential investors. In this respect, the warnings of both men are very much on the mark. The narrator's eventual conclusion, however, once again shifts the discussion to surprising grounds. The rhetoric of liberation does not serve her, she finds, as the world is controlled by men, "and look! while guys don't come to some agreement as to what liberation is, well, we'll be going to hell, because they fix things to their advantage." Her decision is to astutely play the system against itself, refusing to participate any longer in this self-serving rhetoric. Instead, she uses a particular performative enunciation of her femininity to her gain:

> That's why now, when I meet a guy and he asks me, "Do you work or go to school?" I answer, like some bimbo, "Oh, gee, I don't work or go to school!" because that's what they want, idiotic little women who won't think and aren't economically self-sufficient.
> They're finally paying for *everything*. (1994a, 36)

Once again in this story, as in *Barbarella*, sensuality *attacks*, creating an unfamiliar, dislocated space for a feminist intervention in the unlikely staging of a helpless femininity. In each case, awareness of the undercurrents of language and of the shifting ideological frames allows the women in these stories to use men's strategies and expectations against them.

Conde puts us all, puts herself as well, in the position of observers upon these strange and familiar scenes, and the fact of our reading, writing, and thinking about them identifies us ineluctably as outsiders to that space. To some degree her stories rely for their effect upon an implicit bond between the reader and the narrator involving a shared understanding and a shared quirky humor about social representations, a reader–narrator complicity that requires the exclusion of each society's typical self-imaginings. Conde's intimate exploration of the Tijuana underworld, for example, is not a knowledge she can expect all her readers to share; however, we as readers are aligned with the liminal characters in her stories. More broadly, as a border writer, she is displaced by definition with respect to mainstream Mexican concepts of themselves. Monsiváis, in an ambiguously tongue-in-cheek taxonomy of Mexico's self-definition, lists eight different variations on how to imagine the "provinces" in central Mexican thought, among which he includes the northern border states as a provincial entity characterized by international cultural shock and the commercialization of nationalism: "en la frontera norte la mexicanidad es, a un tiempo, selección de lo entrañable, coraza defensiva y disfraz esporádico," 'on the northern border Mexicanness is, at the same time, the choice of the intimate, a defensive shell, and a sporadic disguise' (1992, 201–202). Although Monsiváis's descriptions are meant to be provocative, it is precisely this corrosive attention to marginality as essence, shell, or disguise that is one of the hallmarks of Conde's prose, whether in her oddly inflected domestic scenes or her nuanced portraits of women from the border underworld. Our illusion of complicity with her—of a joke or a delicately phrased insight shared—is undercut by the shifting positionalities of characters and narrators in the borderlands she limns.

I am tempted to end my discussion at precisely this point. However, that would be to ignore the central problem haunting this reading of Conde's work. Strikingly enough, although it seems to me that it is this distancing element that is most likely to earn Conde additional readers in this country, such an appropriation of her work, like this paper, tends to organize itself neatly around theoretical concerns that Conde—unfortunately—might well reject. Her border is not, finally, contained in or defined by Derrida's or Apter's border metaphor, nor by Bhabha's academic homelessness. If indeed the theoretical structure of U.S. literary theory has a long historical connection to thought elaborated through the crucible of displacement and exile (perhaps the same could be said of the most influential variants of French theory as well: thinkers like Derrida, Kristeva, Todorov, and Cixous all carry with them impressive border-crossing credentials as displaced intellectuals), then those elements are precisely the ones that allow us to naturalize Conde within that literary–theoretical establishment without questioning its boundaries. Like Carlos Monsiváis, whose meditations on the central Mexican–northern border axis served as the frame for this paper, Eduardo Barrera has commented on the strangely circular construction of much theorizing on border issues. Referring to one of the most prominent performers of "borderness" for U.S. and European audiences—Mexico City native Guillermo Gómez Peña—Barrera writes: "Gómez Peña fabricates his border by drinking from the same theoretical watering holes as the academics who test their arguments with his texts. This quasi-incestuous relationship has turned into a vicious circle that excludes primary referents. Gómez-Peña's border turns into the Border of . . . Homi Bhabha" (1995, 152). Rosina Conde, too, has commented on the alienation of the border from itself in these cultural productions. Conde was one of the members of the Border Arts Work-shop/Taller de Arte Fronterizo, founded by Gómez Peña. She tells Tabuenca Córdoba in a 1994 interview that she left the workshop, how-ever, because "they wanted to present a border art much different from ours, but this was not a problem. . . . The problem was that they wanted to impose their will. They wanted to turn us into pseudo-Chicanos/as, or into a fronterizo/a that did not represent us" (1995–1996, 164).

Conde and Barrera put their finger on precisely the problem that exer-cises me here, and to which I confess to having no solution. Although imaginatively we can shift our positions, aligning ourselves with Conde's characters and, with a complicitous wink, pretending to step outside both the U.S. and the Mexican mainstream cultural establishments, in fact the presuppositions we bring to our readings inexorably shape our under-standing of them. Neil Larsen poses the conundrum eloquently in his recent book tracing the intersection of North American Latin American-ists and Latin American writing:

> Writing and reading "North by South" has had continually to pose the question of its own authority. Even the most exoticist of gazes presupposes the exotic as an object whose legitimacy must be at least equal to the domestic. Thus, in directing its attention elsewhere, the North necessarily concedes something about its own sense of identity and authority, its own position on the hermeneutic map. The question of the *object's* legitimacy— why read *this* and not something else?—cannot finally be detached from the question of *self*-legitimization: what, at the outset, authorizes or justifies the subject as the reader/writer of this object? (1995, 3)

Larsen's question brings us directly into the realm of the ideological and cultural biases encrypted in the literary canon. He suggests, for exam-ple, that the Boom writers of the 1960s and 1970s became an interna-tional academic phenomenon partly because non-Latin American Latin Americanists found the Boom amenable to readings in which a Euro-pean High Modernist aesthetic coincided fortuitously with a sensibility made acute in opposition to the U.S. involvement in the Vietnam War.

I suspect that the Rosina Conde who resisted being turned into a Gómez Peña/Homi Bhabha pseudo-Chicana nostalgic for a universaliz-ing, utopic, abstract borderness, is equally careful in her stories to resist cooption into another version of the North's hermeneutic map. The unsettling edginess of her stories, the slipperiness of terms and position-alities represent the first place to search for such traces of resistance. In these powerful texts, it is through Conde's reinscription of concepts of gender right that she exposes the weakness and bias of much Mexican, Chicano, and mainstream U.S. theoretical meditations on borders.

NOTES

1. (Hilda) Rosina Conde (Zambada) (b. Mexicali, 1954) is the author of the short story/novella collections *Embotellado de origen* (*Bottled at the Source*, 1994), *El agente secreto* (*The Secret Agent*, 1990), *En la tarima* (*On the Platform*, 1984), *De infancia y adolescencia* (*Of Infancy and Adolescence*, 1982), *Arrieras somos. . . .* (trans. as *Women on the Road. . . .*, 1994). There is a considerable overlap among stories in the collections. She has also published several volumes of poetry: *Poemas de seducción* (*Poems of Seduction*, 1981), *Bolereando el llanto* (*Crying to Boleros*, 1993), *De Amor gozoso* (*textículos*) (*On Pleasurable Love: Texticules*, 1991), has worked in theater: "Cuarto asalto" ("Fourth Assault"; the fourth act of a collaborative play entitled *En esta esquina* [*On this Corner*]), has written a novel, *Genara* (1998), and is coauthor of *Below San Onofre* (1992). It would be impossible to study all her works in this short space, so I will concentrate here on short stories drawn from two collections: *En la tarima* and *Women on the Road. . . .*

2. Barrón Salido (1995) is referring to a specific report on the situation in Tijuana. She quotes Martín de la Rosa's extensive list of marginal persons: "Vamos a ocuparnos en este apartado de los peones, los albañiles, meseros, lavacoches, periodiqueros, las 'marías,' los que 'ya volvieron del otro lado' (metedólares), los que 'quieren ir al otro lado,' las empleadas domésticas, las 'que lavan ajeno,' los yonkeros, los 'cholos,' los barrenderos, los artesanos, los vendedores ambulantes, . . . los desocupados," 'We are going to concern ourselves in this report with the peons, the construction workers, the waiters, the car washers, the newspaper sellers, the indigenous women workers, those who came back from the other side, those who want to go to the other side, the servants, the washerwomen, the junkies, the gang members, the street sweepers, the handicraft makers, the street salespeople, the unemployed.'

3. Apter is referring to Homi Bhabha's coinage of the word "unhomely" as a way of rethinking Freud's classic study of the "Unheimlich" (usually translated as the "uncanny"). For Bhabha, the postcolonial critic/writer's experience of the unhomely follows from "the estranging sense of the relocation of the home and the world in an unhallowed place" and he describes it as a common feature in border culture, in exile literature, and in third world literature in general: "In the stirrings of the unhomely, another world becomes visible. It has less to do with forcible eviction and more to do with the uncanny literary and social effects of enforced social accommodation, or historical migrations and cultural relocations. The home does not remain the domain of domestic life, nor does the world simply become its social or historical counterpart. The unhomely is the shock of recognition of the world-in-the-home, the home-in-the-world" (1992, 141).

4. The titillating anomaly of the virgin–whore follows directly from ambiguous legal status of prostitution in Mexico. Federal law makes procuring illegal, but does not proscribe prostitution per se. The result, as Barrón Salido notes, is that establishments "hide" their most notorious function: "únicamente no se registra

como actividad económica, aún cuando se presenta de manera abierta," 'it is just ignored as an economic activity, even when it occurs in an open manner.' One consequence is an inevitable spillover of function and of public perception. Because the prostitutional economy is "hidden," there is tendency to assume that all women who work in such places are necessarily prostitutes (1995, 39).

WORKS CITED

Apter, Emily. 1995. "Comparative Exile: Competing Margins in the History of Comparative Literature." In *Comparative Literature in the Age of Multiculturalism*, ed. Charles Bernheimer, 86–96. Baltimore, MD: Johns Hopkins University Press.

Barrera, Eduardo. 1995. "Apropriación y tutelaje del la frontera norte." *Puentelibre, revista de literatura* 4 (Spring): 13–17.

Barrón Salido, Patricia. 1995. *Las "María Magdalena": El oficio de la prostitución y su estrategia colectiva de vida*. Draft of bachelor's thesis. Tijuana: Colegio de la Frontera Norte.

Bhabha, Homi. 1992. "The World and the Home." *Social Text* 10: 141–153.

Butler, Judith. 1990. *Gender Trouble: Feminism and the Subversion of Identity*. New York: Routledge.

Conde, Rosina. 1984. *En la tarima*. Mexico: Universidad Autónoma Metropolitana.

———. 1994a. *Arrieras somos. . . .* Culiacán: DIFOCUR. Trans. as *Women on the Road. . . .*, ed. Gustavo V. Segade, intro. Sergio D. Elizondo. San Diego, CA: San Diego State University Press.

———. 1994b. *Embotellado de origen*. Aguascalientes: Instituto Cultural de Aguascalientes.

Derrida, Jacques. 1993. *Aporias*. Trans. Thomas Dutoit. Stanford, CA: Stanford University Press.

Larsen, Neil. 1995. *Reading "North by South": On Latin American Literature, Culture, and Politics*. Minneapolis: University of Minnesota Press.

Menocal, María Rosa. 1994. *Shards of Love: Exile and the Origins of the Lyric*. Durham, NC: Duke University Press.

Monsiváis, Carlos. 1994. "De la cultura mexicana en vísperas del TLC." In *La educación y la cultura ante el Tratado de Libre Comercio*, ed. Julio López, Gilberto Guevara Niebla, and Néstor García Canclini, 189–209. Mexico: Nueva Imagen.

Paz, Octavio. 1961. *Labyrinth of Solitude*. Trans. Lysander Kemp. New York: Grove.

Rangel Gómez, Gudelia. 1996. Untitled, manuscript.

Tabuenca Córdoba, María-Socorro. 1995–1996. "Viewing the Border: Perspectives from 'The Open Wound.' " *Discourse* 18, nos. 1–2: 146–168.

Trinh T. Minh-ha. 1989. *Woman, Native, Other: Writing Postcoloniality and Feminism*. Bloomington and Indianapolis: Indiana University Press.

Trujillo Muñoz, Gabriel. 1990. "La literatura bajacaliforniana contemporánea: El punto de vista femenino." In *Mujer y literatura mexicana y chicana: culturas en contacto*, Vol. 2, ed. Aralia López González, Amelia Malagamba and Elena Urrutia, 177–187. Tijuana: Colegio de la Frontera Norte.

Wittig, Monique. 1985. "The Mark of Gender." *Feminist Issues* 5: 3–12.

10

The Postmodern Hybrid

Do Aliens Dream of Alien Sheep?

Rolando Romero

> **To put [multicultural] concerns into a future (or to locate them in a past) is a classic technique of displacing social "problems."**
>
> Sneja Gunew, "Denaturalizing Cultural Nationalisms: Multicultural Readings of 'Australia'"

ritics have labeled Ridley Scott's *Blade Runner* (1982) the quintessential postmodern film. The plot—set in 2019 Los Angeles—centers around an enslaved group of replicants or humanoids who have escaped from an off-world colony. Laws declare illegal their presence on earth and thus police hire twenty-first-century bounty hunter Rick Deckard (called Blade Runner, played by Harrison Ford) to destroy—or, in the parlance of the film, "retire"—the replicants. The studio changed Scott's original conception of the film as represented in the work print after sneak previews in Denver and Dallas showed that the public did not appreciate the gloomy possibility that Deckard himself might be a humanoid (Kerman 1991, 141). In the San Diego sneak preview, the studio tested a less gloomy ending, which included a voice-over narration

This chapter is a revised version of an article by the same title that originally appeared in the journal *PostScript* 16 (fall 1996): 41–52. Reprinted by permission of *PostScript*.

by the main character. The final version (dubbed by Paul M. Sammon as the domestic cut) released by the studio did not include a sequence in which Deckard dreams of a unicorn in a forest. The last scene shows Deckard and Rachel (Sean Young) flying into the sunset in a hovercraft, although in another version, the script concluded with Deckard taking Rachel out of the city and then, revealing the misogynist strand of film-making, killing her, purportedly so she would not be killed by the police. The distributor pulled out the film from general release when, even with the addition of the happy ending, it still did not fare well commercially. Placed by the studio directly on the secondary markets, the film acquired cult standing. In 1991 the studio released the director's cut. Scott negotiated with the studios to have his original ending restored.[1] The director's cut ends with Deckard and Rachel stepping into the elevator after seeing the origami unicorn built by Gaff.

The studio's cutting of the unicorn sequence in the domestic cut, however, effectively eliminated the structural role Gaff (Edward James Olmos) plays in the film. Repeatedly, Gaff visually hints at the significance of the scenes in the film by building origami figures. Gaff builds the figure of a chicken when Deckard hesitates to accept the Blade Runner assignment. Later when Deckard searches Leon's hotel room, Gaff constructs the figure of a man with an erection, foreshadowing Deckard's and Rachel's physical relationship.

Gaff builds a third figure of a unicorn—the innocent beast lured into a trap by the "purity" of a virgin helping the captors. The unicorn sequence charges Gaff with the structural role of indicating to the audiences the possibility that the naïve Deckard might himself be a replicant:

> The motivation of this unicorn sequence became clear in the final scenes. Gaff leaves behind an origami unicorn, indicating that he knows Deckard's private memories, and the only way this could possibly happen would be if Deckard was a replicant with all his memories nothing more than artificial transplants. (Instrell 1992, 164)

The director's cut clarifies the meaning of the unicorn by leading the audience to believe that Gaff's memories have been implanted on Deckard. The characters' sharing of memories would not only explain Gaff's sympathy toward the couple's relationship, it would also explain why Gaff decides not to pursue Rachel and Deckard.

What were the structural consequences of erasing the unicorn sequence from the final cut? Contemporary audiences perceive Olmos as the archetype of the Chicano character because of his roles in such noted Chicano canonical films as *Zoot Suit* (1982), *The Ballad of Gregorio Cortez* (1983), and *Stand and Deliver* (1988). Thus the studio effectively erased the Chicano/a presence by erasing Gaff's structural role in the first release where Olmos's character functioned as a synecdoche for the Chicano/a population. Olmos's character does not exist in Philip K. Dick's original *Do Androids Dream of Electric Sheep?* (1982) Hampton Fancher, the original scriptwriter, introduced the character and, as he states, "I made him part Mexican because I'm partly Chicano myself" (Sammon 1996, 113). Edward James Olmos subsequently played a large part in developing and fine-tuning the character. Paul Sammon considers Gaff one of the most memorable characters, though, as Edward James Olmos explained to him, "Gaff was so undefined, I was making him up as we went along." Olmos further explains to Sammon:

> First I asked Ridley if I could embellish the character, make him more interesting to the audience. Ridley respected me enough as an artist to trust me with building up an entire history for Gaff. So the back story I came up with was that Gaff was primarily Mexican-Japanese, and that his lineage in America stretched back at least five generations. Gaff was quite proud of that, as well as the sense of his past culture. (1996, 113)

David Peoples, the second scriptwriter Ridley Scott hired to polish Fancher's script, fine-tuned Gaff's character further. Peoples

> created a certain personality for him in order to allow Gaff to express a whole bunch of expository material. Gaff was looking for a promotion and always badgering Deckard about his personal appearance in my scripts. And in the course of all this badgering, he'd tell some of the story to the audience.
>   . . . I felt Gaff's exposition wasn't in any way dull or boring; it was coming from a character who really had an agenda, and it was disguised within this agenda. (Sammon 1996, 114–115)

It is also probable that the director did not deem the Chicano presence important because he had originally planned to film in England. When first filmed, "the street scenes were created on the New York Street set at the Burbank Studios" (Kerman 1991, 186). To add to the location confusion, the *Blade Runner* term is credited to William Burroughs, who secured the rights to a story by Alan Nourse with the same title. In Burroughs's ultimate welfare state, the blade runners were smugglers and runners who would take "the actual drugs, instruments and equipment from the suppliers to the clients and doctors and underground clinics" (Burroughs 1994, n.p.). Burroughs's dystopia associates the "minorities" with decay from the very first sentence:

> Now B.J. you are asking me to tell you in one sentence what this film is about?. . . For starters it's about plain middle-class middle-income bracket Joe, the $15,000-a-year boy, sweating out two jobs, I.R.S. wringing the moon-light dollars out of him to keep the niggers and the spics on welfare and Medicare so they can keep up their strength to mug his grandmother, rape his sister, and bugger his ten-year-old son. (1994, n.p.)

Burroughs sets his *Blade Runner, A Movie* in a Manhattan of the future where mainland Puerto Ricans and African Americans serve the author as props to characterize his American dystopia.

Although critics could argue that the *Blade Runner* script does not include more Chicano/as merely because the story takes place in the Los Angeles Chinatown, the representation of a future Los Angeles that obliterates a great majority of the population is inconceivable. I argue that the studio's ambivalence in releasing the two film versions in fact also reflects an ambivalence toward the Los Angeles Latino/a population, which the discourse of the dominant culture would want to render invisible and nonexistent or, at least, as alien.

My argument as to the causes of this ambivalence goes far beyond material explanations of why the studio or the director opted for different versions. The ambivalence of the ending and of the structural role of Latino/as in the film reflects postmodernism's ambivalence toward hybridity itself. It is not coincidental that *Blade Runner*, as the "quintessential postmodern film" would also show indeterminacy toward the representation of the most visible population in the California landscape.

Critics consider the film a classic of postmodernism no doubt thanks to the director's dystopian vision of the Los Angeles in the year 2019—"a city in the not-very-distant future of Western capitalism" (Kerman 1991, 16). *Blade Runner* turns the earth into a planetary run-down inner city, with "demonic scene[s] of flaming towers, acid rain [suggesting atmospheric changes], and streets jammed with characters in a contemporary *Inferno*" (1991, 42). David Desser compares the Los Angeles of *Blade Runner* with Milton's hell in *Paradise Lost:*

> A Dungeon horrible, on all sides round
> As one great Furnace flam'd, yet from those flames
> No light, but rather darkness visible
> Serve'd only to discover sight of woe,
> Regions of sorrow, doleful shades, where peace
> And rest can never dwell, hope never comes
> That comes to all; but torture without end
> Still urges, and a fiery Deluge, fed
> With ever-burning Sulphur unconsumed. (I: 61–69)

Another critic refers to the city as a Hades (Kerman 171). The people able to afford it "emigrated to the Off-World Colonies, and yet the streets swarm with Orientals, Hispanics and punks" (Kerman 1991, 17). Society has completely fragmented, and as evidenced by the emphasis on the eyes (the green eye of the opening sequence, the owl, the Voight-Kampff test, the photographs, Decker's Esper machine, Chow's laboratory, Tyrell's own death), only the ever-present state control (represented by police vehicles and computers) can reestablish a social order. The film also borrows heavily from the tradition of the private eye film noire and, at least according to one critic, from Roman Polanski's *Chinatown*. As Kerman has noted, Deckard's and Tyrell's privileged panoramic position establishes the relationship between control and the ability to see. Kerman goes as far as to establish that "Tyrell even looks a bit like the Nazi Angel of Death, Dr. Joseph Mengele" (1991, 23). The Esper machine that Deckard uses also allows for the ultimate analysis of any picture taken in by the eye. It is clear from the commentaries that the film uses the mix of ethnicities to suggest the decrepitude of the future Los Angeles:

> In *Blade Runner*, race is structured into the film in both the traditional and the science fictional aspects of the issue. This futuristic Los Angeles is densely populated by a swarming mass of humanity, with a noticeable majority of Orientals, Latinos (the neon lights of a downtown Spanish-language movie theater flash prominently near J.F. Sebastian's apartment) and a smattering of Mediterranean types. The streets are also filled with a variety of midgets, punks and decadent revelers (the latter among the few Caucasians). In fact, the sight of a white person is rare enough . . . for the replicant, Pris, to ask Sebastian why he hasn't emigrated off-world. (1991, 111)

The film portrays visions of the possibilities of cultural contact with the Other. The subliminal need for "space" is another coded message to the dominant culture that sees itself pushed out by the "overbreeding" of the migrant. This fear explains the usage of the replicants as metaphors for oppressed groups who historically have been subjected to exploitation, enslavement, and extermination, and who have been deprived of such human rights as life, liberty, and the pursuit of happiness (Kerman 1991, 9). Clearly the film racializes the replicants as minorities: The viewer is told that the term "skin job" replaces the word "nigger" (1991, 27). In the final scene in which Batty and Deckard square off, Batty "strips down like a Comanche warrior in a kind of tribal ritual" (1991, 168). "The replicants' association with people of color, with the masses at street level, and with frightful sexuality, implicate the dehumanization process necessary at the political level to call forth the possibility of genocide" (1991, 115).[2]

Because Ridley Scott came to direct the film after the success of the 1980 top grossing *Alien*, it is also hard not to view the replicants as subliminal metaphors for the California undocumented workers, especially taking into account that Philip K. Dick lived and worked in Santa Ana, California (the servants' quarters of Orange County). Paul Sammon's subsection "The T-Shirt War" details the ultimate irony, if not explanation, of Scott's sympathy toward the replicants. According to Sammon, Scott had mentioned to a British newspaper that he found it frustrating to work in the United States because the crew often second-guessed his decisions. British crews, on the other hand, would perform as instructed with the words "Yes, Guv'nor." When members of the U.S. crew read the article, they had T-shirts made with the words " 'Yes Guv'nor, My Ass" to wear on the set. Scott and a couple of the producers responded by also having T-shirts made with the words "Xenophobia Sucks" (1996, 218).

The representation of the replicant as alien is also textualized in the film. One of the characters in Dick's *Do Androids Dream of Electric Sheep?* calls the replicants "illegal aliens" (Dick 1982, 119). When Leon and Roy enter the eye shop, Chew tells them: "You not come here! Illegal!" On one of the *faux* newsstands in the set, "The cover of another magazine sported an in joke; a blurb for an article entitled 'Illegal Aliens,' bylined by one 'Ridley Scott' " (Sammon 1996, 104).

In the penultimate scene of the film, as Deckard hangs from the rooftop, Batty tells him: "Quite an experience to live in fear. That's what it is to be a slave." Batty's remarks subtly refer to the illegal immigrant constantly besieged by the threat of being turned in to the Immigration Service. The film depicts the replicants as indistinguishable from their human counterparts, except for their physical perfection and their limited life span. The four-year life span might also be the ultimate dream for a society that uses and abuses the undocumented worker with minimum wages, and would want to discard them before the workplace abuse leads to the use of social services. In the film's earth, only the hybrids remain: the androids, the minorities, the outcast. It is this vision of despair that is intermingled in the plot. The hybrid cop will let the protagonist escape with his humanoid lover because he understands hybridity.

The film also speaks unmistakably to the American dream. Batty quotes William Blake's poem, "America: A Prophecy," which uses the American Revolution as an allegory for personal freedom and independence, according to Kolb (Kerman 1991, 160):

> Fiery the angels rose, and as they rose deep thunder rolled
> Around their shores; indignant burning with the fires of Orc. (Blake 1979, 116)

But Batty changes the poem to read "fiery the angels fell." Instrell believes that "the single alteration from 'rose' to 'fell' completely inverts Blake's original references to the rise of the American democratic Revolution and suggests instead its ultimate demise" (1992, 167). The film allegorizes the demise of the American dream by having the story take place in the Thanksgiving month of November. There is no mistaking the fact that the film attempts to portray the American dream gone awry, especially taking into account the genre of private eye films:

> Most of the characters in L.A. private eye fiction have come to California from somewhere else, often from sleepily innocent Midwestern towns, searching for the new Eden which Los Angeles advertised itself as being. California allowed the immigrants to cast aside their perceived failures and dare to hope for a new beginning, "the myth of a future." (Kerman 1991, 189)

The film puts to rest the myth of the East–West expansion as the ultimate story of doom. The west lies in outer space, now that the minorities have taken over California. Instrell writes:

> Similarly, racism seems to underlie the ethnic composition of the figures in the picture, with its "normal" white hero, and white power figures, contrasted with the large number of exotic, mainly Asian, proletarians of the underclass inhabiting the city. This can all too easily be read as reflecting a white Anglo-Saxon fear of the Western cities of the future being overrun by foreigners of a different skin color. (1992, 169)

The visions of the postmodern dystopia are no doubt helped by the director's previous work directing television commercials for Hovis and Levi Jeans. These visions are also present in *Blade Runner* with the ever-present Coke billboard over the city of Los Angeles.

Hybridity in *Blade Runner* is represented also by Olmos's persona and previous "ethnic" identification. The script quite obviously characterizes the traits of the replicants by their names. Rachel, the replicant with whom Deckard will eventually fall in love, reincarnates the biblical wife of Israel in the Old Testament, the mother of a culture that will rule the Earth: thus Deckard escapes "into a new Eden with a new Eve, hoping to regain at least a personal paradise" (Kerman 1991, 51). Leon Kowalski, by profession a nuclear waste engineer, is the instinctual beast that readily kills in self-defense. Not coincidentally his degree of intelligence and his profession fit the viewers' prejudices about ethnic stereotypes. Pris, the "pleasure model" clearly brings to the surface the ideas that the original French word connotes: "capture, prize, taken." Roy Batty, the bright bad boy and Aryan Superman, represents the original fallen angel.

Thus the viewer can also assume that the word "Gaff" highlights the character's traits. The British define "gaff" as "a public place of entertainment, especially a cheap or disreputable music hall or theater." Additionally, the dictionary defines gaff as "a clumsy social error; a faux pas; a blatant mistake or misjudgment." The word, originally derived from the French, translates into Spanish as "metida de pata." The production notes describe Gaff as "a man of the future, a multilingual bureaucrat with Oriental skin, Japanese eyes, and blue irises. He is an intellectual and a sartorial dandy" (Kerman 1991, 156):

> "Gaff was originally a very minor character in my early scripts," explains Hampton Fancher [the original scriptwriter]. "I's just glommed onto a real word—a 'gaffe' or a mistake—and then came up with a character to match that. I made him part Mexican because I'm partly Chicano myself. Eddie Olmos and David Peoples are the ones who really fleshed him out."
> (Sammon 1996, 113)

Clearly, the audience will perceive Olmos as both director and scriptwriter intended. The filmmakers obviously used Olmos's screen persona to convey the intentions of the script through Gaff, the quintessential figure of the hybrid character.[3]

The filmmakers also obliterated Spanish, the language of the hybrid, from the film. Although other languages are used in *Blade Runner* (German, for example, spoken by a street gang in the scene in which Deckard is about to enter Sebastian's apartment; Chinese, in the scene at the noodle bar; Mandarin in Chew's shop; Urdu in Ben-Hassan's shop), Spanish is conspicuously absent from the film (except in the Marquee of the Million Dollar Movie Theater that shows films in Spanish). Again, although Gaff uses "cityspeak"—a sort of future caló composed by combining the languages spoken in California: Spanish, English, Chinese—Spanish is nowhere to be heard. In fact the script at one point called for the usage of Chicano caló in the film, but the sequence was also cut from the final versions. In the film, even the elevators speak with forked tongues—the elevator in Tyrell's building counts in six different languages; the elevator in Deckard's apartment thanks him in two languages. And yet, whether covertly or subliminally, the film suggests the Chicano/a presence by the architecture of the retrofitted buildings that resemble Mayan pyramids or by the Mayan motifs of Deckard's apartment.

The erasure of hybridity is also textualized in the film. The director visually keeps the audiences off balance by framing the characters, not centered, but screen left or screen right. The erasure of the Chicano/Latino population through the cutting of the unicorn segment also clearly is apparent in the killing of Zhora and Leon in the public square, the space that accommodates most of the minorities represented in the film. Scott described the scene:

> The hundreds of extras reflect the wide variety of people found in this future Times Square—soldiers from many countries, Asian peasants, hard-core punks and slumming society folks. (Kerman 1991, 163)

One of the critics believes that "the thronging population of the streets and the commercial signs suggest a tidal wave of immigration from the Third World" (Kerman 1991, 202). In a scene of total chaos, Zhora runs out of the club trying to escape her pursuer. The Blade Runner will eventually shoot her in the shoulder, and the audience will be exposed to the scene in slow motion from different angles as Zhora crumbles, breaking the panes of glass in the display windows, ultimately resembling one of the store mannequins. Symptomatically, the scene takes place in the sight of everyone, but no one really pays attention to the fact that Deckard pursues Zhora with a gun. People seem unconcerned for their own safety, because no one gets out of the way. Nor is Deckard concerned about the other bystanders, because he does not hesitate to fire his weapon and risk the possibility of injuring innocent people. The shooting is obviously intended as a spectacle of justice, similar to public hangings or tortures. It is intended to arrest the possibility of dissent. And there is no doubt as to who will be the recipient of that message: the minorities who dare to cross the line, who dare to question the status quo.

Blade Runner's existential exploration of hybridity and its "postmodern" quality, in essence, go hand in hand. Although characterizations of postmodernism vary, Rick Instrell believes that the postmodernism of the film stems largely from a stylistic excess that provides the public with surfaces on which to exercise its cultural knowledge: "This illustrates a key feature of post-modern texts, the deliberate construction of a 'double reader,' one 'naïve' and the other 'smart.' Intertextuality then becomes the key method for engaging the 'smart' reader in this play upon 'encyclopedic competence' " (1992, 168).

The association of hybridity with postmodernism is commonplace. Néstor García Canclini's *Culturas híbridas: Estrategias para entrar y salir de la modernidad* (1990) stands as the most salient example of the proximity of the two issues. Although postcolonial theorists, such as Homi Bhabha, Marie Louise Pratt, and José Rabasa, also have engaged this issue, because of the common strands between postcolonialism and postmodernism, their definition of the hybrid coincides in the deferral if not in the tropes of its narration.[4] Postcolonialism, concerned as it is with exposing power relations within the issues of cultural contact, does not provide a model that explains how finally different cultures come together. García Canclini entitles the chapter on hybridity "Hybrid Cultures, Oblique Powers" and he concludes that dominant political discourse and its material practices have difficulty incorporating hybridity because its "theatrical and ritual aspects . . . make evident what there is of the oblique, the simulated and the deferred in any interaction" (1990, 327). García Canclini's explanation of hybridity implies that the hybrid never speaks face to face but always undermines the status quo with what appears to be, rather than cultural syncretism, cultural duplicity.

García Canclini believes that real communication in the postmodern space comes about as a result of illusions, similar to the Tijuana zebra everybody knows is really a donkey: The hiding games of undocumented immigrants that are "tolerated" by U.S. police become a resource for defining identity and communicating with others (1990, 237). Roger Bartra also seems to believe in this "don't ask, don't tell" philosophy. He writes:

> The border is a line that demands straightforward behavior; a red alarm lights if we "approximate it tangentially" (as in *irse por la tangente*), in the sense that this phrase can have in Spanish of cleverly evading or escaping trouble. The border is anathema to the ambiguity of people like Guillermo Gómez-Peña, who approximate borders tangentially as a way of life and a mode of expression. (1993, 11)

The dictionary defines "tangential" as "irrelevant," although in all fairness both García Canclini and Bartra focus on the strict codification of behavior colonial discourse demands. In this sense, colonial discourse considers persons who deviate from the norm as "irrelevant." But this oblique representation of hybridity, focused on the point of view of the status quo, repudiates a self-representation that would deny characterizations of deviancy, tangentiality, and cultural irrelevancy.

Postmodernism also suggests that hybridity is forever deferred, pushed back, postponed. Homi K. Bhabha, for example, believes that contemporary culture always is located "beyond," although, especially, "the discriminated subject or community occupies a contemporary moment that is historically untimely, forever belated" (1996, 56). Bhabha makes the same point in his *Location of Culture:*

> It is the trope our of our times to locate the question of culture in the realm of the *beyond*. At the century's edge, we are less exorcised by annihilation— the death of the author—or epiphany—the birth of the "subject." Our existence today is marked by a tenebrous sense of survival, living on the borderlines of the "present," for which there seems to be no proper name other than the current and controversial shiftiness of the prefix "post": *postmodernism, postcolonialism, postfeminism.* (1994, 1)

Postmodernism provides a recipe for cultural contact in which the ingredients never mix. These issues clearly are textualized in what I would term the "future perfect" and "past imperfect" nature of the descriptions of postmodernism. In the "future perfect" mode cultural contact has already occurred: Guillermo Gómez Peña, a critic who relates questions of contact to questions of power, for example, describes himself as "postmexica" and "postpunk." In the other, cultural contact has not occurred, as when Gómez Peña uses the term "prechicano" (quoted in García Canclini 1990, 238). Most of the terminology suggests the inability to live anywhere, all real contact having already occurred as the "post" prefix suggests, or has not yet occurred as the prefix "pre" intimates. Postmodern grammar of cultural interaction lacks a present tense because the narrators situate themselves either after or before the actual cultural contact.

Postmodern cartography mimics postmodern grammar, narrating the hybrid in tropes of displacements and movements, with words such as "transterrado," "transplanted," "transculturation," and "translation." The word "trans" derives from Latin to mean "across," "beyond," "through," although postmodernism also ties the geography quite closely to the earth or "terra" (trans*terra*do, *terri*torializado). Gómez Peña's heavy reliance on geographical metaphors stresses the physical nature of the border. He frequently uses words with the root "cross": "crossing the border," "crosscultural thinking," and "crisscross[ing] from the past to the present."

Gómez Peña does not consider the border a state of mind or a place a person inhabits, but a place of crossing, like a bridge, that will take the person somewhere else. The representation of the border as a place of crossing and not one of habitation relies on dominant models that characterize the border akin to the River Styx.

The common narrative of hybridity relies on words such as "displacement," "discontinuity," and "dislocation," whose prefix derives from the roots "apart" or "asunder," further establishing postmodernism's inability to stare hybridity in the face. Fredric Jameson exemplifies the trend of avoidance in his study of postmodernism by focusing on Philip K. Dick, the original author of *Do Androids Dream of Electric Sheep?* Jameson argues that just as history becomes a projection into the past of contemporary concerns, science fiction projects present concerns into the future. Thus seen, science fiction reflects more about the present than about the events to come. The inability to focus on hybridity directly explains why numerous science fiction films, most of which take place in a mythical future, have dealt with the issue, from *Star Trek* to *Star Wars*, from *Alien* to *Alien Nation.* Jameson calls the genre "nostalgia for the present" in his *Postmodernism or the Cultural Logic of Late Capitalism.* He writes:

> For if the historical novel "corresponded" to the emergence of historicity, of a sense of history in its strong modern post-eighteenth-century sense, science fiction equally corresponds to the waning or the blockage of that historicity, and, particularly in our own time (in the postmodern era), to its crisis and paralysis, its enfeeblement and repression. Only by means of a violent formal and narrative dislocation could a narrative apparatus come into being capable of restoring life and feeling to this only intermittently functioning organ that is our capacity to organize and live time historically. Nor should it be thought overhastily that the two forms are symmetrical on the grounds that the historical novel stages the past and science fiction the future. (1991, 284)

This "future present" mode explains the anxiety of postmodernism in dealing with cultural contact. The future present tense creates a virtual reality that avoids the pitfalls of present characterizations.

Where does hybridity end and postmodernism begin? Often the postmodern condition, especially as it pertains to fragmentation, is made one with the issue of hybridity. Hybridity, for García Canclini, is postmodernism itself:

> Postmodernism is not a style but the tumultuous copresence of all styles, the place where the chapters in the history of art and folklore are crossed with each other and with new cultural technologies. (1990, 244)

Canclini calls Tijuana, which cultural materialism has turned into the prototype of postmodernism, "one of the biggest laboratories of postmodernity" (1990, 233).

The deferral of cultural contact is made clear by the way in which postmodernism narrates the hybrid. Canclini relies on verbs such as *fragmentar* (fragment), *agrupar* (group), *combinar* (combine), *mezclar* (mix), *relacionar* (relate), *intercambiar* (interchange), *coexistir* (coesist), *entretejer* (intertwine); on nouns such as *continuidad* (continuity), *discontinuidad* (discontinuity), *pluralidad* (plurality), *interacciones* (interaction), *dualidad* (duality), *ambivalencia* (ambivalence), *cruces* (crosses), *mezclas* (mixes), *deslizamientos* (slide), *desplazamientos* (displacements); and on adjectives such as *múltiple* (multiple), *mestizo* (mestizo), *impuro* (impure), *móvil* (mobile). García Canclini, similar to most postmodern critics, relies on the technique of enumeration. Gómez Peña states that he considers himself "Postmexica, prechicano, panlatino, land crossed [*transterrado*], Artamerican . . . it depends on the day of the week or the project in question" (quoted in García Canclini 1990, 238).

Postmodernism also constantly relies on tropes of fragmentation. Gómez Peña frequently follows the same lines of narration postmodern theories dictate. He calls himself the "half and half" (1993, 16), and sees himself as a person with a personality disorder: He speaks of a multiplicity of voices, each speaking "from a different part of my self" (1993, 21). He refers to himself as being Mexican, part of the year and Chicano the other part, although he also considers himself Latin American.

The strategy of contemporary negations of hybridity is not new to nondominant groups. Güido Podestá's reading of the Harlem Renaissance (1991), Ramón Gutiérrez's (1989) reading of the construction of the myth of Aztlán by an Anglo American governor who wanted to attract residents from the East Coast into New Mexico, Richard Rodríguez's reading of the mythification of pre-Columbian culture in Mexico, all indicate that the inability to accept contemporary hybridity in the here and now might in fact be nothing more than the subliminal psychological cover to racism and discrimination. Elizabeth Burgos writes in the introduction to *I, Rigoberta Menchú*:

> Los latinoamericanos están siempre dispuestos a asumir como suyos los grandes momentos de las culturas precolombinas, azteca, inca, maya, pero no establecen ningún nexo entre este esplendor pretérito y los indios pobres, explotados, despreciados, que les sirven como esclavos. (1985, 14)
> [Latinamericans are always willing to claim as theirs the great moments of the pre-Columbian cultures—Aztec, Inca, Mayan—but they do not establish

any link between that past splendor and the poor, exploited, ignored Indians who serve them as slaves.]

In the eyes of colonial discourse, Africa, Tenochtitlán, or Aztlán serve as the rhetorical tropes of contained purity that by implication point to a degradation. In this colonial discourse the rebellion in Chiapas, Rosario Castellanos and the Popol-Vuh can coincide. In this colonial discourse, English Only, Proposition 187, and the California missions share the same semantic space of exclusion.

It is no coincidence that the criticism of the film has focused on the genre that produced *Dr. Jekyll and Mr. Hyde*, as well as *Frankenstein*. For the replicants' monstrosity lies in their close proximity to their Other, as expressed in the replicants' similarity to the hunters. Scott obviously manipulates the audience's sympathy toward the replicants, because the script does not properly justify their persecution (they are not allowed to be on earth), and thus they simply defend themselves, albeit brutally, against the persons trying to eliminate them. Roy Batty saves Deckard because he values life and cannot see it being wasted. Deckard does not defeat Batty, who just drifts away having reached the end of his limited lifespan. When Batty shows compassion, Deckard understands that replicants are also capable of love, a realization that allows him then to understand that he can also love a replicant—Rachel, the replicant whom Deckard cannot kill and with whom he falls in love. The ultimate communication has taken place; there is no difference between humans and nonhumans, no difference between self and other. Thus normalization never occurs, as the characters find out. Perhaps in the end the persecutors understand that they, just like the people they pursue, share in the same experiences. There is an uncanny moment in which the I's confront alterity and staring at its eyes watch only their own reflection. As Joseph Campbell writes:

> The hero, whether god or goddess, man or woman, the figure in a myth or the dreamer of a dream, discovers and assimilates his opposite (his own unsuspected self) either by swallowing it or by being swallowed. One by one the resistances are broken. He must put aside his pride, his virtue, beauty, and life, and bow or submit to the absolutely intolerable. Then he finds that he and his opposite are not of differing species, but one flesh. (1968, 108)

If memory makes humankind, why are the replicants with their implanted memories not human? If poetry inhabits the realm of the spirit, why does the replicant Roy Batty quote William Blake? The monstrosity of these characters lies in their similarity to their creators.

Their fall from grace is caused by the knowledge of their existential condition. Ultimately a film like *Blade Runner* reminds us that the hybrid is always within us and that it shares with the audience the dream that one day it will be judged only by the contents of its character.

NOTES

1. Paul Sammon has determined that the studios released as many as six different versions of the film: (1) the work print; (2) the San Diego sneak preview; (3) the domestic cut; (4) the international cut; (5) the director's cut; and (6) the television broadcast version. His "Appendix B: Different Faces of *Blade Runner*—How Many Versions?" details the differences among them (1996, 394–408). The work print was used to test the market; the San Diego sneak preview incorporated the changes made to the work print. Changes to the San Diego sneak preview, the domestic cut, the international cut, and the television broadcast version—all similar among themselves—were made to accommodate the different markets without necessarily changing the film's structure. (Studios deem international audiences less prudish to violence, sex, and language than American audiences.) *Blade Runner: The Director's Cut* (1992), structurally closer to the work print, approximates Ridley Scott's original intentions.

2. *Blade Runner*, by sexualizing the alien, suggests, if not the close connection between self/another, at least the attraction of self to other. The script equates Zhora (a representation of temptation) to the mannequins when she becomes an object of the male gaze. The film associates the character with the serpent. Not only does the serpent's scale allow Deckard to find her (in a strip joint called "The Snake Pit"), but while Deckard drinks at the bar, symptomatically swallowing worms with his drink, the announcer introduces Zhora with the words: "Taffey Lewis presents Miss Salome and the snake. Watch her take the pleasure from the serpent that once corrupted men."

3. The script characterizes Gaff as part Chicano and part Japanese. Olmos made Gaff "more Asian." His skin was madeup in yellowish tones, according to the actor (Sammon 1996, 114). Linking Asian American culture to Chicano culture simply reflects a California reality. Richard Rodríguez's *Days of Obligation* (1992) also ties Chicano/a culture to Asian American concerns.

4. See José Rabasa's *Inventing America* (1993), Mary Louise Pratt's *Imperial Eyes* (1992), and Homi Bhabha's *The Location of Culture* (1994).

WORKS CITED

Bartra, Roger. 1993. "Introduction." In *Warrior for Gringostroika*, Guillermo Gómez Peña, 11–12. Saint Paul, MN: Greywolf.

Bhabha, Homi K. 1994. *The Location of Culture*. New York: Routledge.

———. 1996. "Culture's In-Between." In *Questions of Cultural Identity*, ed. Stuart Hall and Paul du Gay, 53–60. London: Sage.

Blake William. 1979. *America: A Prophecy*, ed. Mary Lynn Johnson and John E. Grant, 106–119. New York: Norton.

Burgos, Elizabeth. 1985. "Introduction." In *Me llamo Rigoberta Menchú y así me nació la conciencia*, Rigoberta Menchú. Mexico: Siglo Veintiuno Editores.

Burroughs, William. 1994. *Blade Runner (a Movie)*. Berkeley, CA: Blue Wind Press.

Campbell, Joseph. 1968. *The Hero with a Thousand Faces*. Princeton, NJ: Princeton University Press.

Dick, Philip K. 1982. *Blade Runner (Do Androids Dream of Electric Sheep?)*. New York: Ballantine Books.

García Canclini, Néstor. 1990. *Culturas híbridas: Estrategias para entrar y salir de la modernidad*. México: Grijalbo.

Gómez Peña, Guillermo. 1993. *Warrior for Gringostroika*. Saint Paul, MN: Greywolf.

Gunew, Sneja. 1990. "Denaturalizing Cultural Nationalisms: Multicultural Readings of 'Australia.' " In *Nation and Narration*, ed. Homi Bhabha, 99–120. London: Routledge.

Gutiérrez, Ramón. 1989. "Aztlán, Montezuma, and New Mexico: The Political Uses of American Indian Mythology." In *Aztlán, Essays on the Chicano Homeland*, ed. Rudolfo Anaya and Francisco Lomelí, 172–187. Albuquerque, NM: El Norte.

Instrell, Rick. 1992. "*Blade Runner:* The Economic Shaping of a Film." *Cinema and Fiction: New Modes of Adapting, 1950–1990*, ed. John Orr and Colin Nicholson, 160–170. Edinburgh: Edinburgh University Press.

Jameson, Fredric. 1991. *Postmodernism, or, The Cultural Logic of Late Capitalism*. Durham, NC: Duke University Press.

Kerman, Judith, ed. 1991. *Retrofitting* "Blade Runner." Bowling Green, OH: Bowling Green University Press.

Podestá, Guido. 1991. "An Ethnographic Reproach to the Theory of the Avant-Garde: Modernity and Modernism in Latin America and the Harlem Renaissance." *Modern Language Notes* 106: 395–422.

Pratt, Mary Louise. 1992. *Imperial Eyes*. New York: Routledge.

Rabasa, José. 1993. *Inventing America: Spanish Historiography and the Formation of Eurocentrism*. Norman: University of Oklahoma Press.

Sammon, Paul M. 1996. *Future Noir: The Making of* "Blade Runner." New York: Harper Collins.

Scott, Ridley. 1982. *Blade Runner*. Videocassette. New Line Home Video, 1992.

———. 1992. *Blade Runner: The Director's Cut*. Videocassette. Warner Brothers Home Video, 1993.

About the Contributors

Danny J. Anderson is a professor of Spanish at the University of Kansas, where he teaches Mexican literature, Mexican cultural studies, and the Latin American novel. His contribution to this volume grew out of his history of the Joaquín Mortiz publishing house, which appeared in the *Latin American Research Review* in 1996. Anderson has published a book entitled *Vicente Leñero: The Novelist as Critic* (1989). He is currently at work on a social history of literary reading in Mexico from the dictatorship of Porfirio Díaz to the present.

Rebecca E. Biron is an associate professor of Spanish at the University of Miami. Her areas of writing and research include Latin American literature and critical theory. She is the author of *Murder and Masculinity: Violent Fictions of Twentieth Century Latin America* (2000) and is currently working on a second book manuscript, *Haunting Romances: Elena Garro and Mexican Literary Culture.*

Juan Bruce-Novoa is a professor of Spanish at the University of California, Irvine. He is author of many articles, books, editions, and anthologies on Mexican and Chicano literature and culture. He has done extensive work on Mexican writers of the midcentury in Mexico, particularly on the relation between the textual and visual arts. He was awarded the *Plural* prize for literary criticism and the Lopez Fuentes prize for literature. In addition to writing criticism, he is also a novelist and poet.

Debra A. Castillo is Stephen H. Weiss Presidential Fellow and professor of Romance studies and comparative literature at Cornell University, where she also serves as director of the Latin American Studies Program.

213

She is author of *The Translated World: A Postmodern Tour of Libraries in Literature* (1984), *Talking Back: Strategies for a Latin American Feminist Literary Criticism* (1992), and translator of Federico Campbell's *Tijuana: Stories on the Border* (1994). Her most recent book is *Easy Women: Sex and Gender in Modern Mexican Fiction* (1998).

Karen Cordero Reiman is a professor in the department of art history at the Universidad Iberoamericana in Mexico City and a founding member of Curare, an alternative center for the study and discussion of contemporary art. She has authored numerous studies of twentieth-century Mexican art and has long been involved in museum work as curator, advisor, and researcher; her exhibit "Anatomies and Constructions: The Representation of the Body in Mexico, 19th to 20th Centuries," opened at the National Museum of Art in Mexico City in October 1998.

Olivier Debroise is a writer and art historian based in Mexico City. He is the founding director of Curare, an alternative center for the study and discussion of contemporary art, and has published many books on the history of art, including *Diego de Montparnasse* (1979), *Figuras en el trópico: Plástica mexicana, 1920–1940* (1984) and *Fuga mexicana: Un recorrido por la fotografía en México* (1994; English translation, *Mexican Suite*, forthcoming.) He has curated many expositions of Mexican art. He is also the author of three novels and is currently directing his first film, *A Banquet at Tetlapayac*.

Montserrat Galí Boadella is a research professor at the University of Puebla, Mexico. She served as director of the Museo del Chopo in Mexico City from 1989 to 1994 and has written six books on Mexican and Catalan art, including *El arte en la era de los medios de comunicación* (1988) and *Imatges de la Memoria* (1999).

Carl Good is an assistant professor of Spanish at Emory University, where he specializes in Latin American poetry, Mexican literature, baroque poetics, and the theory of literature. He is currently writing a book that reimagines the relationship between poetry and narration in Latin American literature.

Rolando Romero is an associate professor of Spanish and Latina/Latino Studies at the University of Illinois Urbana-Champagne. He has written on Mexican and U.S. Latino literature, poststructuralism, border theory, and postdeconstructive historiography in a wide variety of publications and is currently general editor of the journal *Discourse*. His book *EdgeWise*, a study of historical constructions of Latinos, is in publication by Duke University Press.

Susan C. Schaffer teaches in the Spanish Department at the University of California, Los Angeles, where she specializes in Mexican literature. She has published numerous studies of contemporary Mexican prose, in particular on the work of José Agustín and Carlos Fuentes.

Jacobo Sefamí is associate professor and chair of the Department of Spanish and Portuguese at the University of California, Irvine. He specializes in twentieth-century Latin American poetry. His books include: *El destierro apacible y otros ensayos* (1987), *Contemporary Spanish American Poets* (1992), *El espejo trizado: La poesía de Gonzalo Rojas* (1992), *De la imaginación poética* (1996), and *Medusario: Muestra de poesía latinoamericana* (with R. Echavarren and J. Kozer).

John V. Waldron is an independent scholar living in Hartford, Connecticut. He wrote his doctoral dissertation on the avant-garde in Mexico and has written on Mexican and Chicano literature.

Index